DEADPOOL
VS
CARNAGE

D1157188

DEADPOOL VS. CARNAGE. Contains material originally published in magazine form as DEADPOOL VS. CARNAGE #1-4 and SUPERIOR CARNAGE ANNUAL #1. First printing 2014. ISBN# 978-0-7851-9015-8. Published by MARVEL WORLDWIDE, INC., a subsidiary of MARVEL ENTERTAINMENT, LLC. OFFICE OF PUBLICATION: 135 West 50th Street, New York, NY 10020. Copyright © 2014 Marvel Characters, Inc. All rights reserved. All characters featured in this issue and the distinctive names and likenesses thereof, and all related indicia are trademarks of Marvel Characters, Inc. No similarity between any of the names, characters, persons, and/or institutions in this magazine with those of any living or dead person or institution is intended, and any such similarity which may exist is purely coincidental. **Printed in Canada.** ALAN FINE, EVP - Office of the President, Marvel Worldwide, Inc. and EVP & CMO Marvel Characters B.V.; DAN BUCKLEY, Publisher & President - Print, Animation & Digital Divisions; JOE QUESADA, Chief Creative Officer; TOM BREVOORT, SVP of Publishing; DAVID BOGART, SVP of Operations & Procurement, Publishing; C.B. CEBULSKI, SVP of Creator & Content Development; DAVID GABRIEL, SVP Print, Sales & Marketing; JIM O'KEEFE, VP of Operations & Logistics; DAN CARR, Executive Director of Publishing Technology; SUSAN CRESPI, Editorial Operations Manager; ALEX MORALES, Publishing Operations Manager; STAN LEE, Chairman Emeritus. For information regarding advertising in Marvel Comics or on Marvel.com, please contact Niza Disla, Director of Marvel Partnerships, at ndisla@marvel.com. For Marvel subscription inquiries, please call 800-217-9158. **Manufactured between 7/4/2014 and 8/11/2014 by SOLISCO PRINTERS, SCOTT, QC, CANADA.**

10 9 8 7 6 5 4 3 2 1 0

WRITER:
CULLEN BUNN

SUPERIOR CARNAGE ANNUAL
ARTISTS:
KIM JACINTO (P. 1-20)
& MIKE HENDERSON (P. 21-30)
COLOR ARTIST:
JAY DAVID RAMOS
LETTERER:
VC'S JOE CARAMAGNA
COVER ARTIST:
RAFA GARRES

ASSISTANT EDITOR: DEVIN LEWIS
EDITOR: SANA AMANAT
SENIOR EDITOR: STEPHEN WACKER

DEADPOOL VS. CARNAGE #1-4
ARTIST:
SALVA ESPIN
COLORIST:
VERONICA GANDINI
LETTERER:
VC'S JOE SABINO
COVER ARTISTS:
GLENN FABRY & ADAM BROWN

ASSISTANT EDITOR: FRANKIE JOHNSON
EDITOR: JORDAN D. WHITE
X-MEN GROUP EDITOR: MIKE MARTS

DEADPOOL CREATED BY ROB LIEFELD & FABIAN NICIEZA

COLLECTION EDITOR: ALEX STARBUCK
ASSISTANT EDITOR: SARAH BRUNSTAD
EDITORS, SPECIAL PROJECTS: JENNIFER GRÜNWALD & MARK D. BEAZLEY
SENIOR EDITOR, SPECIAL PROJECTS: JEFF YOUNGQUIST
SVP PRINT, SALES & MARKETING: DAVID GABRIEL
BOOK DESIGNER: NELSON RIBEIRO

EDITOR IN CHIEF: AXEL ALONSO
CHIEF CREATIVE OFFICER: JOE QUESADA
PUBLISHER: DAN BUCKLEY
EXECUTIVE PRODUCER: ALAN FINE

POSSIBLY THE WORLD'S MOST SKILLED MERCENARY, DEFINITELY THE WORLD'S MOST ANNOYING, WADE WILSON WAS CHOSEN FOR A TOP-SECRET GOVERNMENT PROGRAM THAT GAVE HIM A HEALING FACTOR ALLOWING HIM TO HEAL FROM ANY WOUND. NOW, WADE MAKES HIS WAY AS A GUN FOR HIRE, SHOOTING HIS PREY'S FACES OFF WHILE TALKING HIS FRIENDS' EARS OFF. CALL HIM THE MERC WITH THE MOUTH...CALL HIM THE REGENERATIN' DEGENERATE...CALL HIM...

CLETUS KASADY WAS A SERIAL KILLER LOCKED UP IN RYKERS ISLAND AND SHARING A CELL WITH A MAN NAMED EDDIE BROCK. BROCK HAD BONDED WITH AN ALIEN SYMBIOTE THAT GRANTED HIM INCREDIBLE SUPER-POWERS, ALLOWING HIM TO BECOME THE SUPER VILLAIN VENOM. VENOM'S ALIEN SYMBIOTE SPAWNED AN OFFSPRING THAT BONDED WITH KASADY, TURNING HIM INTO THE MURDEROUS MADMAN...

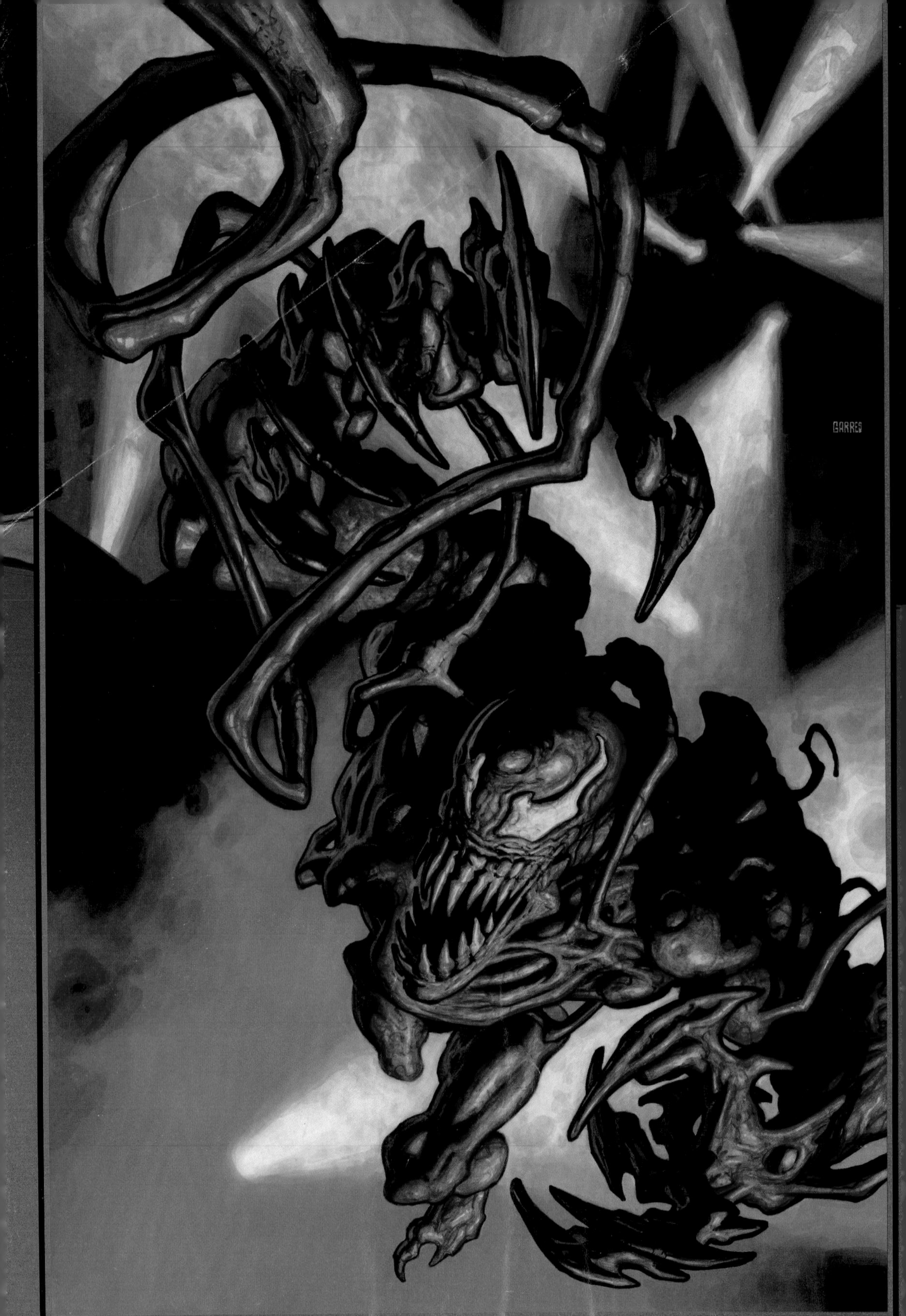

Superior Carnage Annual #1

FINAL ☆☆☆☆

DAILY BUGLE®

NEW YORK'S FINEST DAILY NEWSPAPER

SINCE 1897 ☆☆☆☆
$1.00 (in NYC)
$1.50 (outside city)

INSIDE: RECENT ATTACKS IN ENGLAND REMAIN MYS-TERY; NEW MS. MARVEL SPOTTED IN NEW JERSEY?; BLACK WIDOW SPINS SOLO IN DUBAI

CARNAGEY HALL

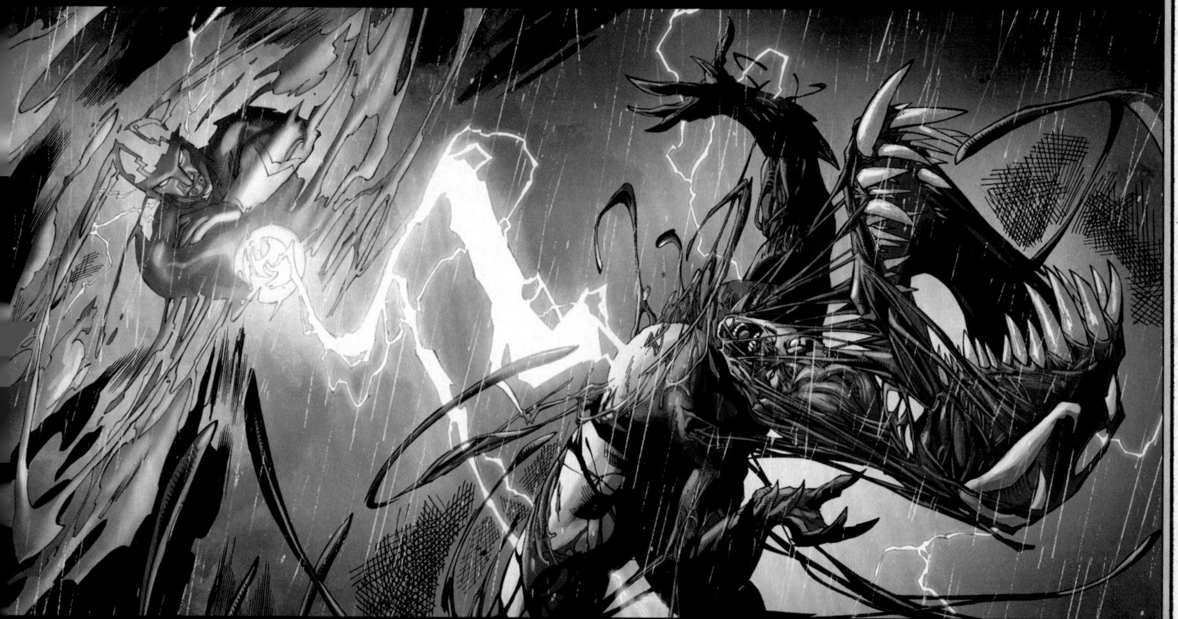

Recently, the Carnage symbiote was stolen by the Wizard, who used to it launch a super villain attack on City Hall. Spider-Man was able to stop the Wizard and Carnage, but only by offering the alien its former host – Cletus Kasady. Before the pair could fully bond, a stray bolt of lightning struck them both, knocking them out to be captured safely.

KASADY BACK BEHIND BARS

After his contact with the symbiote at City Hall, Cletus Kasady has seemingly regained some brain function. Prosecutors are currently determining if he is fit to stand trial.

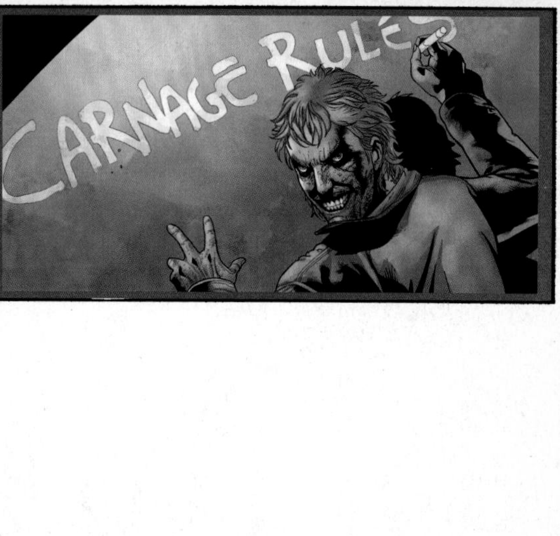
CARNAGE RULES
CARNAGE

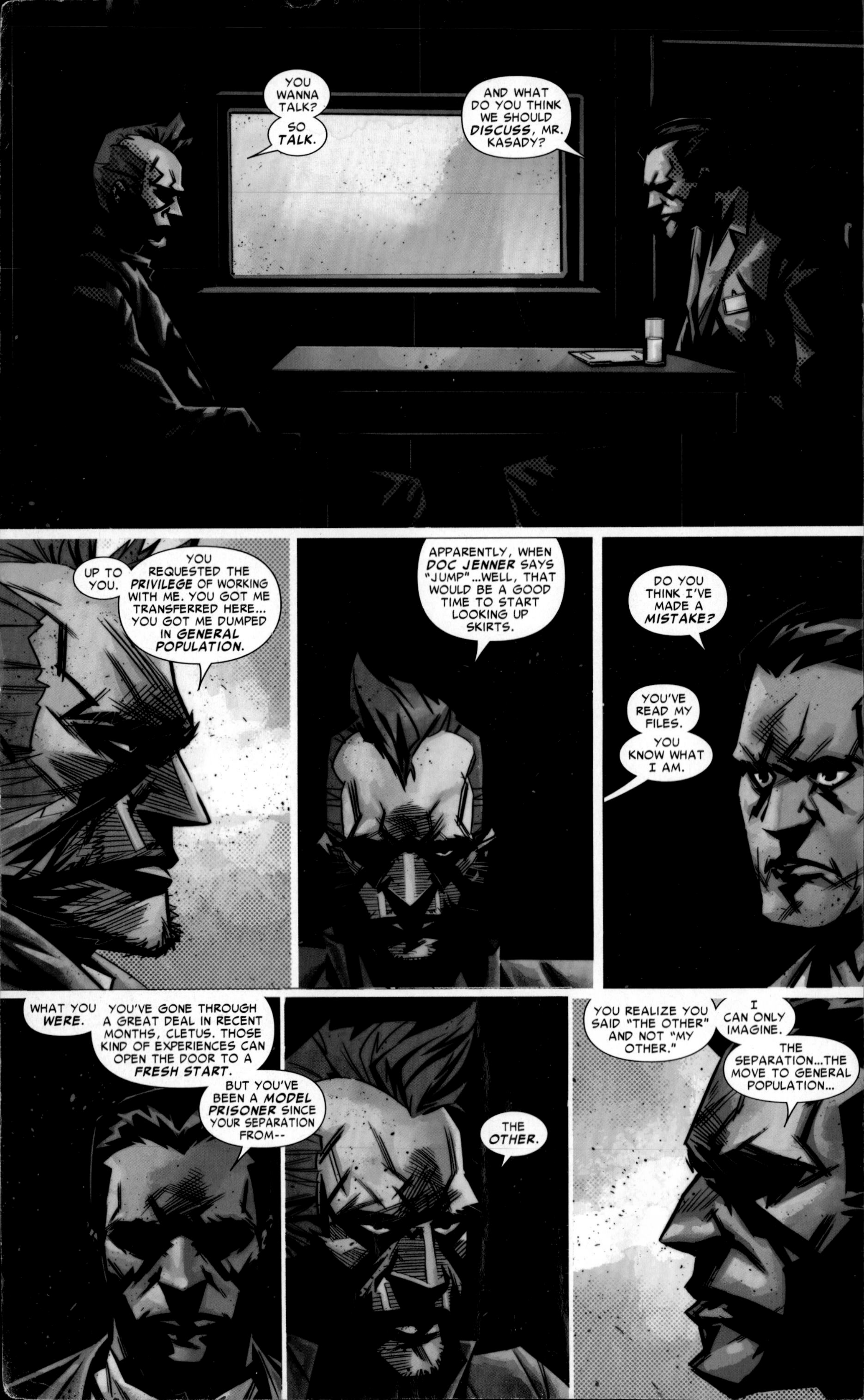
YOU WANNA TALK?
SO TALK.
AND WHAT DO YOU THINK WE SHOULD DISCUSS, MR. KASADY?
UP TO YOU.
YOU REQUESTED THE PRIVILEGE OF WORKING WITH ME. YOU GOT ME TRANSFERRED HERE... YOU GOT ME DUMPED IN GENERAL POPULATION.
APPARENTLY, WHEN DOC JENNER SAYS "JUMP"...WELL, THAT WOULD BE A GOOD TIME TO START LOOKING UP SKIRTS.
DO YOU THINK I'VE MADE A MISTAKE?
YOU'VE READ MY FILES.
YOU KNOW WHAT I AM.
WHAT YOU WERE.
YOU'VE GONE THROUGH A GREAT DEAL IN RECENT MONTHS, CLETUS. THOSE KIND OF EXPERIENCES CAN OPEN THE DOOR TO A FRESH START.
BUT YOU'VE BEEN A MODEL PRISONER SINCE YOUR SEPARATION FROM--
THE OTHER.
YOU REALIZE YOU SAID "THE OTHER" AND NOT "MY OTHER."
I CAN ONLY IMAGINE.
THE SEPARATION...THE MOVE TO GENERAL POPULATION...

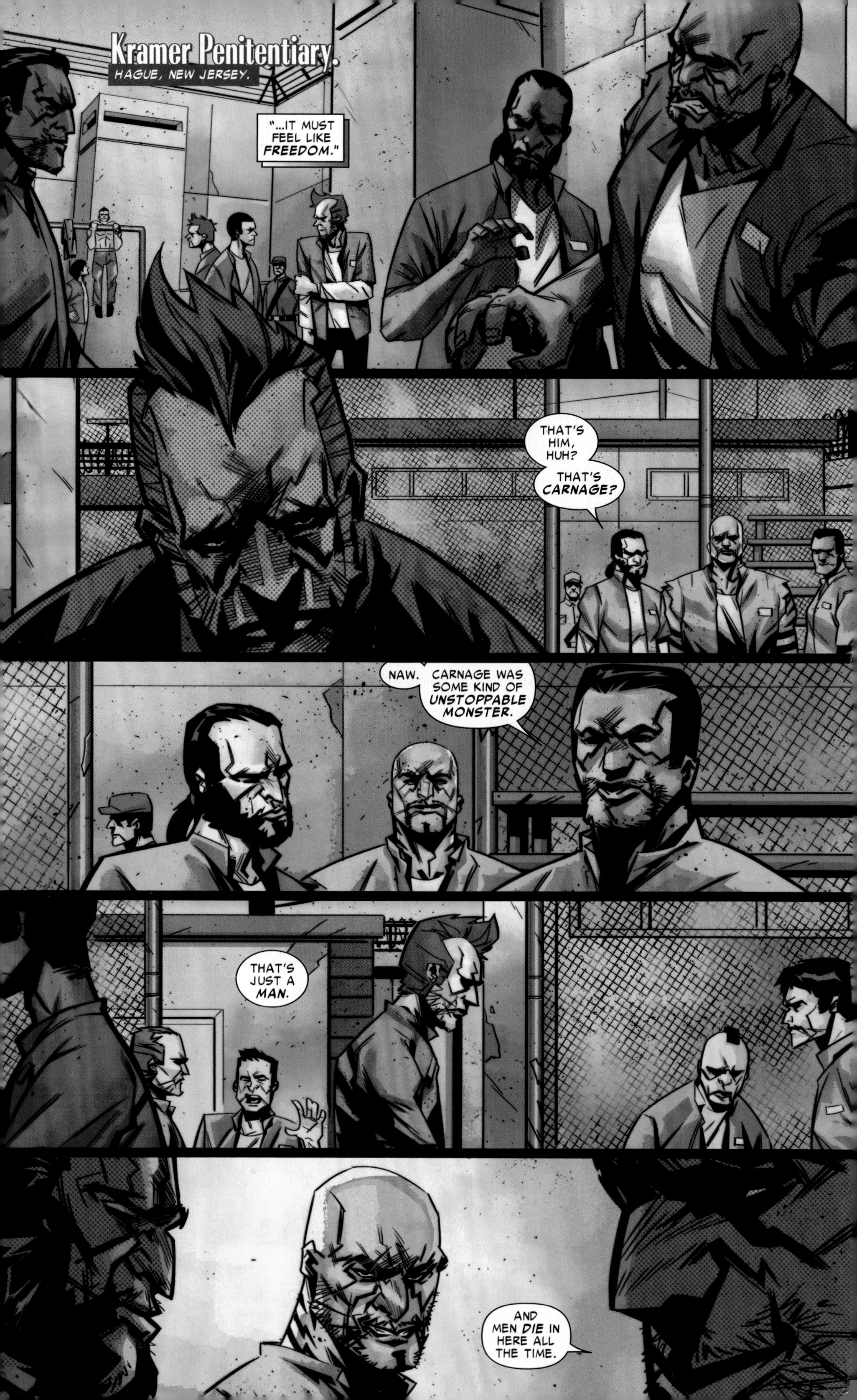
Kramer Penitentiary.
HAGUE, NEW JERSEY.
"...IT MUST FEEL LIKE FREEDOM."
THAT'S HIM, HUH?
THAT'S CARNAGE?
NAW. CARNAGE WAS SOME KIND OF UNSTOPPABLE MONSTER.
THAT'S JUST A MAN.
AND MEN DIE IN HERE ALL THE TIME.

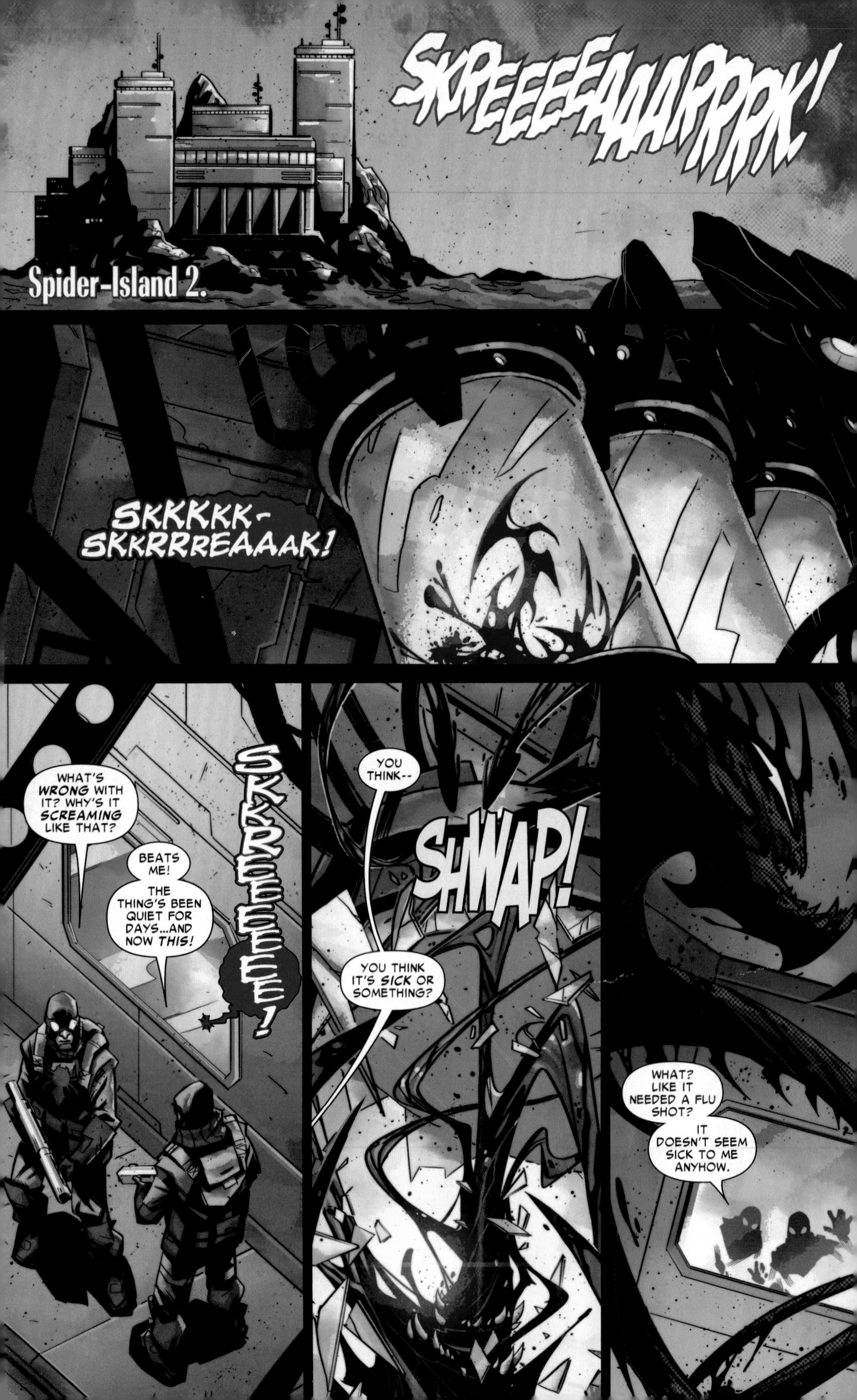
SKREEEEEAAARRRK!
Spider-Island 2.
SKKKKK-SKKRRREAAAK!
WHAT'S WRONG WITH IT? WHY'S IT SCREAMING LIKE THAT?
SKKREEEEEE!
BEATS ME!
THE THING'S BEEN QUIET FOR DAYS...AND NOW THIS!
YOU THINK--
SHWAP!
YOU THINK IT'S SICK OR SOMETHING?
WHAT? LIKE IT NEEDED A FLU SHOT?
IT DOESN'T SEEM SICK TO ME ANYHOW.

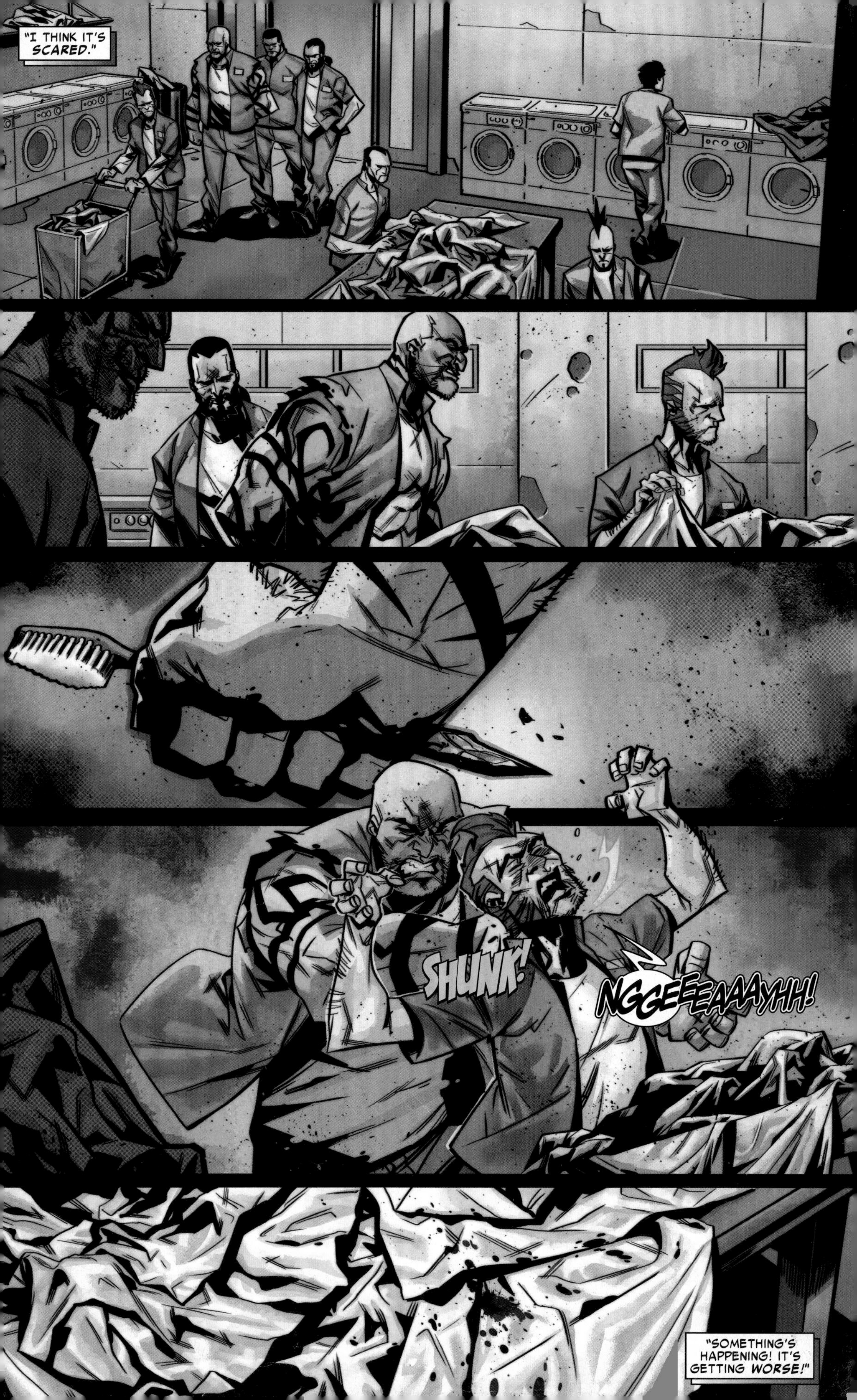
"I THINK IT'S SCARED."
SHUNK!
NGGEEEAAAYHH!
"SOMETHING'S HAPPENING! IT'S GETTING WORSE!"

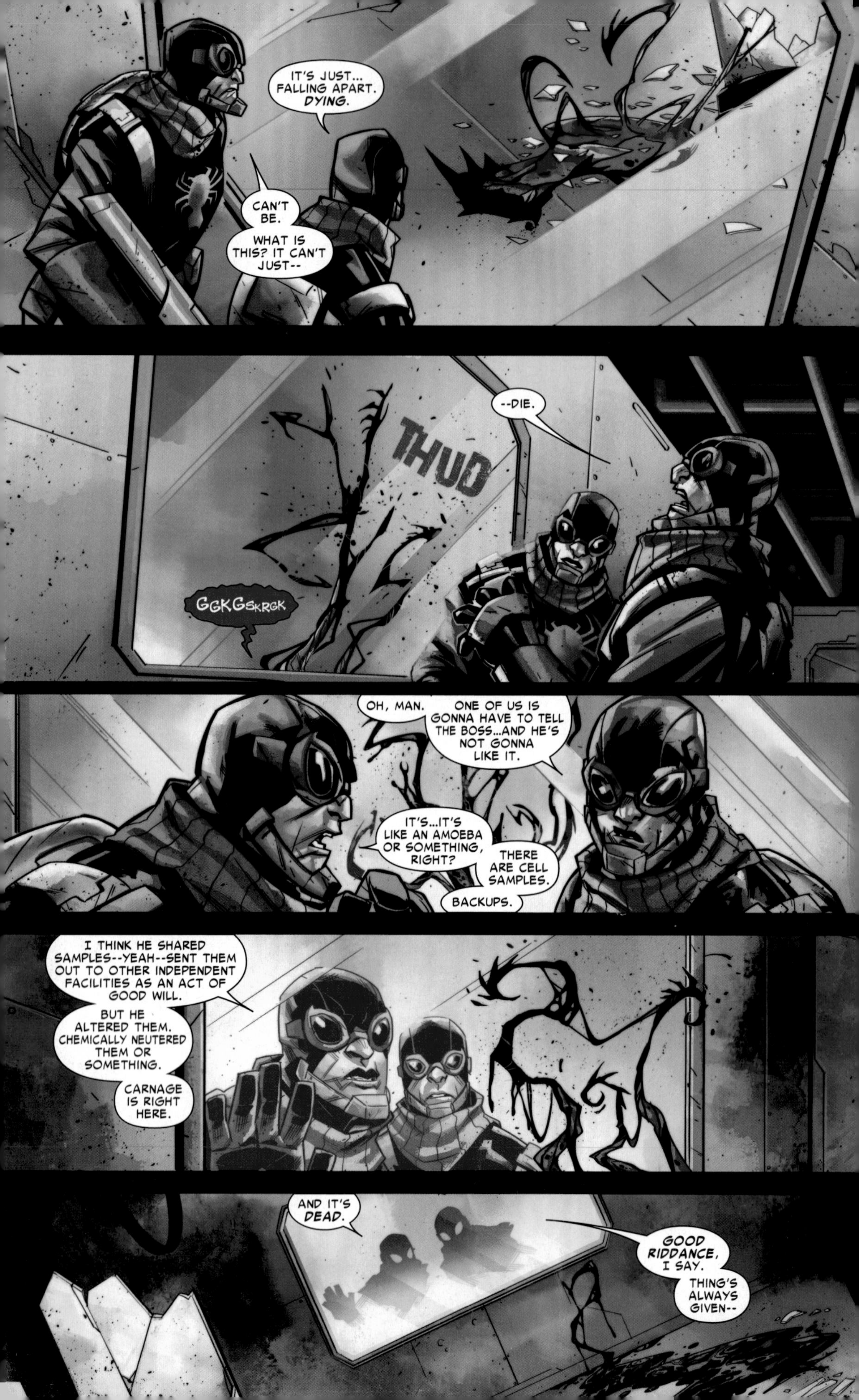
IT'S JUST... FALLING APART. DYING.
CAN'T BE.
WHAT IS THIS? IT CAN'T JUST--
--DIE.
THUD
GGKGSKRGK
OH, MAN.
ONE OF US IS GONNA HAVE TO TELL THE BOSS...AND HE'S NOT GONNA LIKE IT.
IT'S...IT'S LIKE AN AMOEBA OR SOMETHING, RIGHT?
THERE ARE CELL SAMPLES.
BACKUPS.
I THINK HE SHARED SAMPLES--YEAH--SENT THEM OUT TO OTHER INDEPENDENT FACILITIES AS AN ACT OF GOOD WILL.
BUT HE ALTERED THEM. CHEMICALLY NEUTERED THEM OR SOMETHING.
CARNAGE IS RIGHT HERE.
AND IT'S DEAD.
GOOD RIDDANCE, I SAY.
THING'S ALWAYS GIVEN--

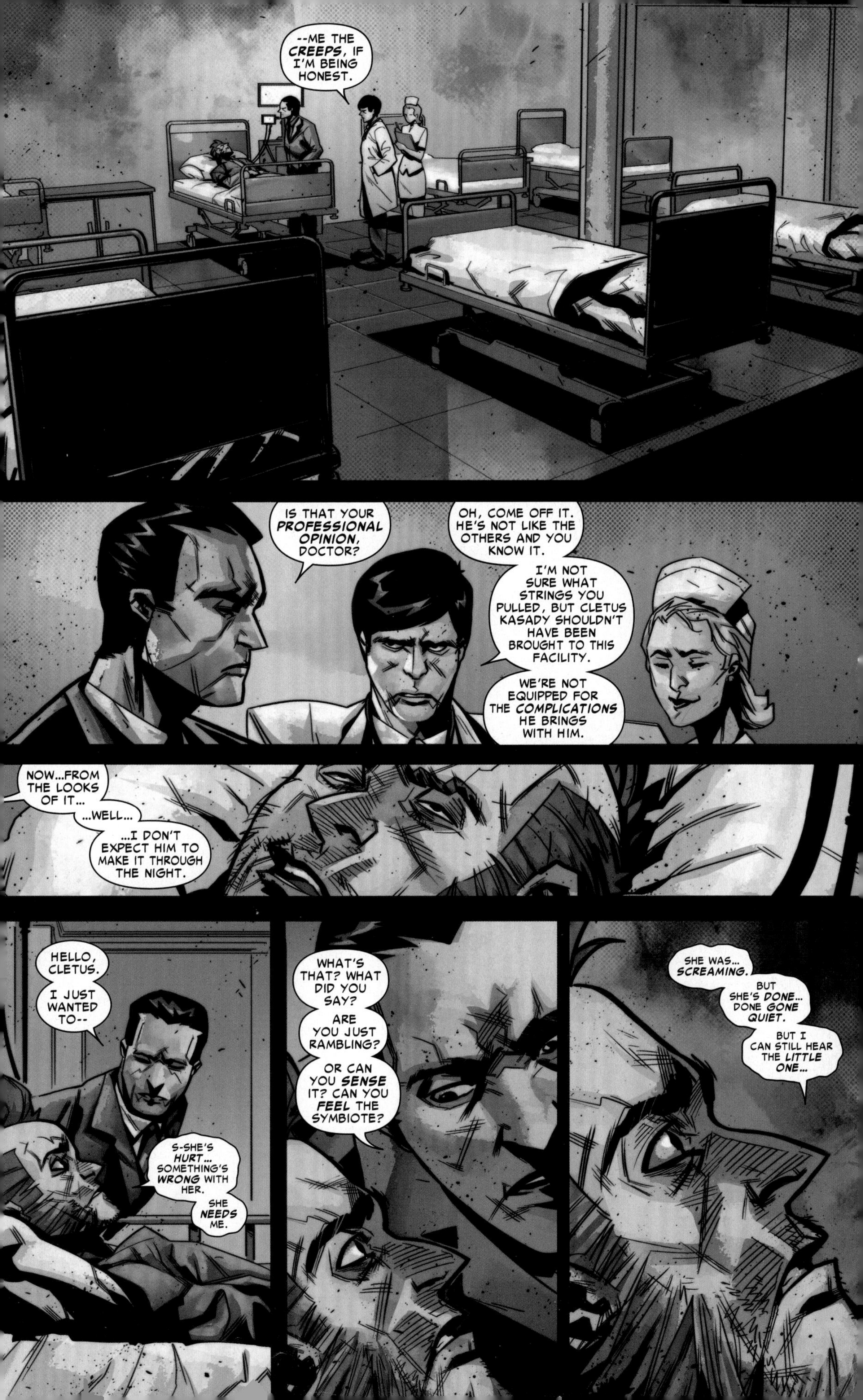
--ME THE CREEPS, IF I'M BEING HONEST.
IS THAT YOUR PROFESSIONAL OPINION, DOCTOR?
OH, COME OFF IT. HE'S NOT LIKE THE OTHERS AND YOU KNOW IT.
I'M NOT SURE WHAT STRINGS YOU PULLED, BUT CLETUS KASADY SHOULDN'T HAVE BEEN BROUGHT TO THIS FACILITY.
WE'RE NOT EQUIPPED FOR THE COMPLICATIONS HE BRINGS WITH HIM.
NOW...FROM THE LOOKS OF IT...
...WELL...
...I DON'T EXPECT HIM TO MAKE IT THROUGH THE NIGHT.
HELLO, CLETUS.
I JUST WANTED TO--
S-SHE'S HURT... SOMETHING'S WRONG WITH HER.
SHE NEEDS ME.
WHAT'S THAT? WHAT DID YOU SAY?
ARE YOU JUST RAMBLING?
OR CAN YOU SENSE IT? CAN YOU FEEL THE SYMBIOTE?
SHE WAS... SCREAMING.
BUT SHE'S DONE... DONE GONE QUIET.
BUT I CAN STILL HEAR THE LITTLE ONE...

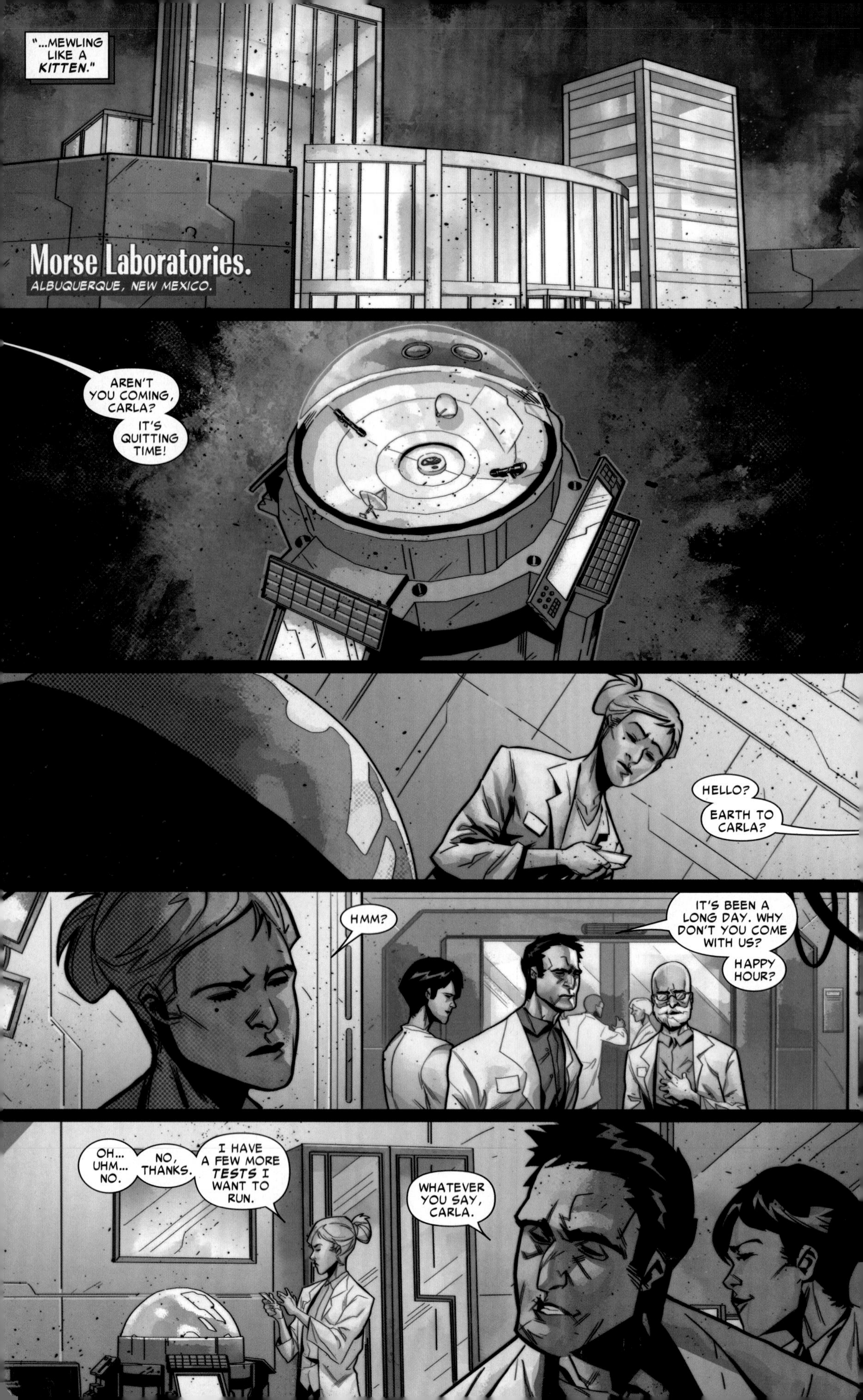
"...MEWLING LIKE A KITTEN."
Morse Laboratories.
ALBUQUERQUE, NEW MEXICO.
AREN'T YOU COMING, CARLA?
IT'S QUITTING TIME!
HELLO?
EARTH TO CARLA?
HMM?
IT'S BEEN A LONG DAY. WHY DON'T YOU COME WITH US?
HAPPY HOUR?
OH... UHM... NO.
NO, THANKS.
I HAVE A FEW MORE TESTS I WANT TO RUN.
WHATEVER YOU SAY, CARLA.

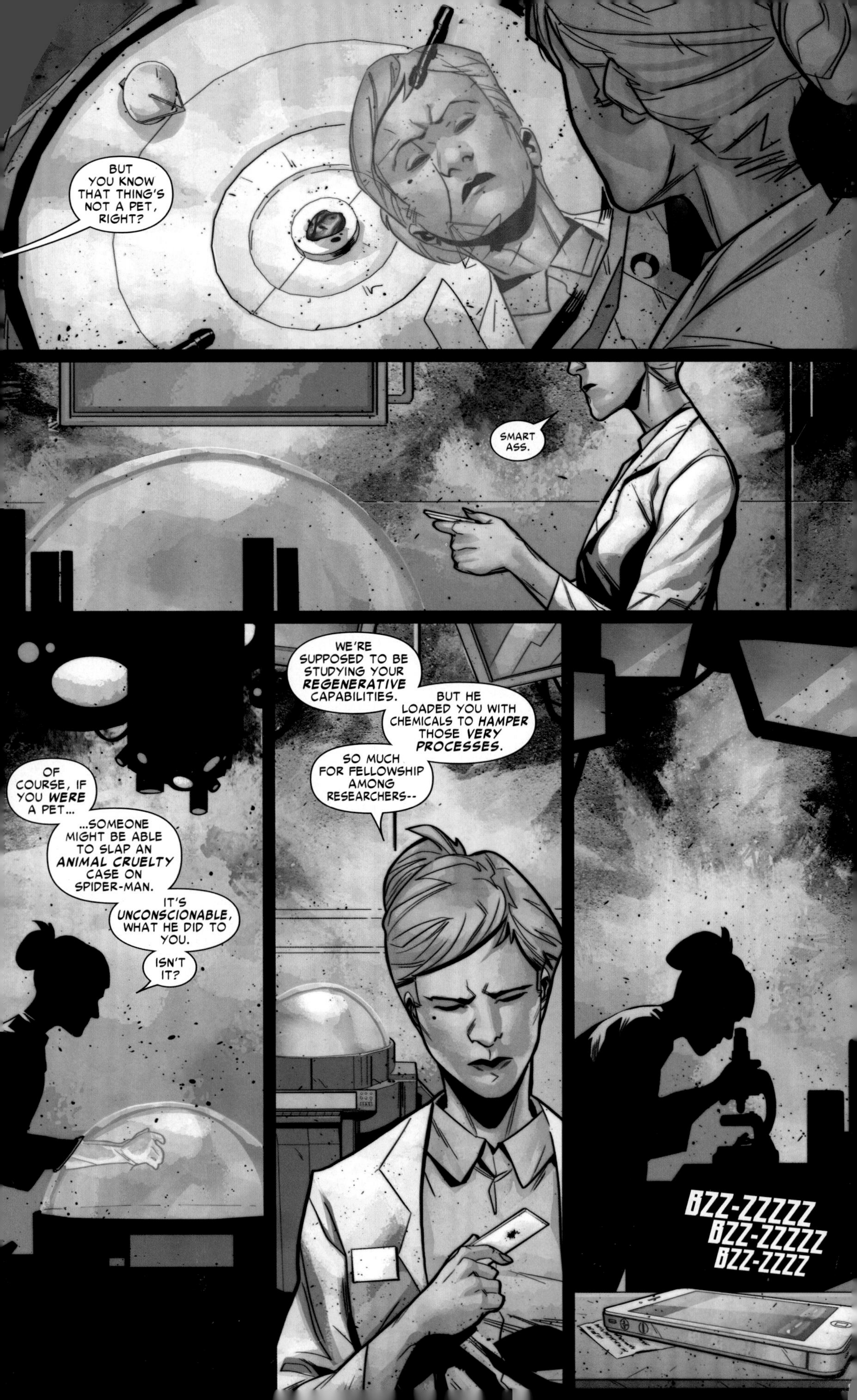
BUT YOU KNOW THAT THING'S NOT A PET, RIGHT?
SMART ASS.
OF COURSE, IF YOU WERE A PET...
...SOMEONE MIGHT BE ABLE TO SLAP AN ANIMAL CRUELTY CASE ON SPIDER-MAN.
IT'S UNCONSCIONABLE, WHAT HE DID TO YOU.
ISN'T IT?
WE'RE SUPPOSED TO BE STUDYING YOUR REGENERATIVE CAPABILITIES.
BUT HE LOADED YOU WITH CHEMICALS TO HAMPER THOSE VERY PROCESSES.
SO MUCH FOR FELLOWSHIP AMONG RESEARCHERS--
BZZ-ZZZZZ
BZZ-ZZZZZ
BZZ-ZZZZ

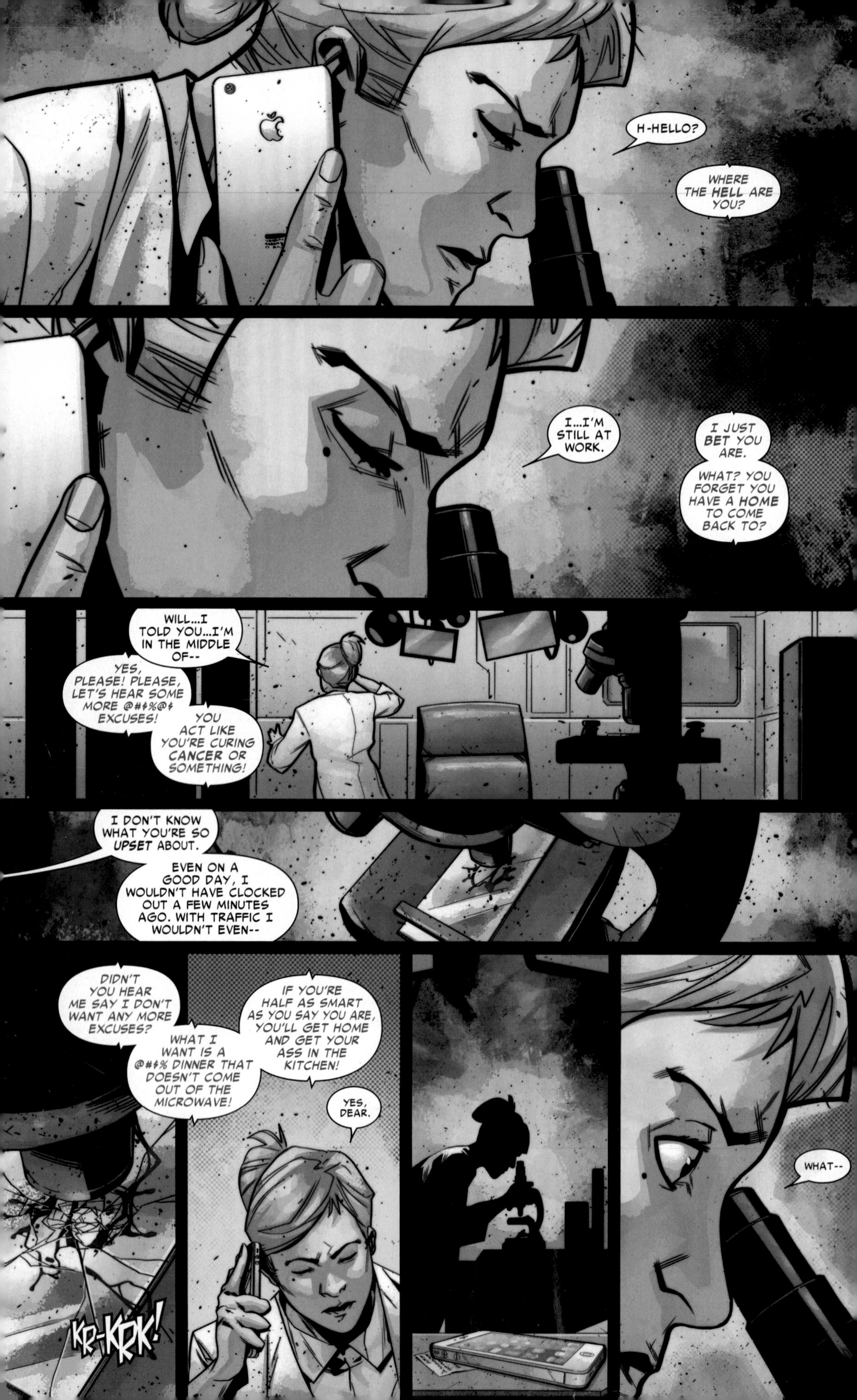
H-HELLO?
WHERE THE HELL ARE YOU?
I...I'M STILL AT WORK.
I JUST BET YOU ARE.
WHAT? YOU FORGET YOU HAVE A HOME TO COME BACK TO?
WILL...I TOLD YOU...I'M IN THE MIDDLE OF--
YES, PLEASE! PLEASE, LET'S HEAR SOME MORE @#$%@$ EXCUSES!
YOU ACT LIKE YOU'RE CURING CANCER OR SOMETHING!
I DON'T KNOW WHAT YOU'RE SO UPSET ABOUT.
EVEN ON A GOOD DAY, I WOULDN'T HAVE CLOCKED OUT A FEW MINUTES AGO. WITH TRAFFIC I WOULDN'T EVEN--
DIDN'T YOU HEAR ME SAY I DON'T WANT ANY MORE EXCUSES?
WHAT I WANT IS A @#$% DINNER THAT DOESN'T COME OUT OF THE MICROWAVE!
IF YOU'RE HALF AS SMART AS YOU SAY YOU ARE, YOU'LL GET HOME AND GET YOUR ASS IN THE KITCHEN!
YES, DEAR.
KR-KRK!
WHAT--

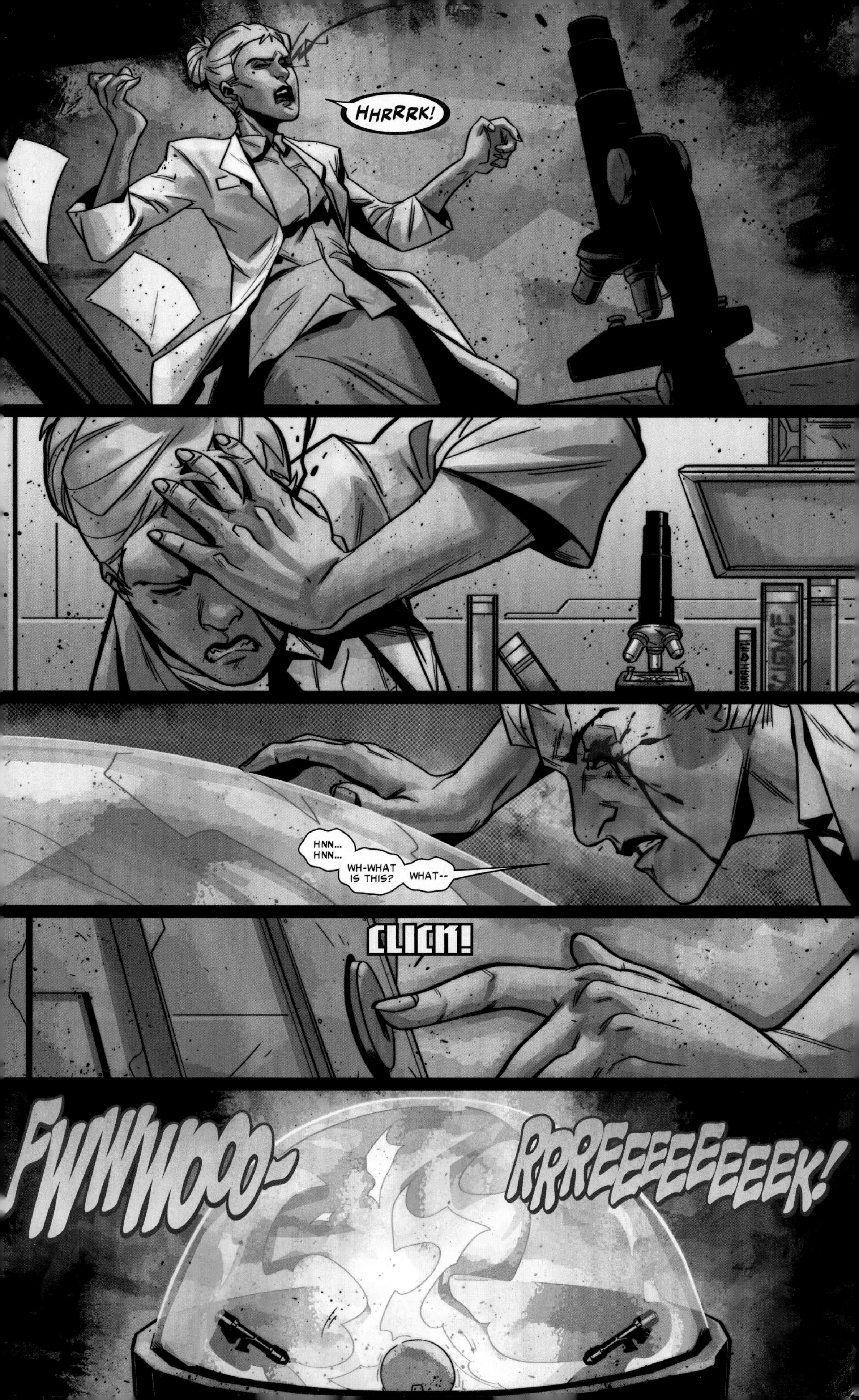
HHRRRK!
SARAH ♥ ...
SCIENCE
HNN... HNN...
WH-WHAT IS THIS?
WHAT--
CLICK!
FWWHOOO-
RRRREEEEEEEEEK!

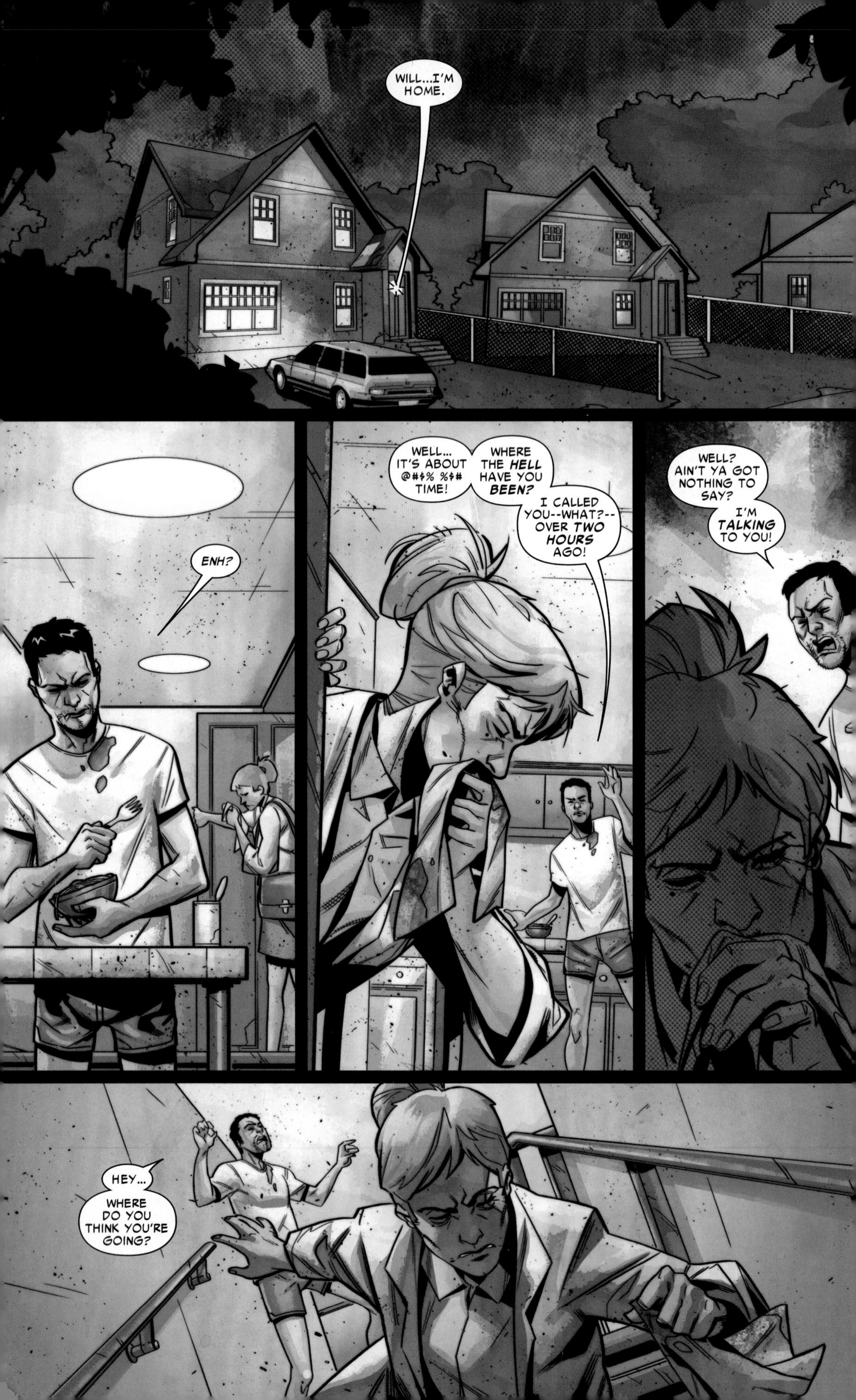
WILL...I'M HOME.
ENH?
WELL... IT'S ABOUT @#$% %$# TIME!
WHERE THE HELL HAVE YOU BEEN?
I CALLED YOU--WHAT?--OVER TWO HOURS AGO!
WELL? AIN'T YA GOT NOTHING TO SAY?
I'M TALKING TO YOU!
HEY...
WHERE DO YOU THINK YOU'RE GOING?

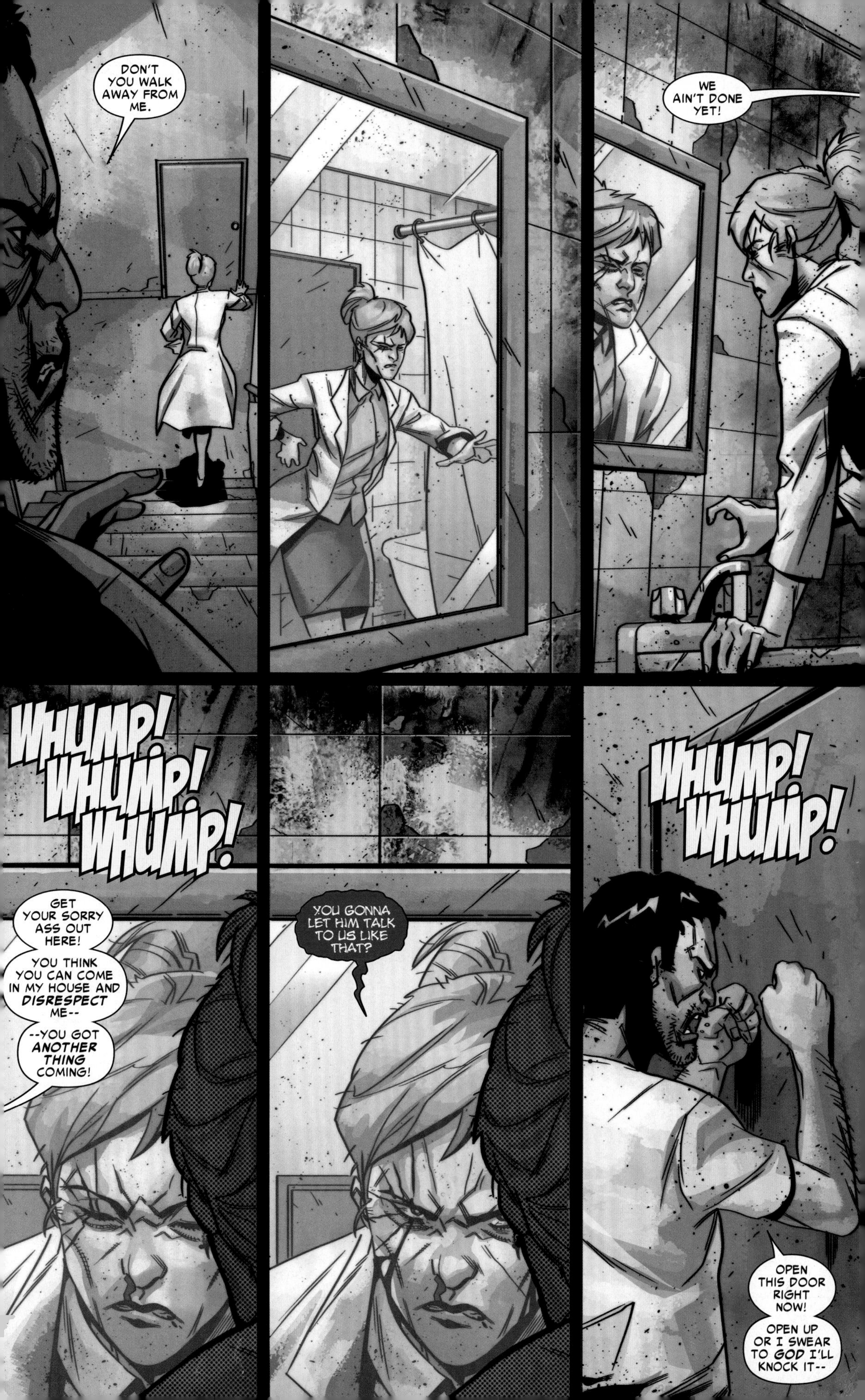
DON'T YOU WALK AWAY FROM ME.
WE AIN'T DONE YET!
WHUMP! WHUMP! WHUMP!
GET YOUR SORRY ASS OUT HERE!
YOU THINK YOU CAN COME IN MY HOUSE AND DISRESPECT ME--
--YOU GOT ANOTHER THING COMING!
YOU GONNA LET HIM TALK TO US LIKE THAT?
WHUMP! WHUMP!
OPEN THIS DOOR RIGHT NOW!
OPEN UP OR I SWEAR TO GOD I'LL KNOCK IT--

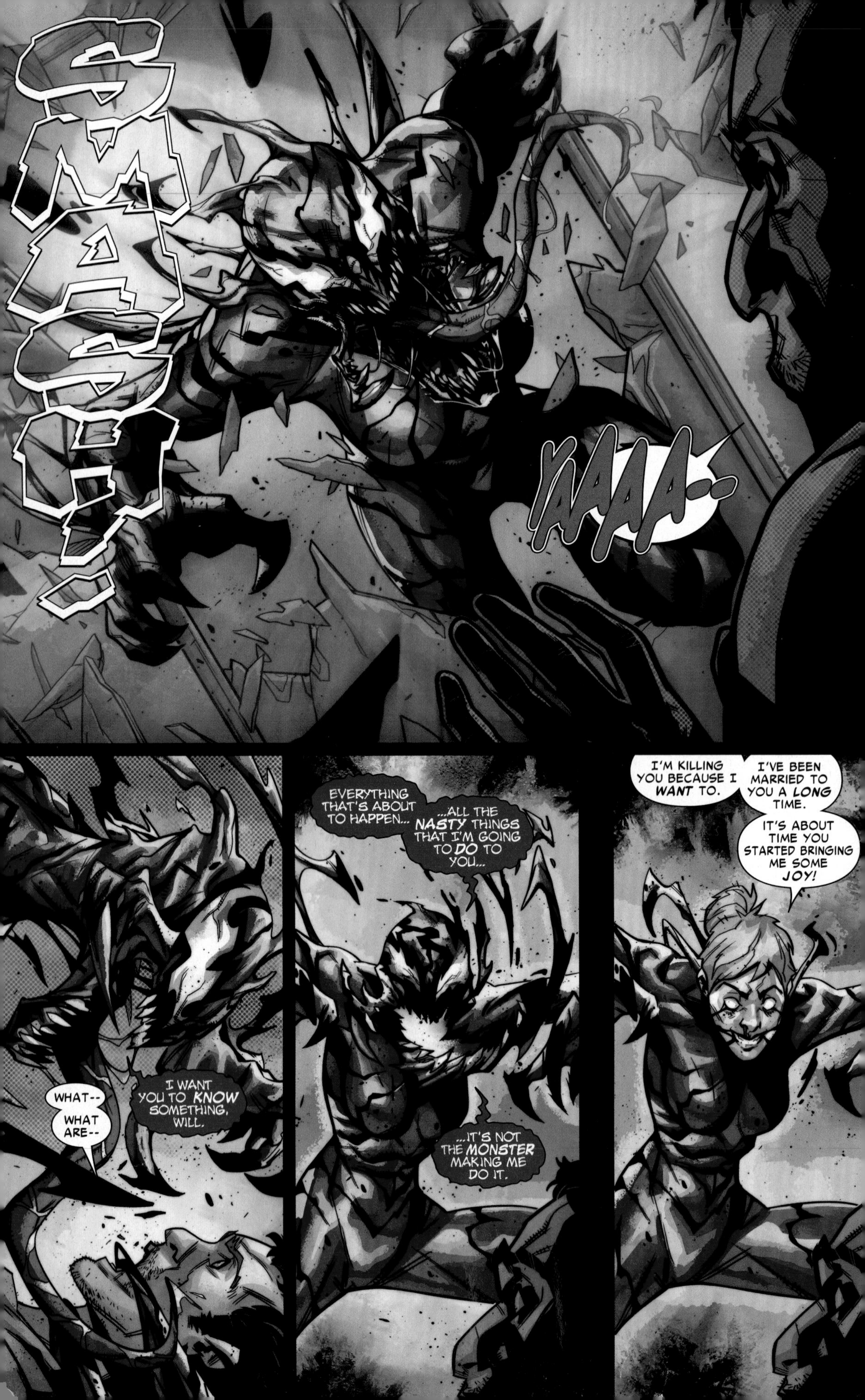
SMASH!
YAAAA--
WHAT--
WHAT ARE--
I WANT YOU TO KNOW SOMETHING, WILL.
EVERYTHING THAT'S ABOUT TO HAPPEN...
...ALL THE NASTY THINGS THAT I'M GOING TO DO TO YOU...
...IT'S NOT THE MONSTER MAKING ME DO IT.
I'M KILLING YOU BECAUSE I WANT TO.
I'VE BEEN MARRIED TO YOU A LONG TIME.
IT'S ABOUT TIME YOU STARTED BRINGING ME SOME JOY!

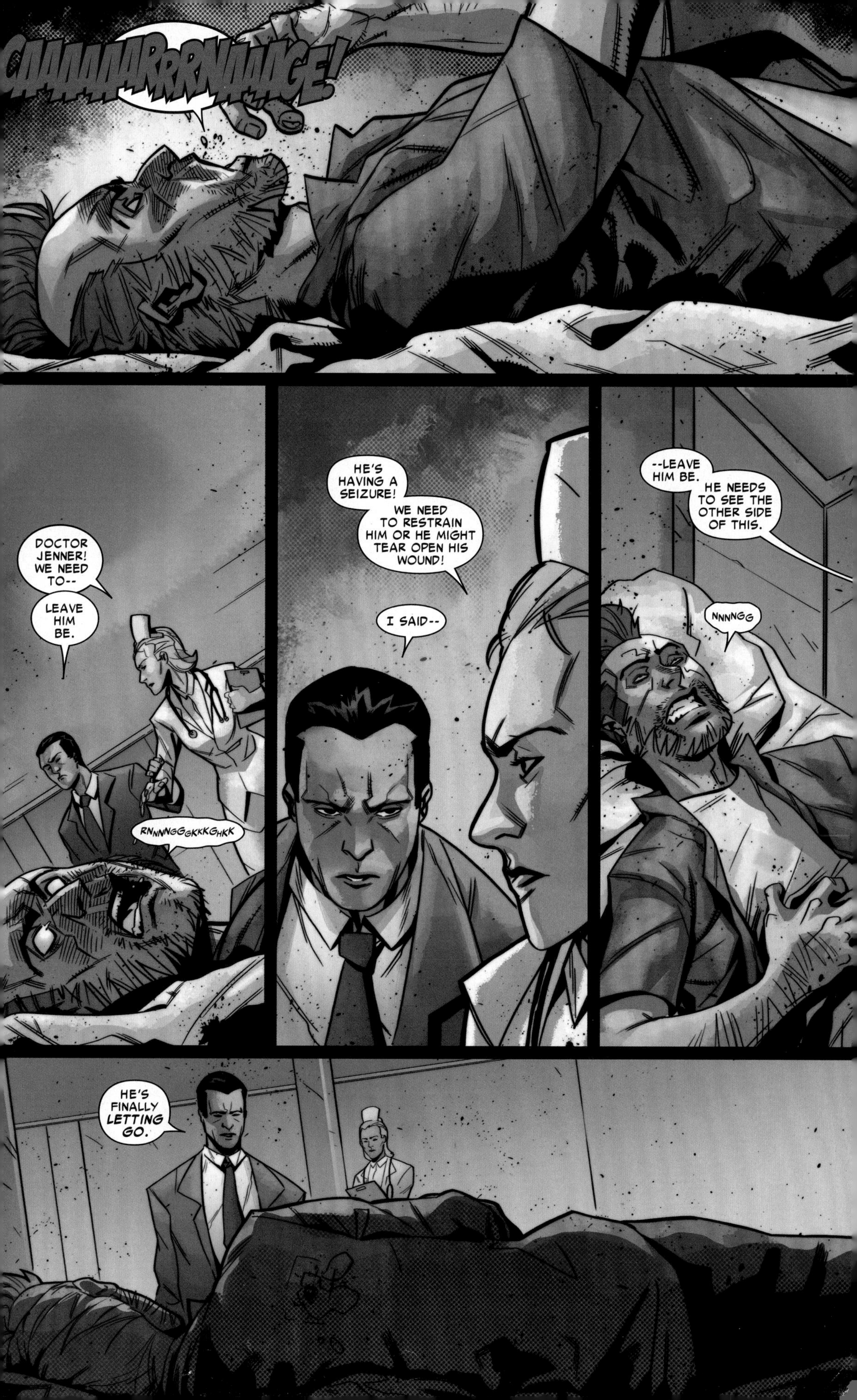
GAAAAARRRNAAAGE!
DOCTOR JENNER! WE NEED TO--
LEAVE HIM BE.
RNNNNGGGKKKGHKK
HE'S HAVING A SEIZURE!
WE NEED TO RESTRAIN HIM OR HE MIGHT TEAR OPEN HIS WOUND!
I SAID--
--LEAVE HIM BE.
HE NEEDS TO SEE THE OTHER SIDE OF THIS.
NNNNGG
HE'S FINALLY LETTING GO.

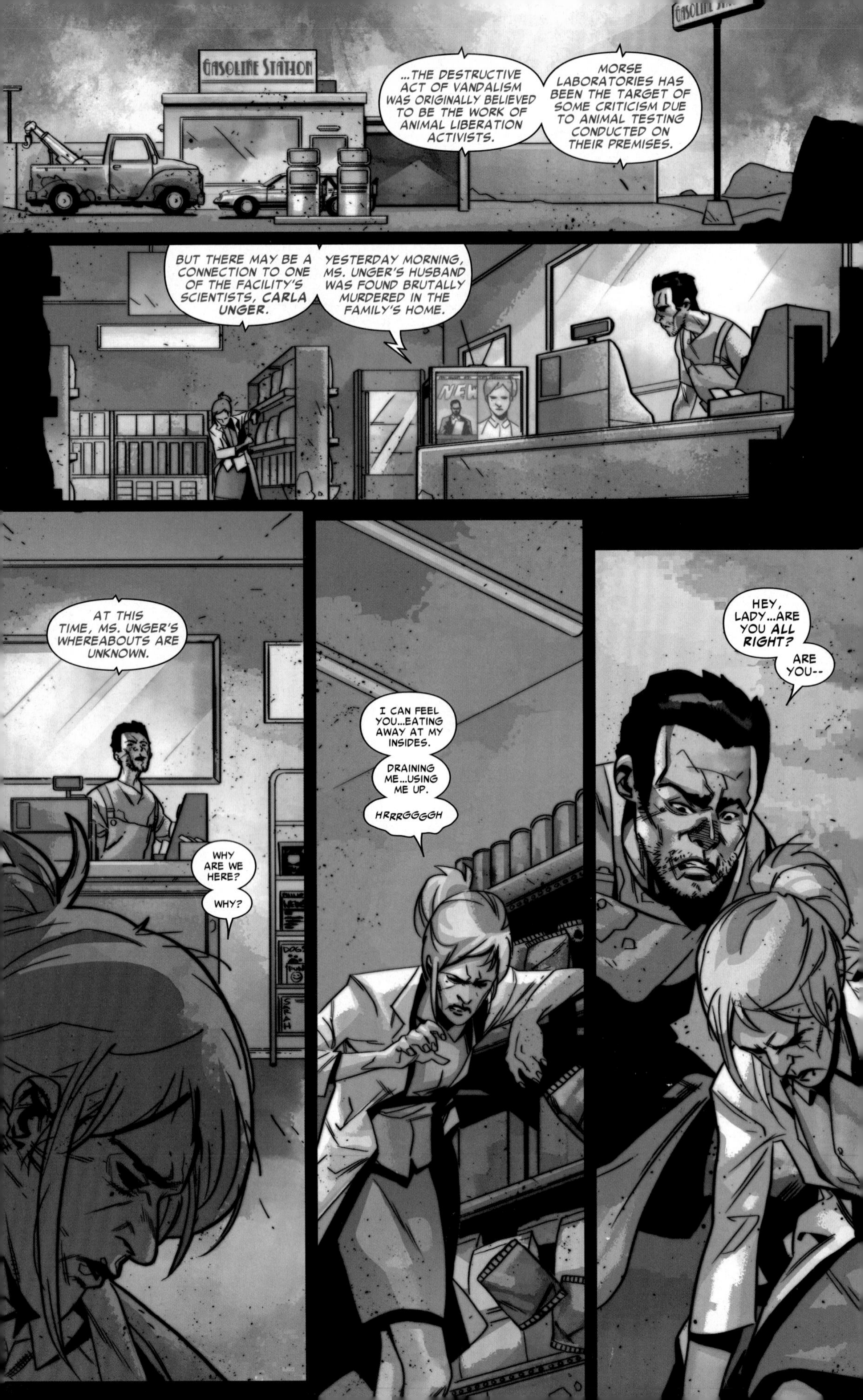

GASOLINE STATION
...THE DESTRUCTIVE ACT OF VANDALISM WAS ORIGINALLY BELIEVED TO BE THE WORK OF ANIMAL LIBERATION ACTIVISTS.
MORSE LABORATORIES HAS BEEN THE TARGET OF SOME CRITICISM DUE TO ANIMAL TESTING CONDUCTED ON THEIR PREMISES.
BUT THERE MAY BE A CONNECTION TO ONE OF THE FACILITY'S SCIENTISTS, CARLA UNGER.
YESTERDAY MORNING, MS. UNGER'S HUSBAND WAS FOUND BRUTALLY MURDERED IN THE FAMILY'S HOME.
NEW
AT THIS TIME, MS. UNGER'S WHEREABOUTS ARE UNKNOWN.
WHY ARE WE HERE?
WHY?
I CAN FEEL YOU...EATING AWAY AT MY INSIDES.
DRAINING ME...USING ME UP.
HRRRGGGGH
HEY, LADY...ARE YOU ALL RIGHT?
ARE YOU--

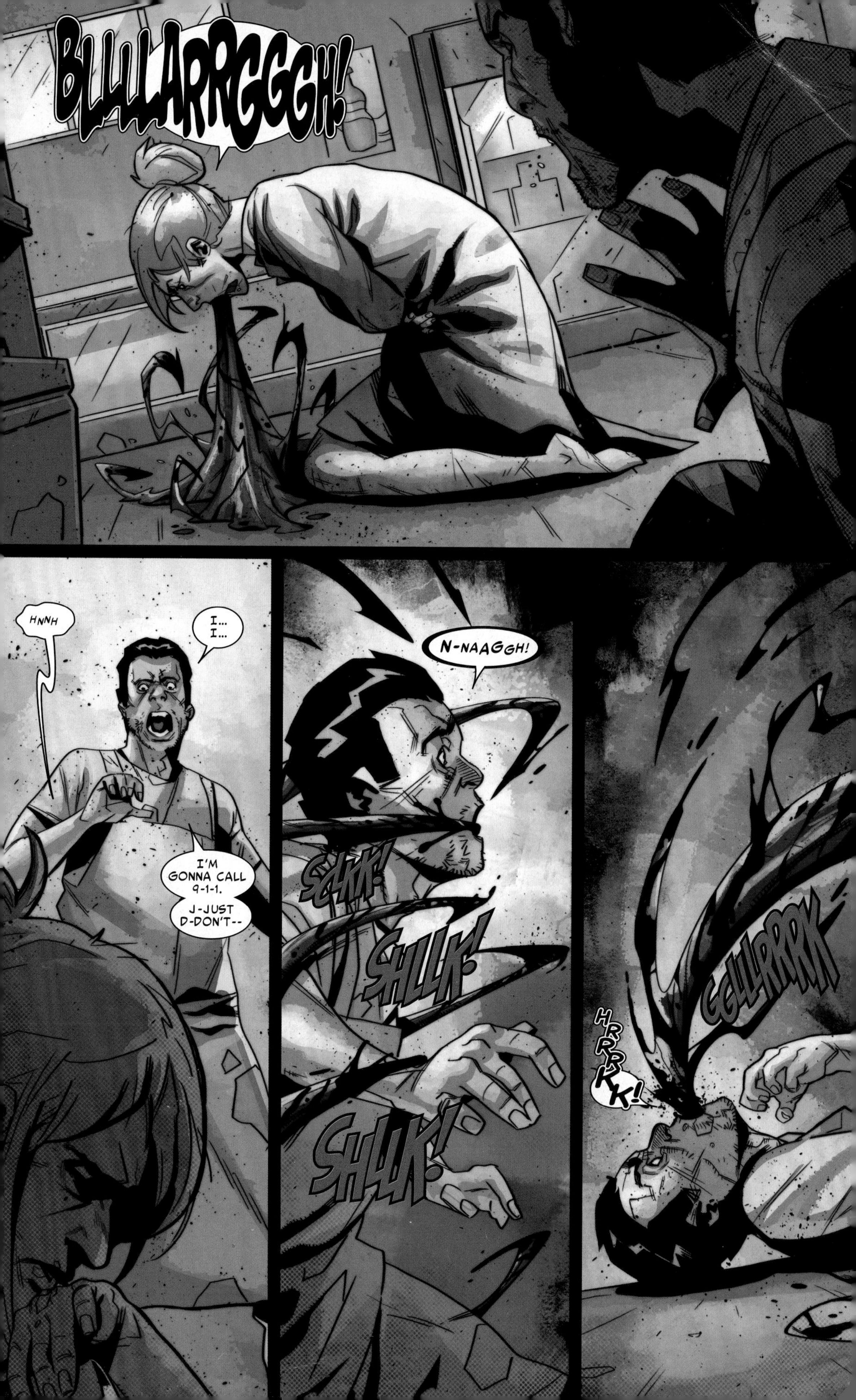
BLLLARRGGGH!
HNNH
I... I...
I'M GONNA CALL 9-1-1. J-JUST D-DON'T--
N-NAAGGH!
SCLKK!
SHLLK!
SHLLK!
GCLLRRRK
HRRRKK!

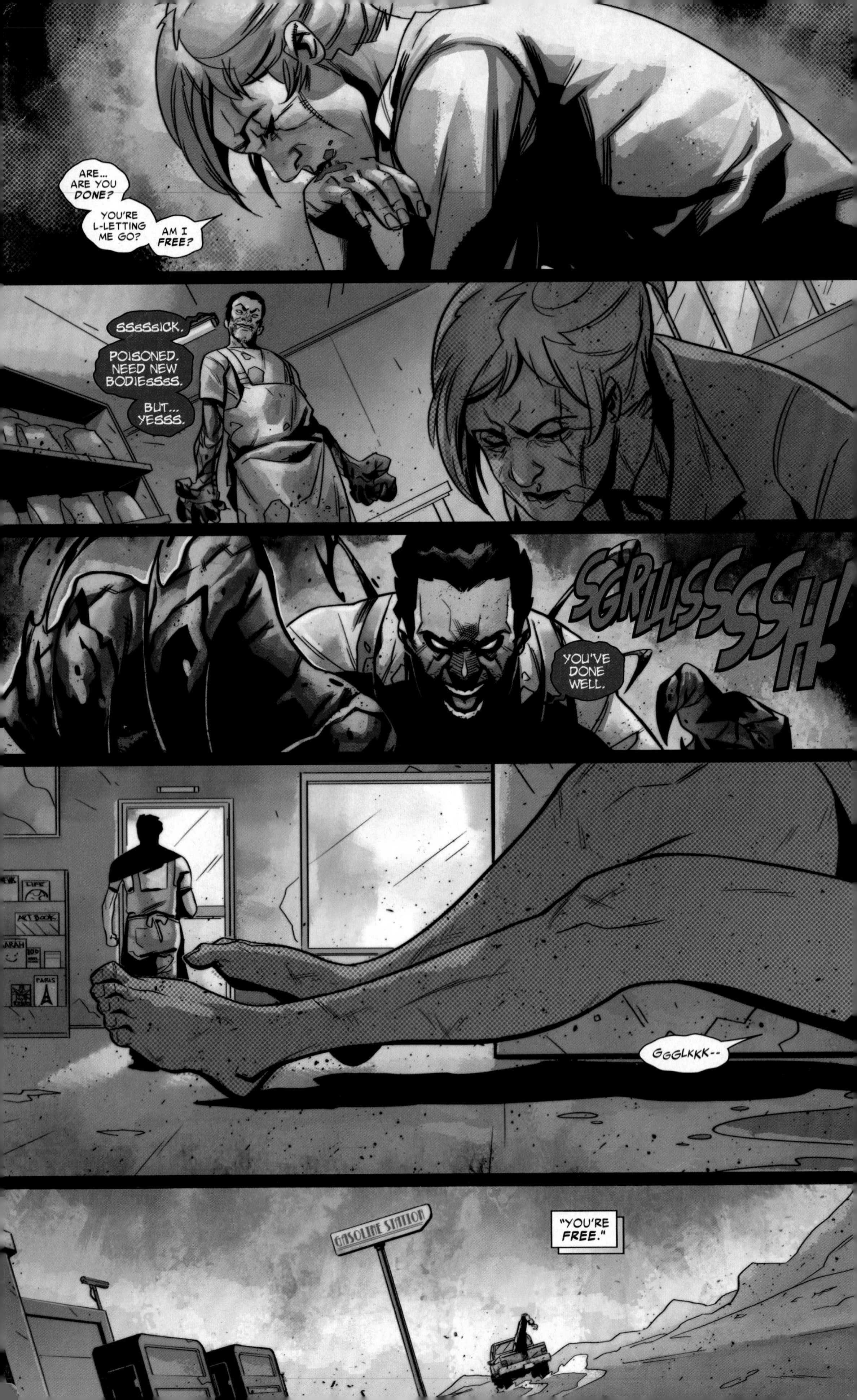
ARE... ARE YOU DONE?
YOU'RE L-LETTING ME GO?
AM I FREE?
SSSSSICK.
POISONED. NEED NEW BODIESSSS.
BUT... YESSS.
SGRLLLSSSSH!
YOU'VE DONE WELL.
GGGLKKK--
GASOLINE STATION
"YOU'RE FREE."

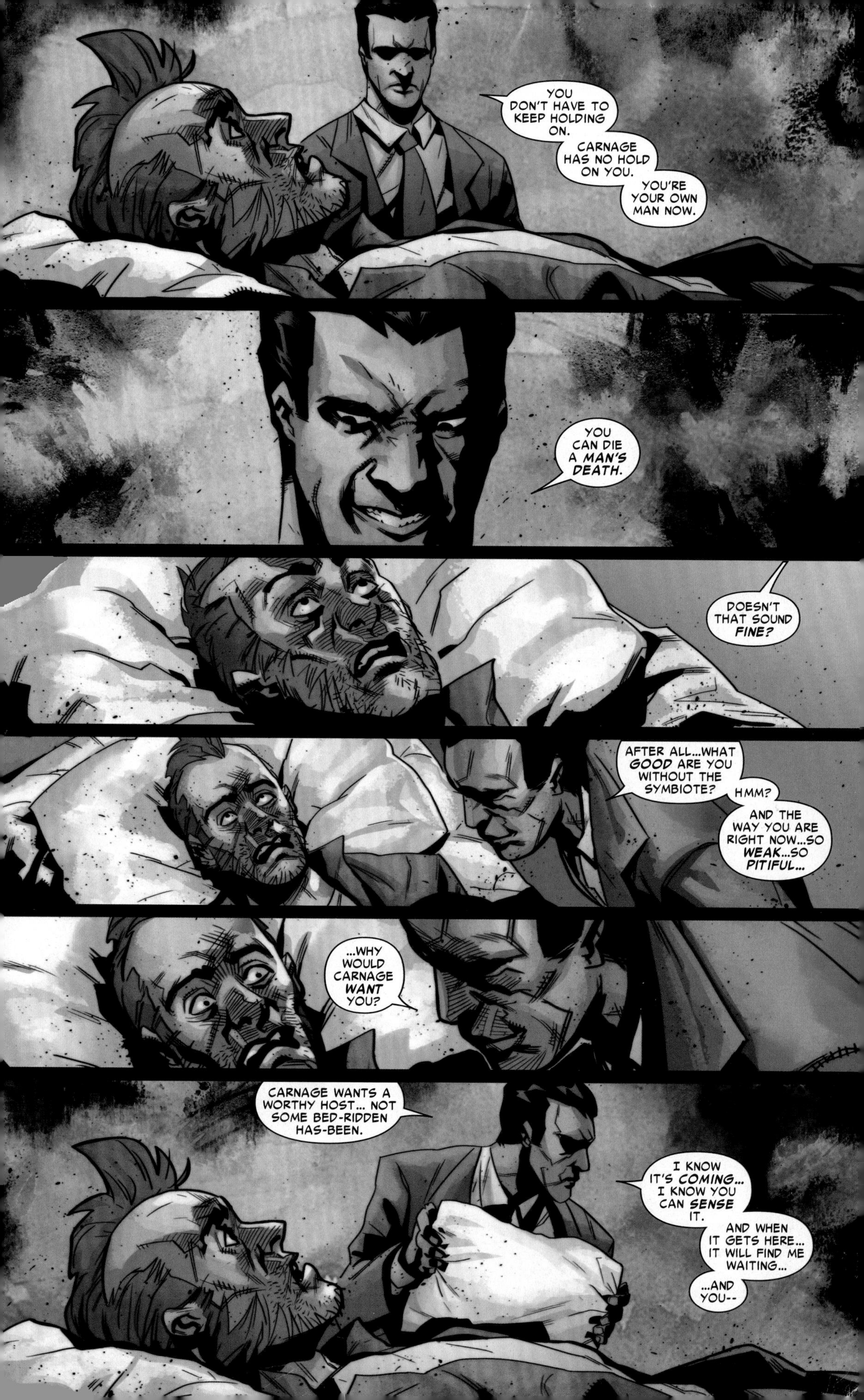
YOU DON'T HAVE TO KEEP HOLDING ON.
CARNAGE HAS NO HOLD ON YOU.
YOU'RE YOUR OWN MAN NOW.
YOU CAN DIE A MAN'S DEATH.
DOESN'T THAT SOUND FINE?
AFTER ALL...WHAT GOOD ARE YOU WITHOUT THE SYMBIOTE?
HMM?
AND THE WAY YOU ARE RIGHT NOW...SO WEAK...SO PITIFUL...
...WHY WOULD CARNAGE WANT YOU?
CARNAGE WANTS A WORTHY HOST... NOT SOME BED-RIDDEN HAS-BEEN.
I KNOW IT'S COMING... I KNOW YOU CAN SENSE IT.
AND WHEN IT GETS HERE... IT WILL FIND ME WAITING...
...AND YOU--

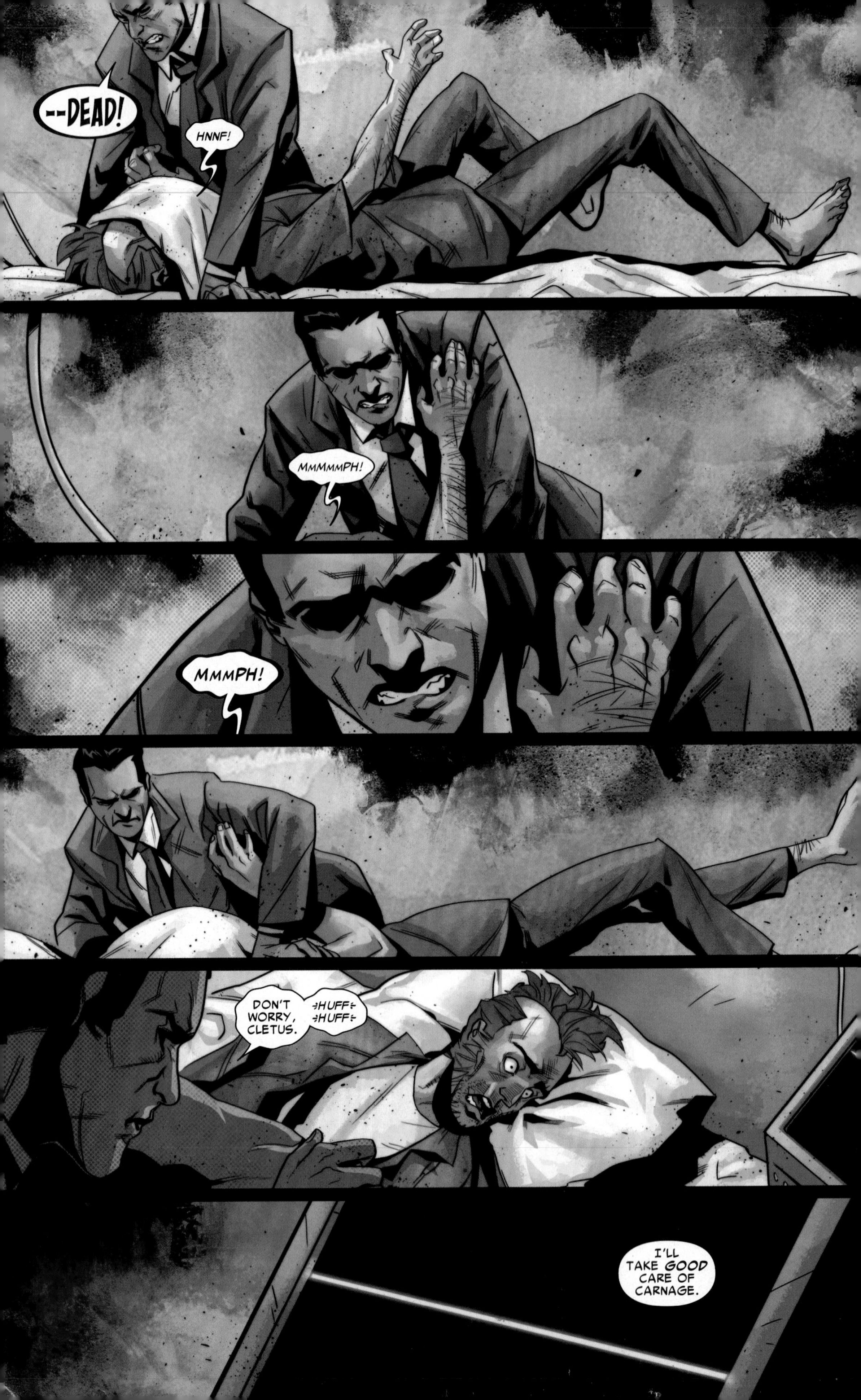
--DEAD!
HNNF!
MMMMMPH!
MMMPH!
DON'T WORRY, CLETUS.
≑HUFF≑ ≑HUFF≑
I'LL TAKE GOOD CARE OF CARNAGE.

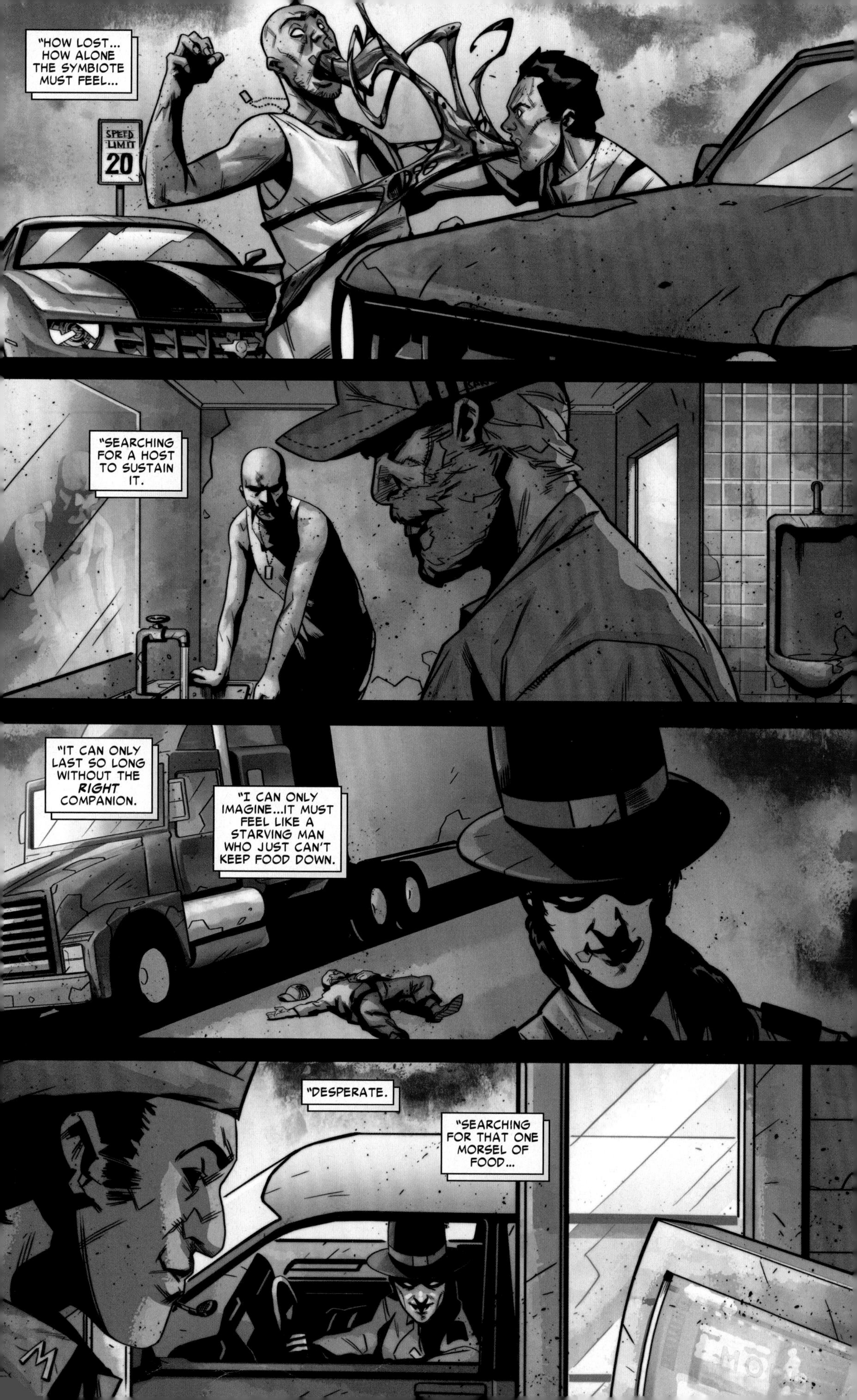
"HOW LOST... HOW ALONE THE SYMBIOTE MUST FEEL...
SPEED LIMIT 20
"SEARCHING FOR A HOST TO SUSTAIN IT.
"IT CAN ONLY LAST SO LONG WITHOUT THE *RIGHT* COMPANION.
"I CAN ONLY IMAGINE...IT MUST FEEL LIKE A STARVING MAN WHO JUST CAN'T KEEP FOOD DOWN.
"DESPERATE.
"SEARCHING FOR THAT ONE MORSEL OF FOOD...

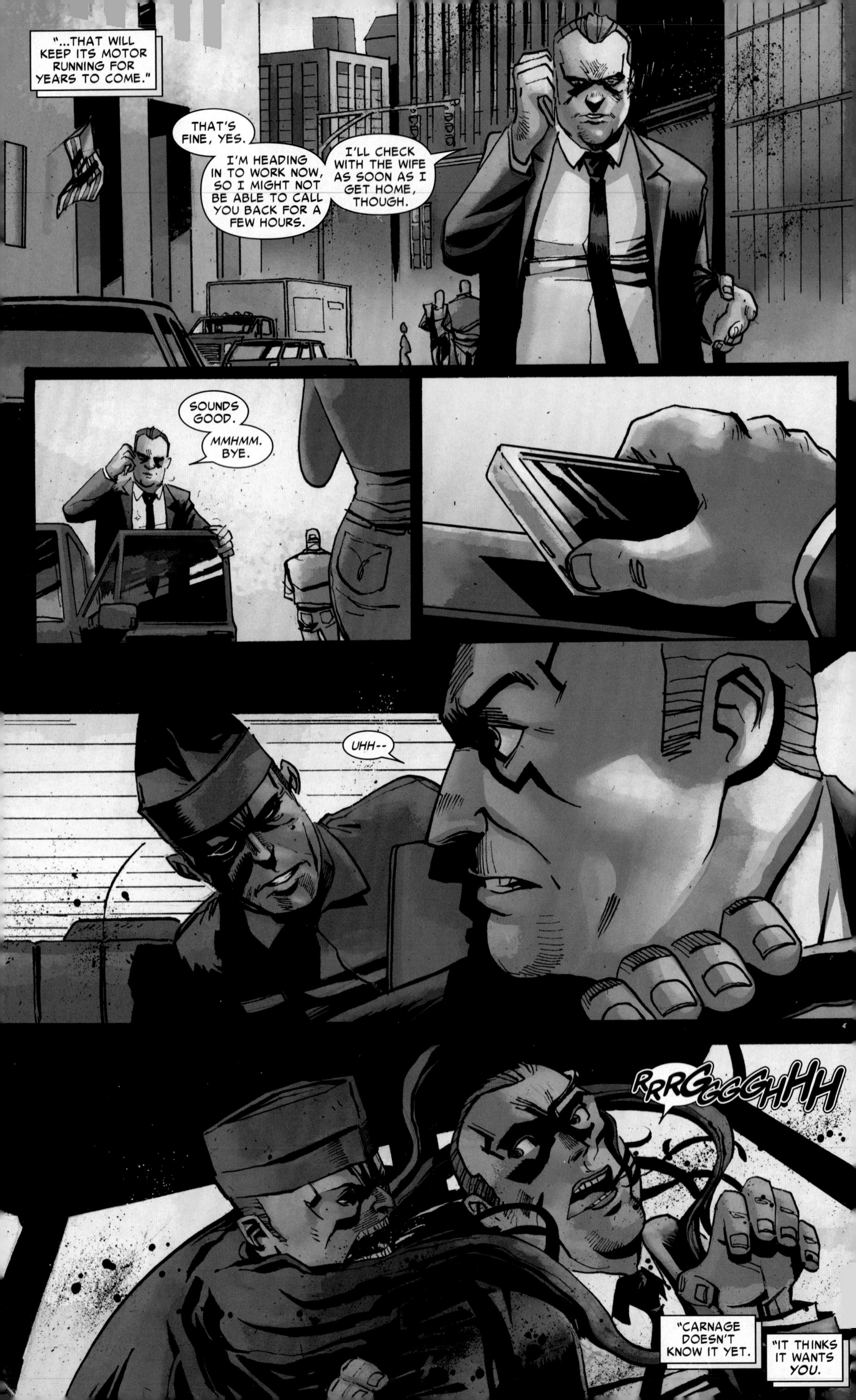
"...THAT WILL KEEP ITS MOTOR RUNNING FOR YEARS TO COME."
THAT'S FINE, YES.
I'M HEADING IN TO WORK NOW, SO I MIGHT NOT BE ABLE TO CALL YOU BACK FOR A FEW HOURS.
I'LL CHECK WITH THE WIFE AS SOON AS I GET HOME, THOUGH.
SOUNDS GOOD.
MMHMM. BYE.
UHH--
RRRGGGGHHH
"CARNAGE DOESN'T KNOW IT YET.
"IT THINKS IT WANTS YOU.

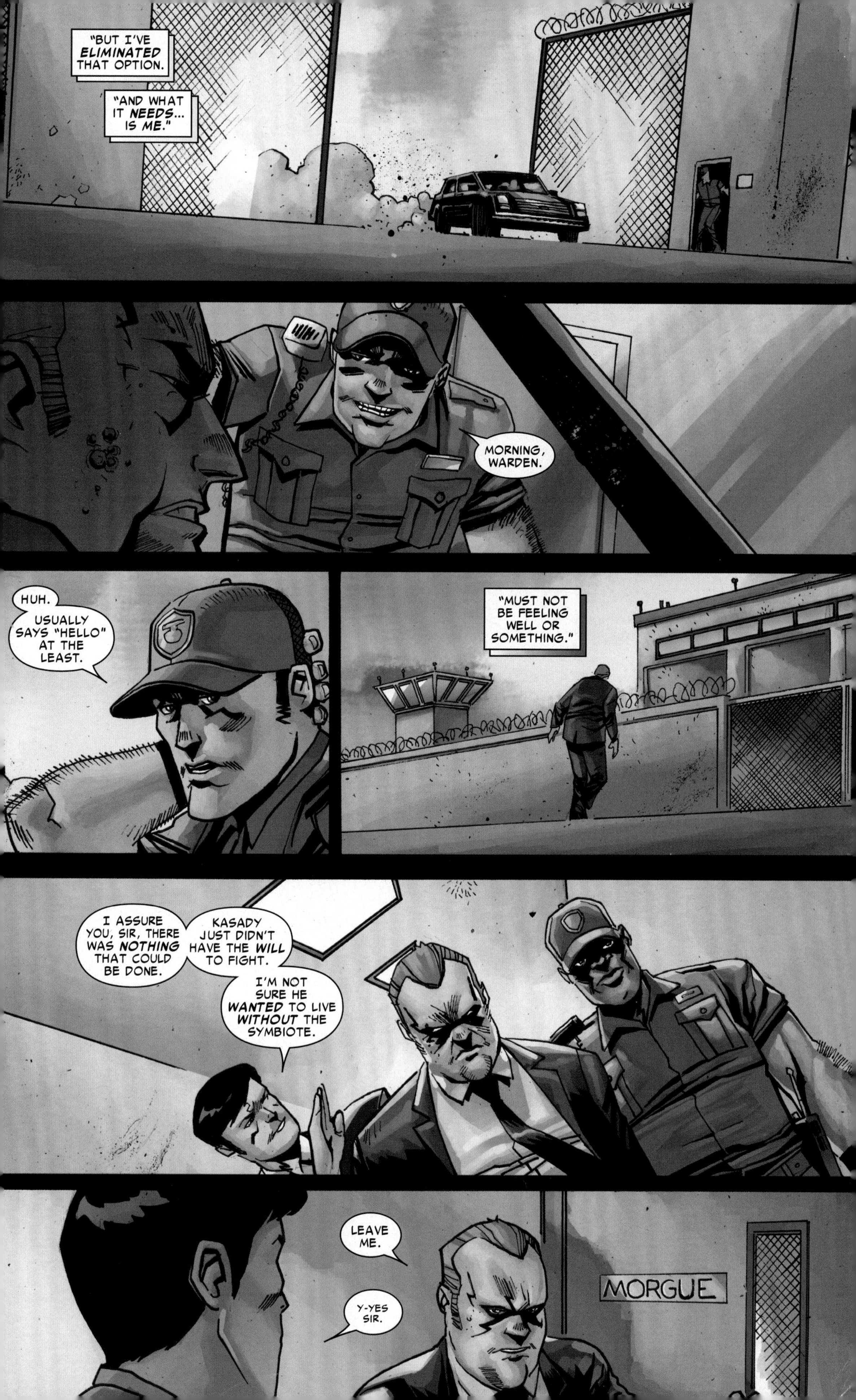
"BUT I'VE ELIMINATED THAT OPTION.
"AND WHAT IT NEEDS... IS ME."
MORNING, WARDEN.
HUH.
USUALLY SAYS "HELLO" AT THE LEAST.
"MUST NOT BE FEELING WELL OR SOMETHING."
I ASSURE YOU, SIR, THERE WAS NOTHING THAT COULD BE DONE.
KASADY JUST DIDN'T HAVE THE WILL TO FIGHT.
I'M NOT SURE HE WANTED TO LIVE WITHOUT THE SYMBIOTE.
LEAVE ME.
Y-YES SIR.
MORGUE

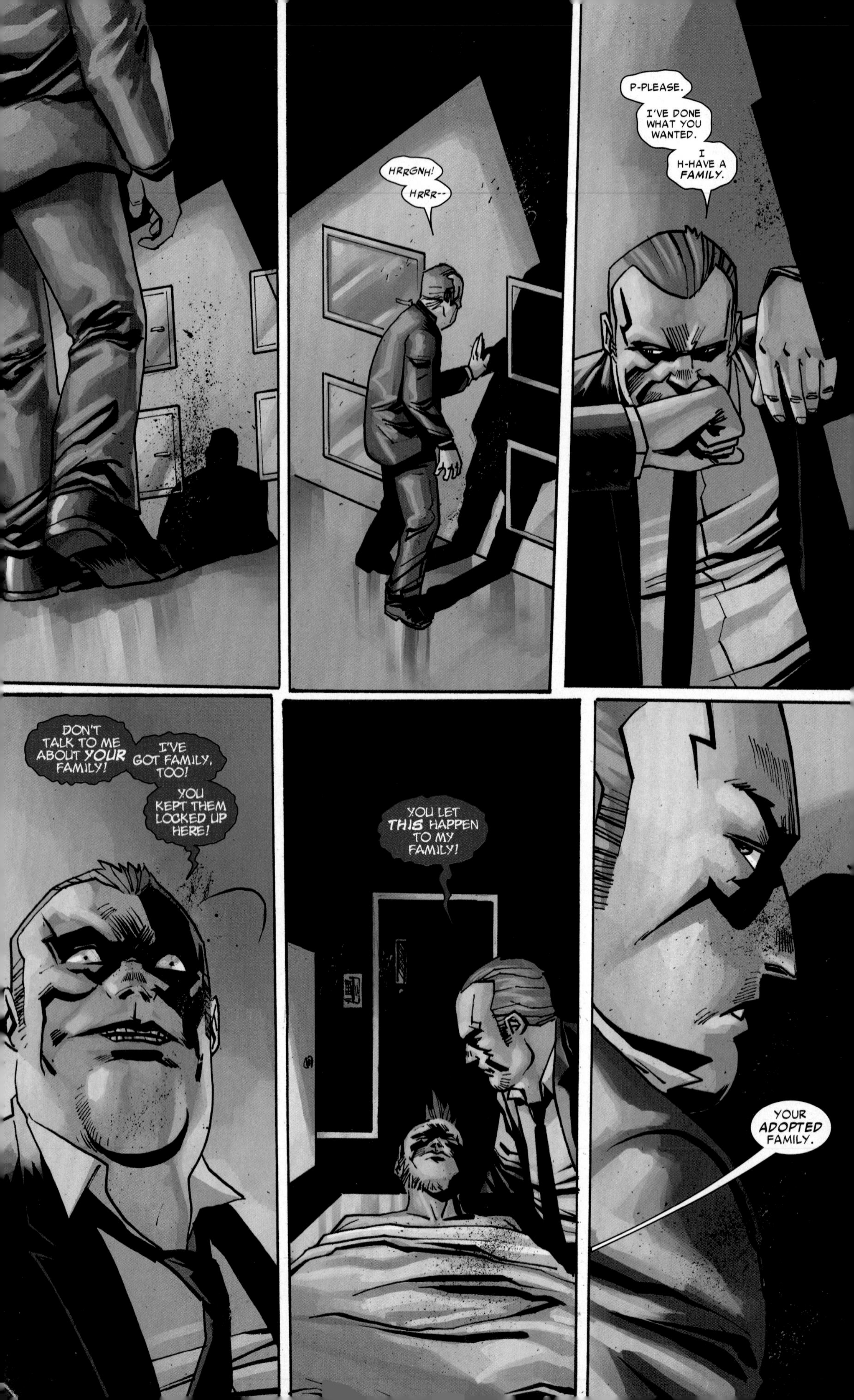
HRRGNH!
HRRR--
P-PLEASE.
I'VE DONE WHAT YOU WANTED.
I H-HAVE A FAMILY.
DON'T TALK TO ME ABOUT YOUR FAMILY!
I'VE GOT FAMILY, TOO!
YOU KEPT THEM LOCKED UP HERE!
YOU LET THIS HAPPEN TO MY FAMILY!
YOUR ADOPTED FAMILY.

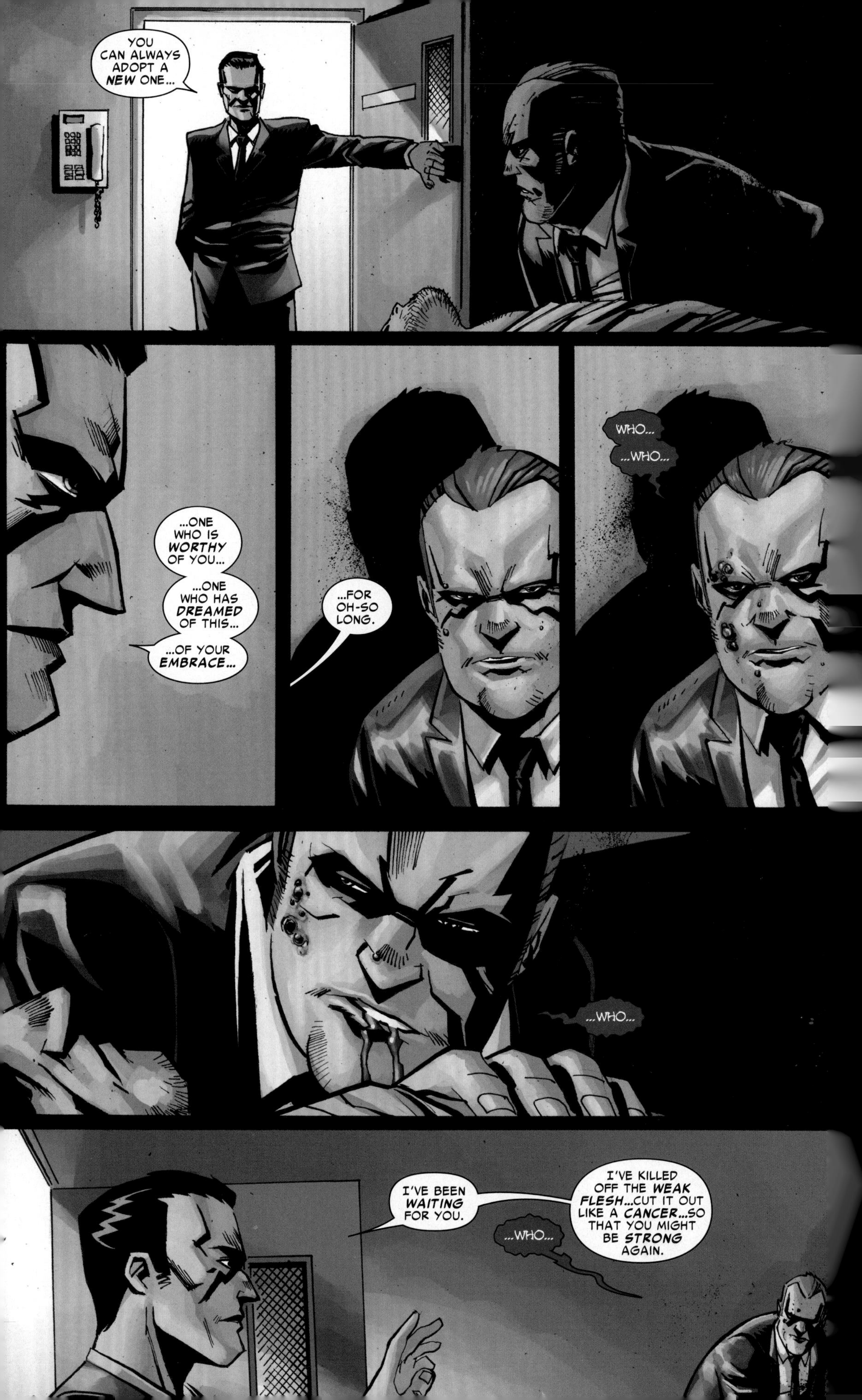
YOU CAN ALWAYS ADOPT A NEW ONE...
...ONE WHO IS WORTHY OF YOU...
...ONE WHO HAS DREAMED OF THIS...
...OF YOUR EMBRACE...
...FOR OH-SO LONG.
WHO...
...WHO...
...WHO...
I'VE BEEN WAITING FOR YOU.
I'VE KILLED OFF THE WEAK FLESH...CUT IT OUT LIKE A CANCER...SO THAT YOU MIGHT BE STRONG AGAIN.
...WHO...

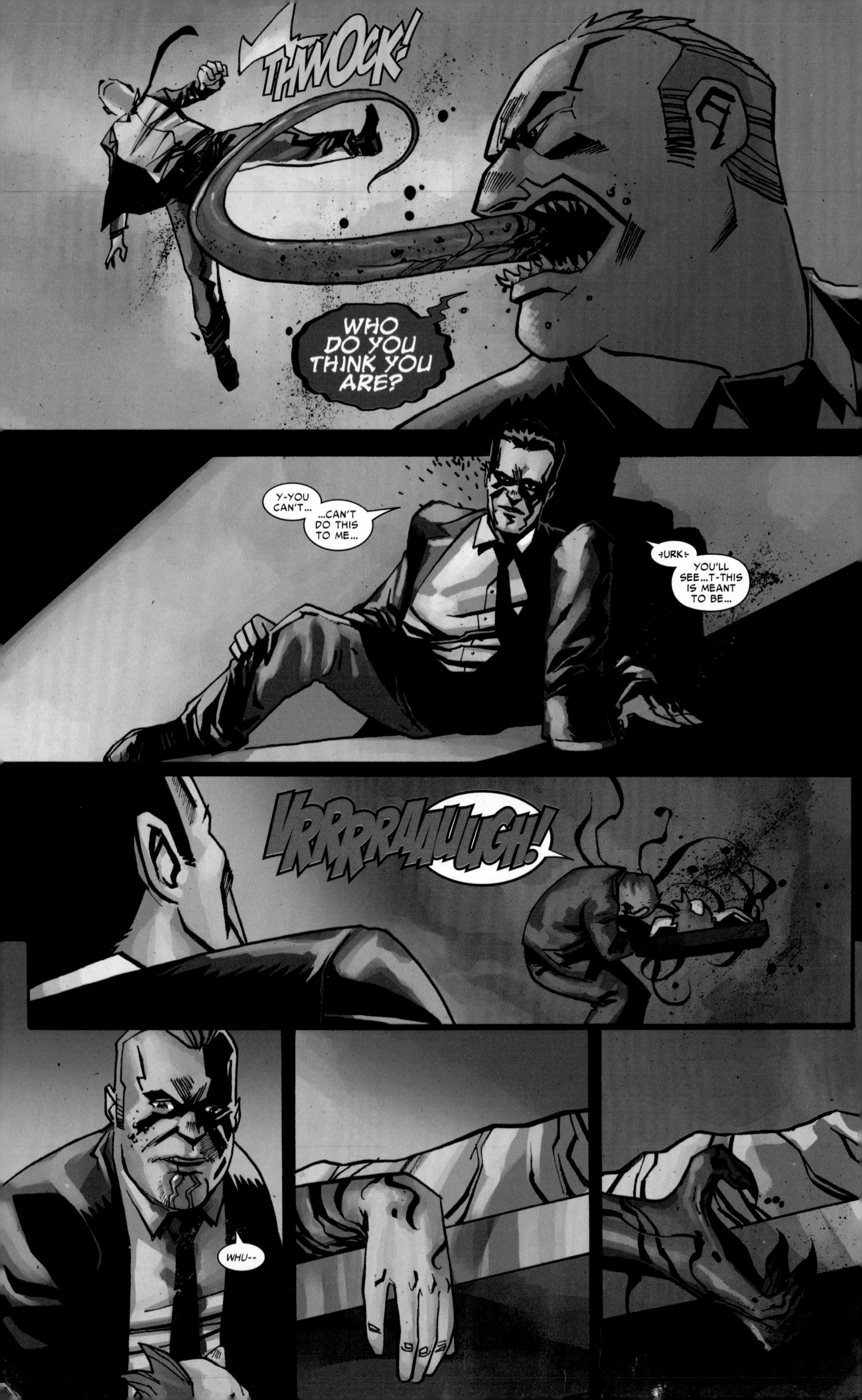
THWOCK!
WHO DO YOU THINK YOU ARE?
Y-YOU CAN'T...
...CAN'T DO THIS TO ME...
URK
YOU'LL SEE...T-THIS IS MEANT TO BE...
VRRRRAAUUGH!
WHU--

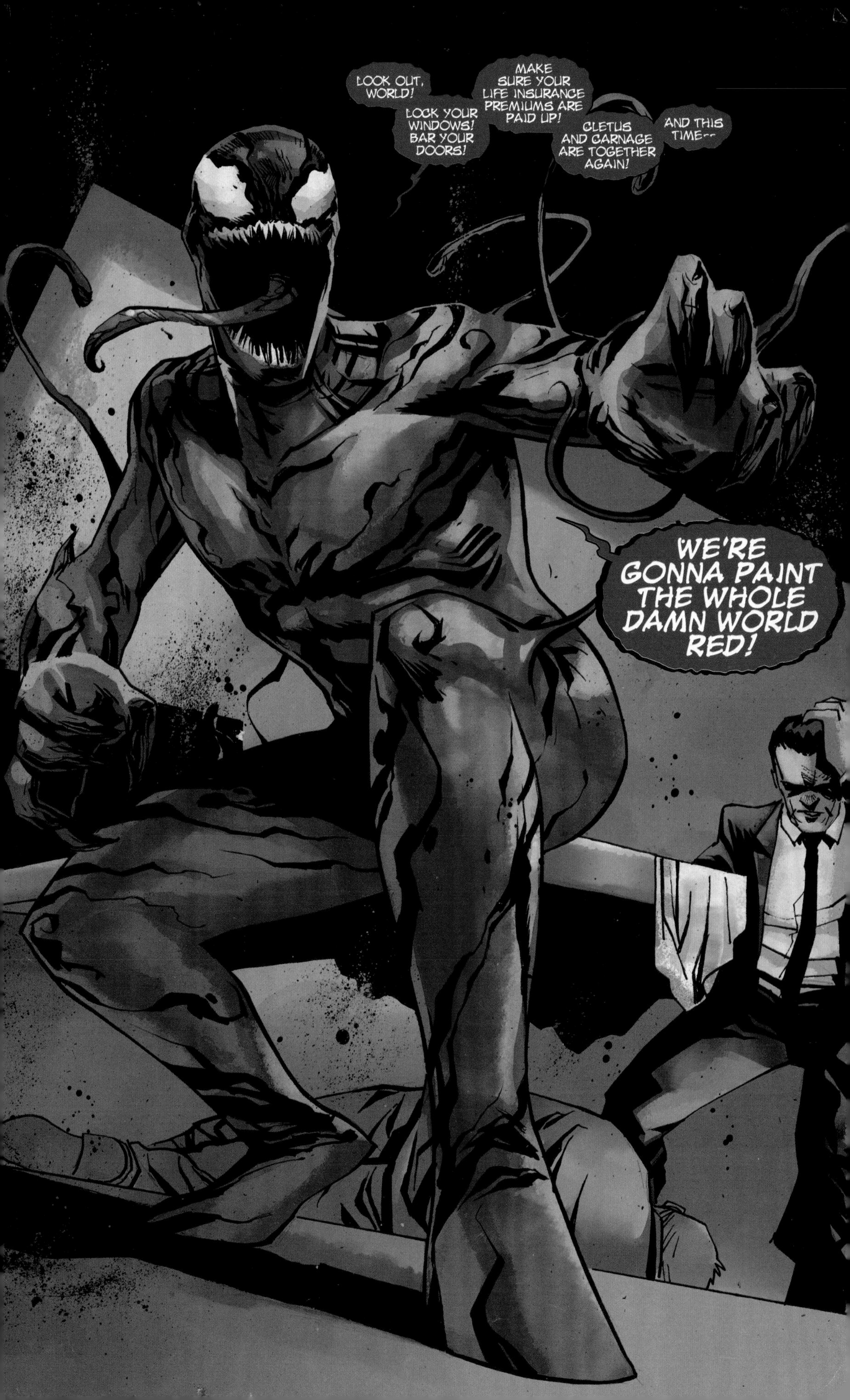
LOOK OUT, WORLD!
LOCK YOUR WINDOWS! BAR YOUR DOORS!
MAKE SURE YOUR LIFE INSURANCE PREMIUMS ARE PAID UP!
CLETUS AND CARNAGE ARE TOGETHER AGAIN!
AND THIS TIME--
WE'RE GONNA PAINT THE WHOLE DAMN WORLD RED!

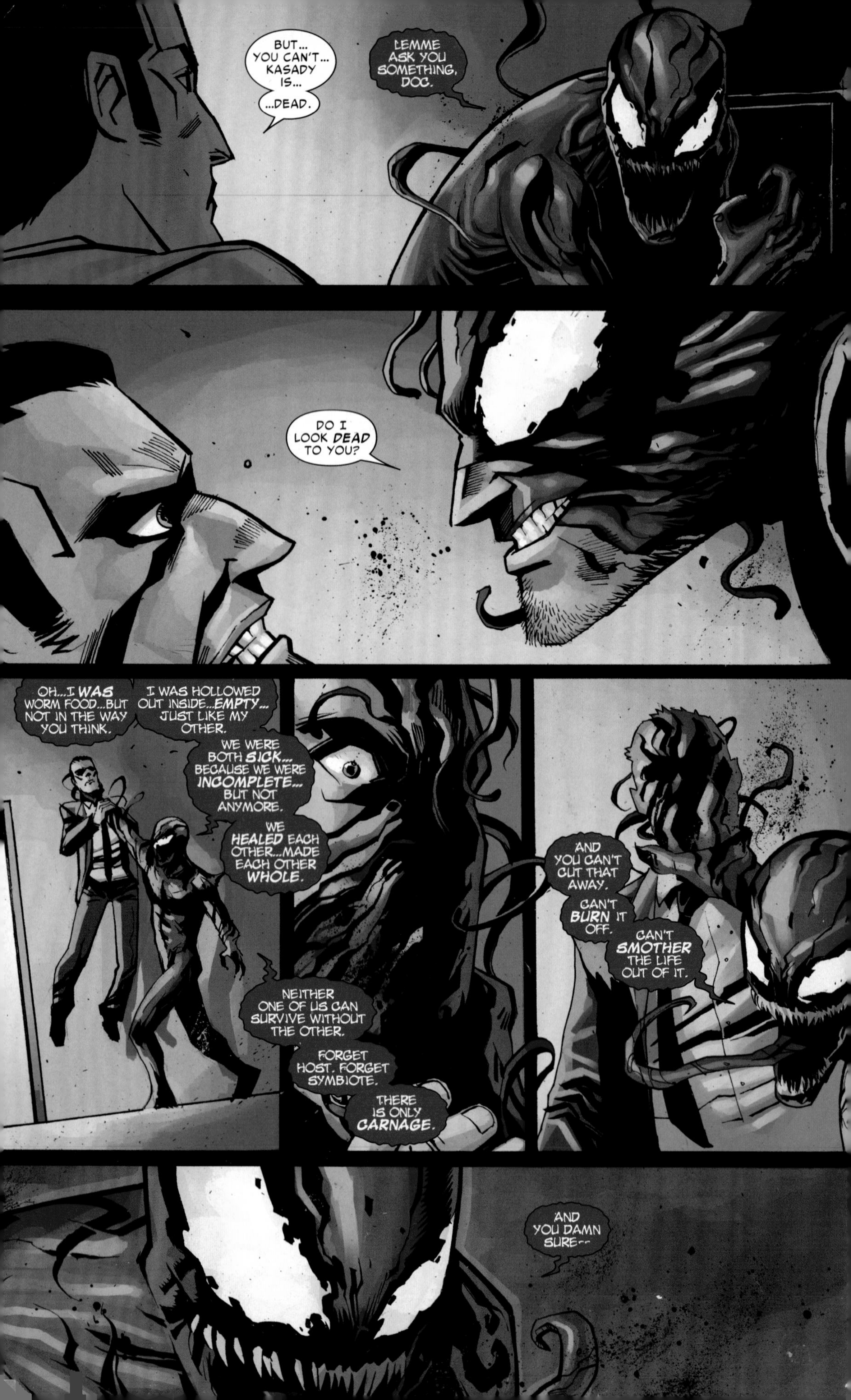

BUT... YOU CAN'T... KASADY IS...
...DEAD.
LEMME ASK YOU SOMETHING, DOC.
DO I LOOK DEAD TO YOU?
OH...I WAS WORM FOOD...BUT NOT IN THE WAY YOU THINK.
I WAS HOLLOWED OUT INSIDE...EMPTY... JUST LIKE MY OTHER.
WE WERE BOTH SICK... BECAUSE WE WERE INCOMPLETE... BUT NOT ANYMORE.
WE HEALED EACH OTHER...MADE EACH OTHER WHOLE.
NEITHER ONE OF US CAN SURVIVE WITHOUT THE OTHER.
FORGET HOST. FORGET SYMBIOTE.
THERE IS ONLY CARNAGE.
AND YOU CAN'T CUT THAT AWAY.
CAN'T BURN IT OFF.
CAN'T SMOTHER THE LIFE OUT OF IT.
AND YOU DAMN SURE--

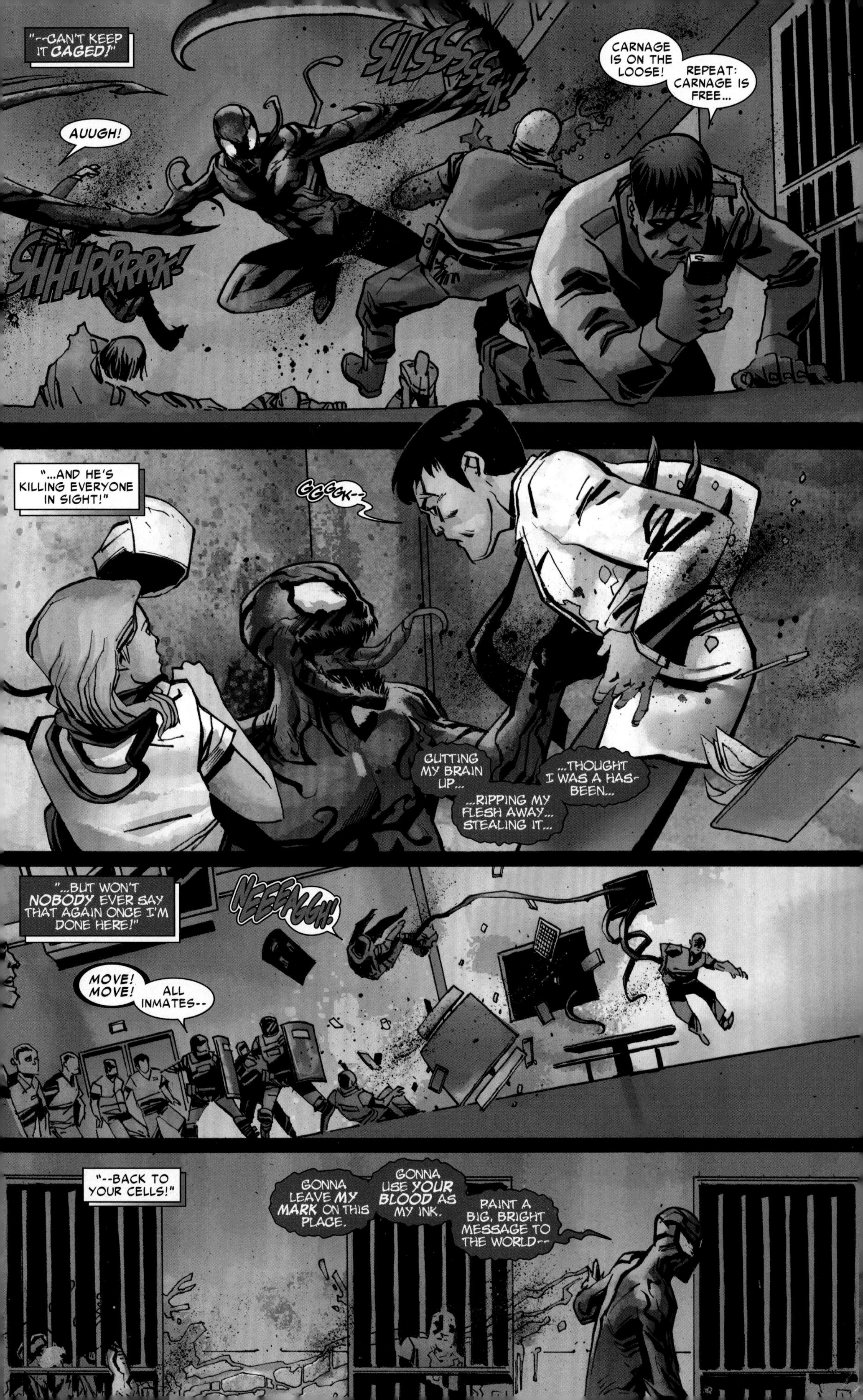
"--CAN'T KEEP IT CAGED!"
SLISSSSSK!
AUUGH!
SHHHRRRRK!
CARNAGE IS ON THE LOOSE!
REPEAT: CARNAGE IS FREE...
"...AND HE'S KILLING EVERYONE IN SIGHT!"
GGGGK--
CUTTING MY BRAIN UP...
...RIPPING MY FLESH AWAY... STEALING IT...
...THOUGHT I WAS A HAS-BEEN...
"...BUT WON'T NOBODY EVER SAY THAT AGAIN ONCE I'M DONE HERE!"
NEEEAGGH!
MOVE! MOVE!
ALL INMATES--
"--BACK TO YOUR CELLS!"
GONNA LEAVE MY MARK ON THIS PLACE.
GONNA USE YOUR BLOOD AS MY INK.
PAINT A BIG, BRIGHT MESSAGE TO THE WORLD--

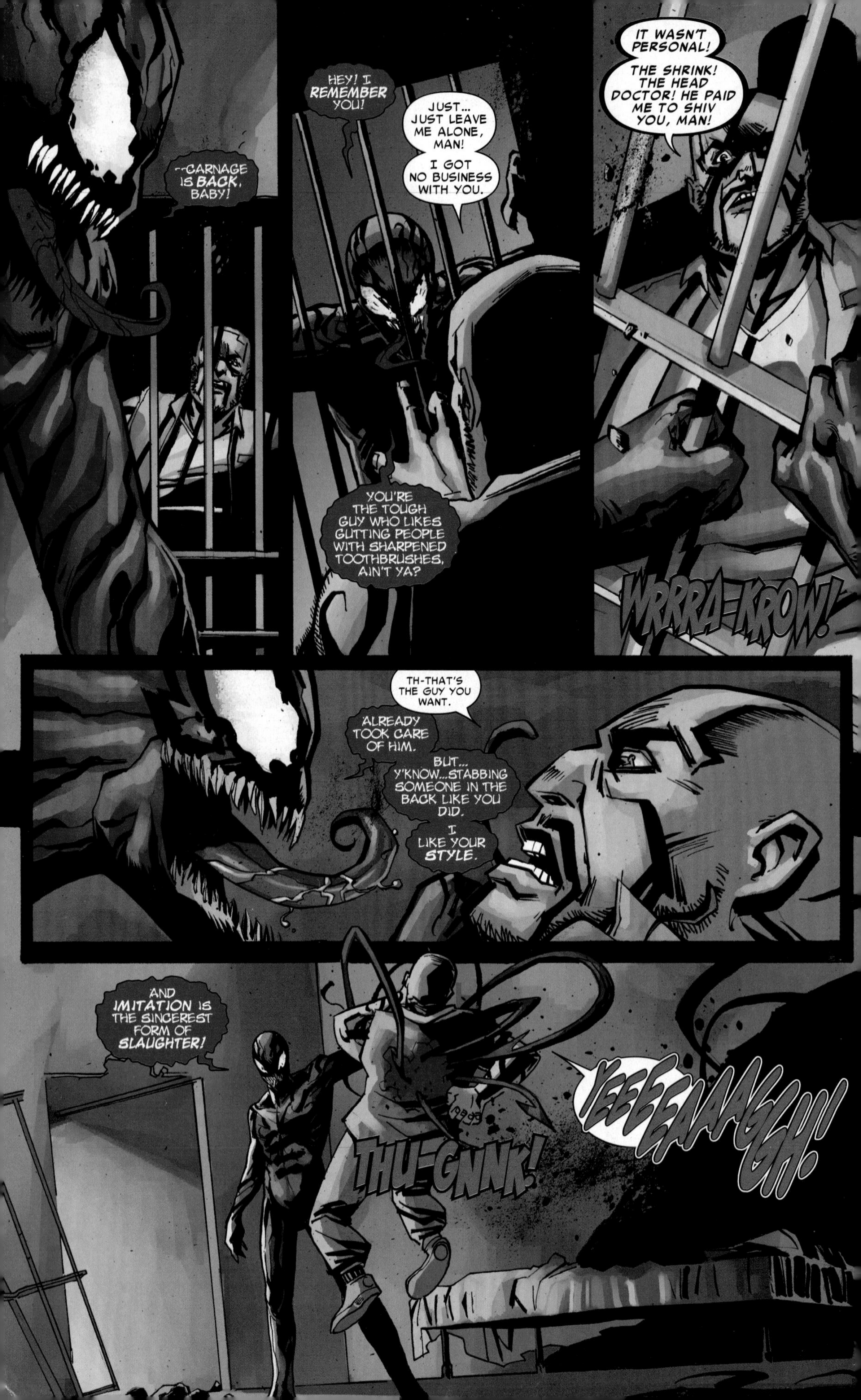
--CARNAGE IS BACK, BABY!
HEY! I REMEMBER YOU!
JUST... JUST LEAVE ME ALONE, MAN!
I GOT NO BUSINESS WITH YOU.
YOU'RE THE TOUGH GUY WHO LIKES GUTTING PEOPLE WITH SHARPENED TOOTHBRUSHES, AIN'T YA?
IT WASN'T PERSONAL!
THE SHRINK! THE HEAD DOCTOR! HE PAID ME TO SHIV YOU, MAN!
WRRRA-KROW!
TH-THAT'S THE GUY YOU WANT.
ALREADY TOOK CARE OF HIM.
BUT... Y'KNOW...STABBING SOMEONE IN THE BACK LIKE YOU DID.
I LIKE YOUR STYLE.
AND IMITATION IS THE SINCEREST FORM OF SLAUGHTER!
THU-GNNK!
YEEEEAAAGGH!

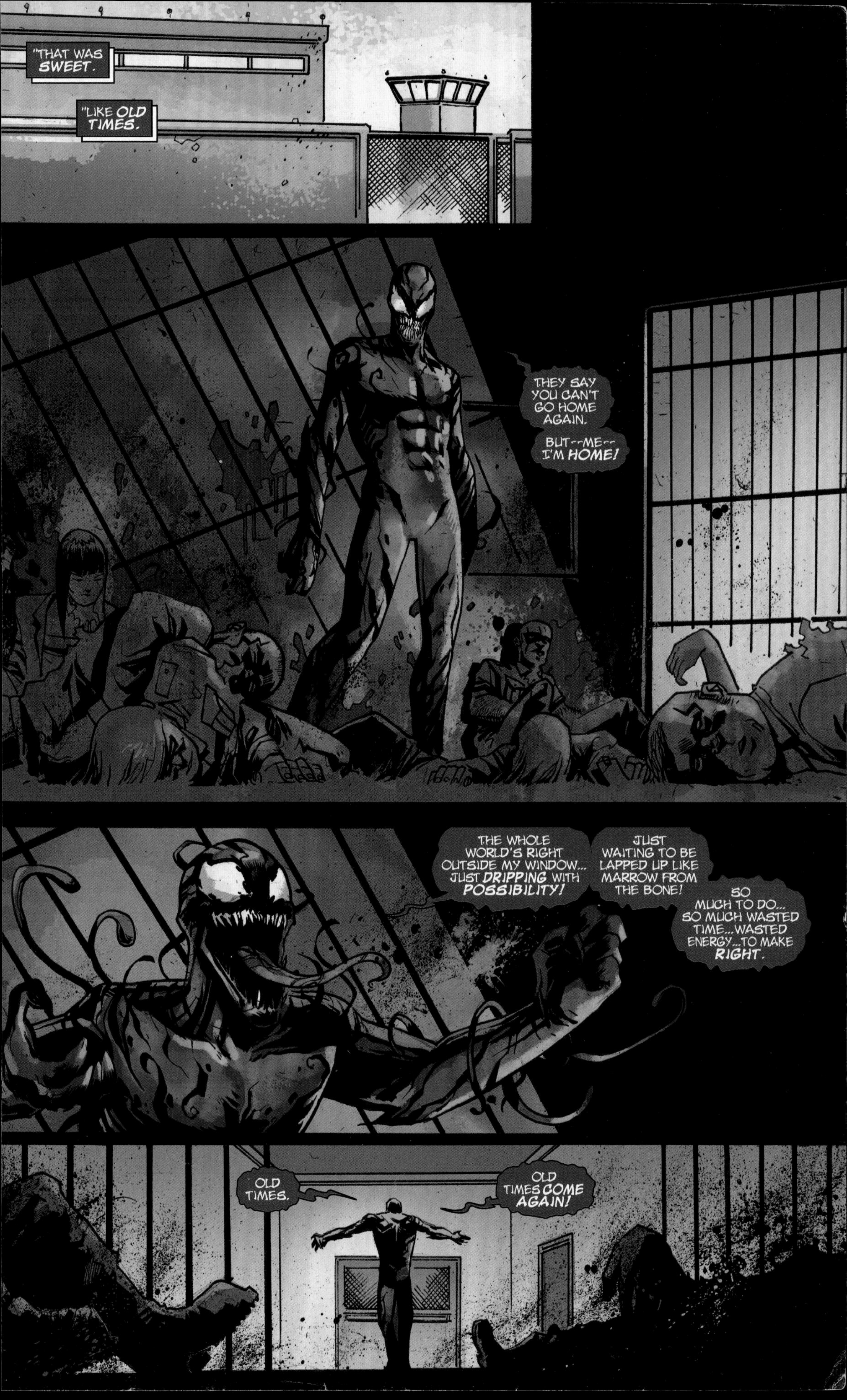
"THAT WAS SWEET.
"LIKE OLD TIMES.
THEY SAY YOU CAN'T GO HOME AGAIN.
BUT--ME-- I'M HOME!
THE WHOLE WORLD'S RIGHT OUTSIDE MY WINDOW... JUST DRIPPING WITH POSSIBILITY!
JUST WAITING TO BE LAPPED UP LIKE MARROW FROM THE BONE!
SO MUCH TO DO... SO MUCH WASTED TIME...WASTED ENERGY...TO MAKE RIGHT.
OLD TIMES.
OLD TIMES COME AGAIN!

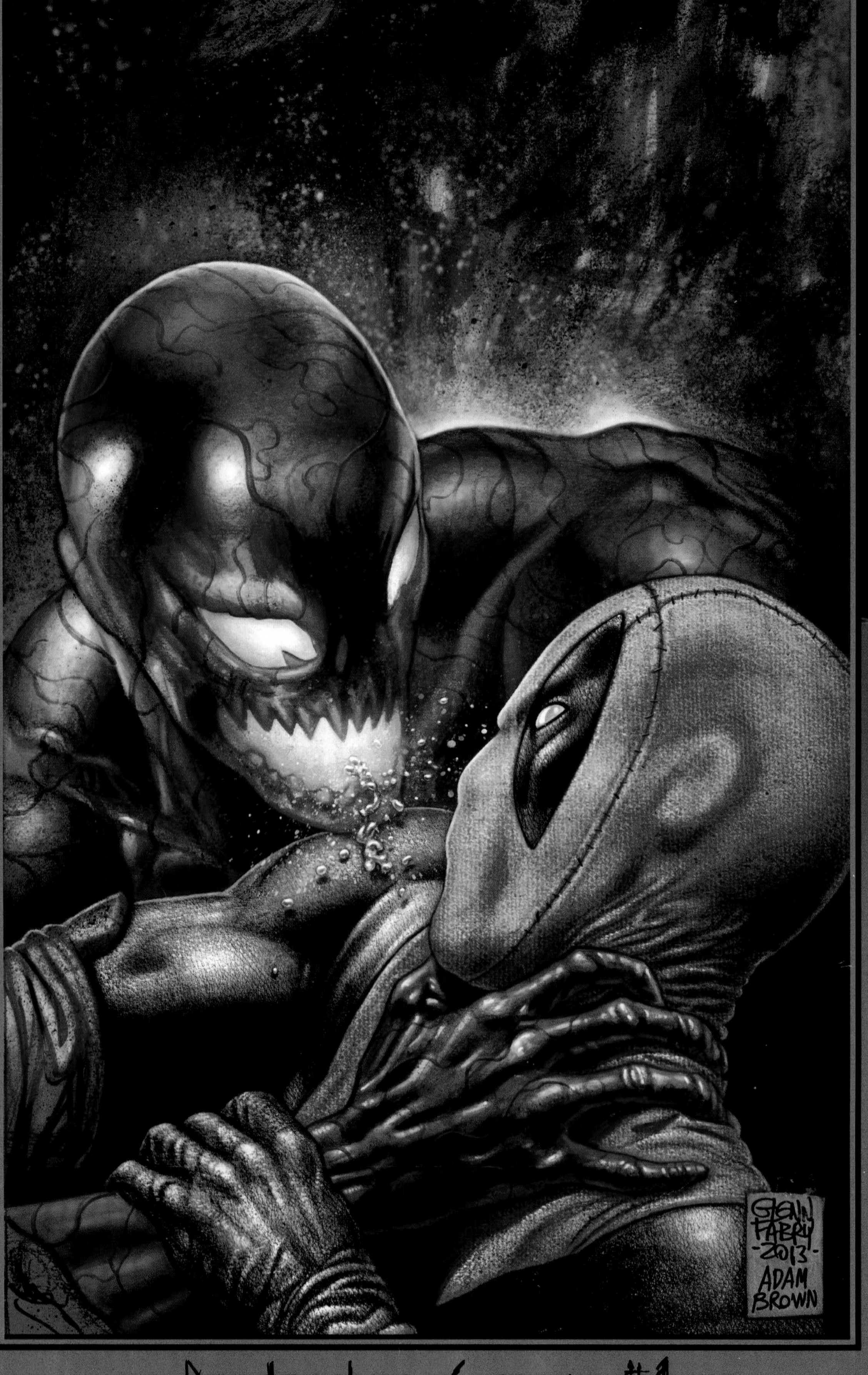
GLENN FABRY -2013-
ADAM BROWN

Deadpool vs. Carnage #1

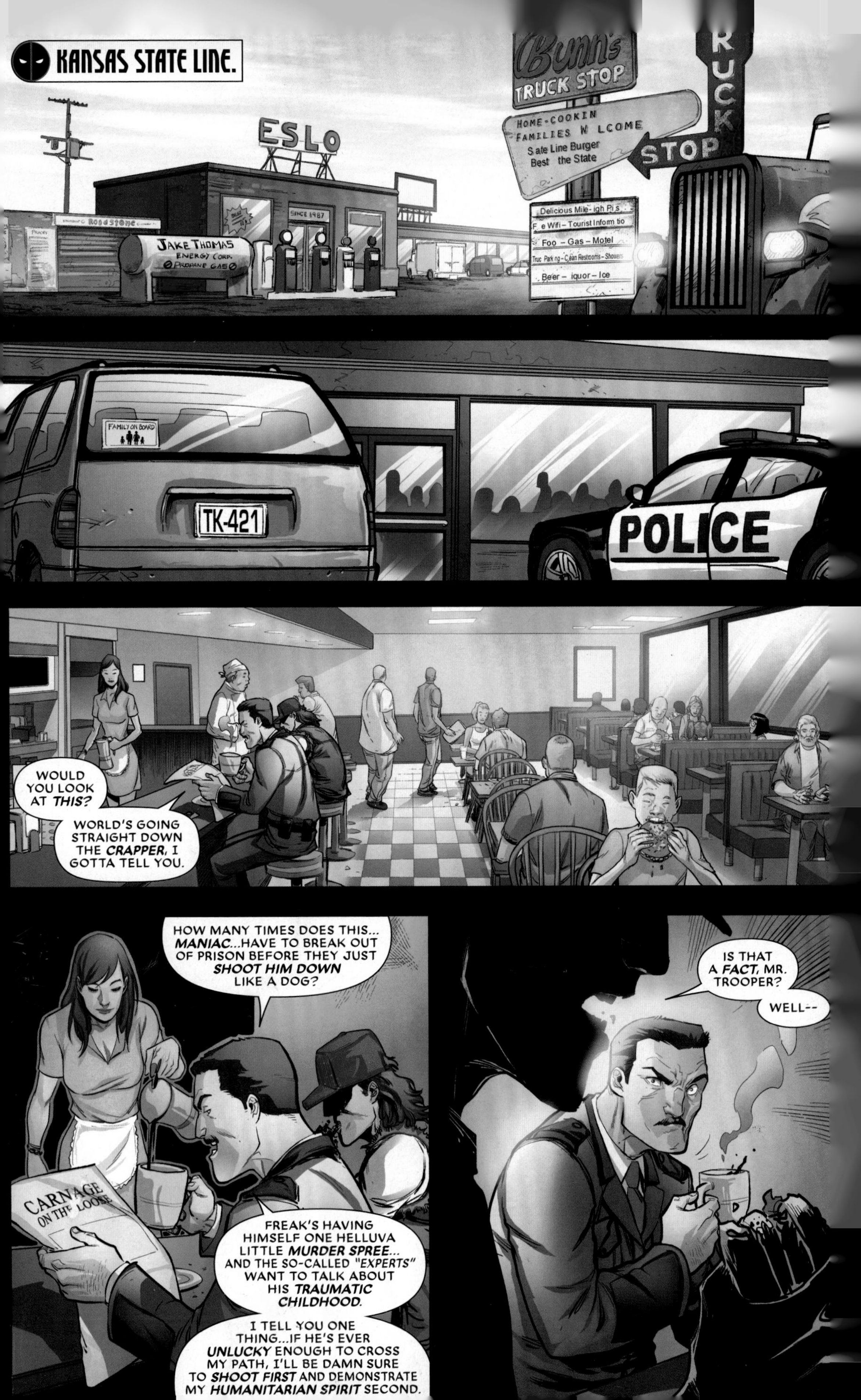
KANSAS STATE LINE.
WOULD YOU LOOK AT THIS?
WORLD'S GOING STRAIGHT DOWN THE CRAPPER, I GOTTA TELL YOU.
HOW MANY TIMES DOES THIS... MANIAC...HAVE TO BREAK OUT OF PRISON BEFORE THEY JUST SHOOT HIM DOWN LIKE A DOG?
FREAK'S HAVING HIMSELF ONE HELLUVA LITTLE MURDER SPREE... AND THE SO-CALLED "EXPERTS" WANT TO TALK ABOUT HIS TRAUMATIC CHILDHOOD.
I TELL YOU ONE THING...IF HE'S EVER UNLUCKY ENOUGH TO CROSS MY PATH, I'LL BE DAMN SURE TO SHOOT FIRST AND DEMONSTRATE MY HUMANITARIAN SPIRIT SECOND.
IS THAT A FACT, MR. TROOPER?
WELL--

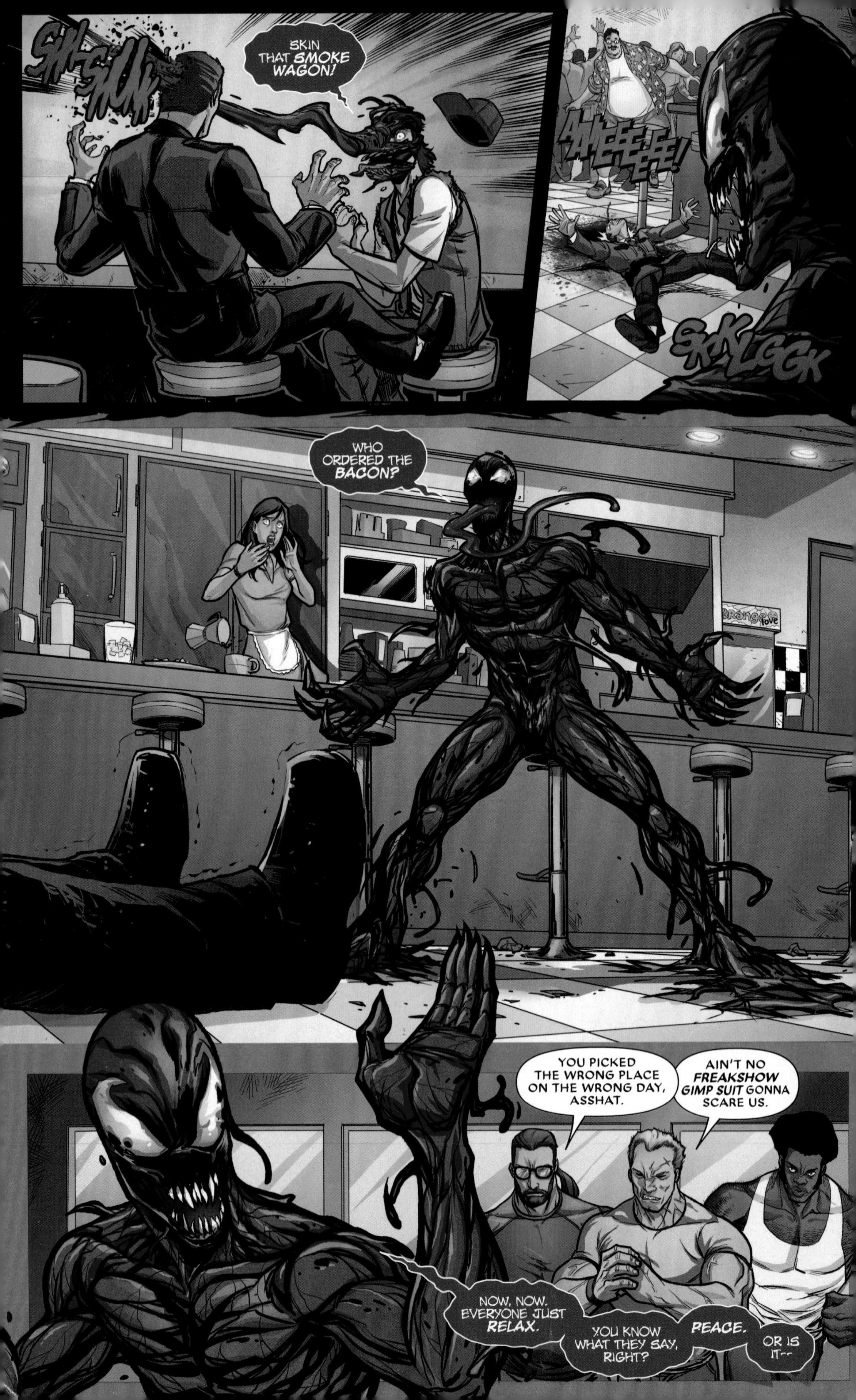
SH-SHUK
SKIN THAT SMOKE WAGON!
AAIEEEE-E-EEE!
SKKLGGK
WHO ORDERED THE BACON?
YOU PICKED THE WRONG PLACE ON THE WRONG DAY, ASSHAT.
AIN'T NO FREAKSHOW GIMP SUIT GONNA SCARE US.
NOW, NOW. EVERYONE JUST RELAX.
YOU KNOW WHAT THEY SAY, RIGHT?
PEACE.
OR IS IT--

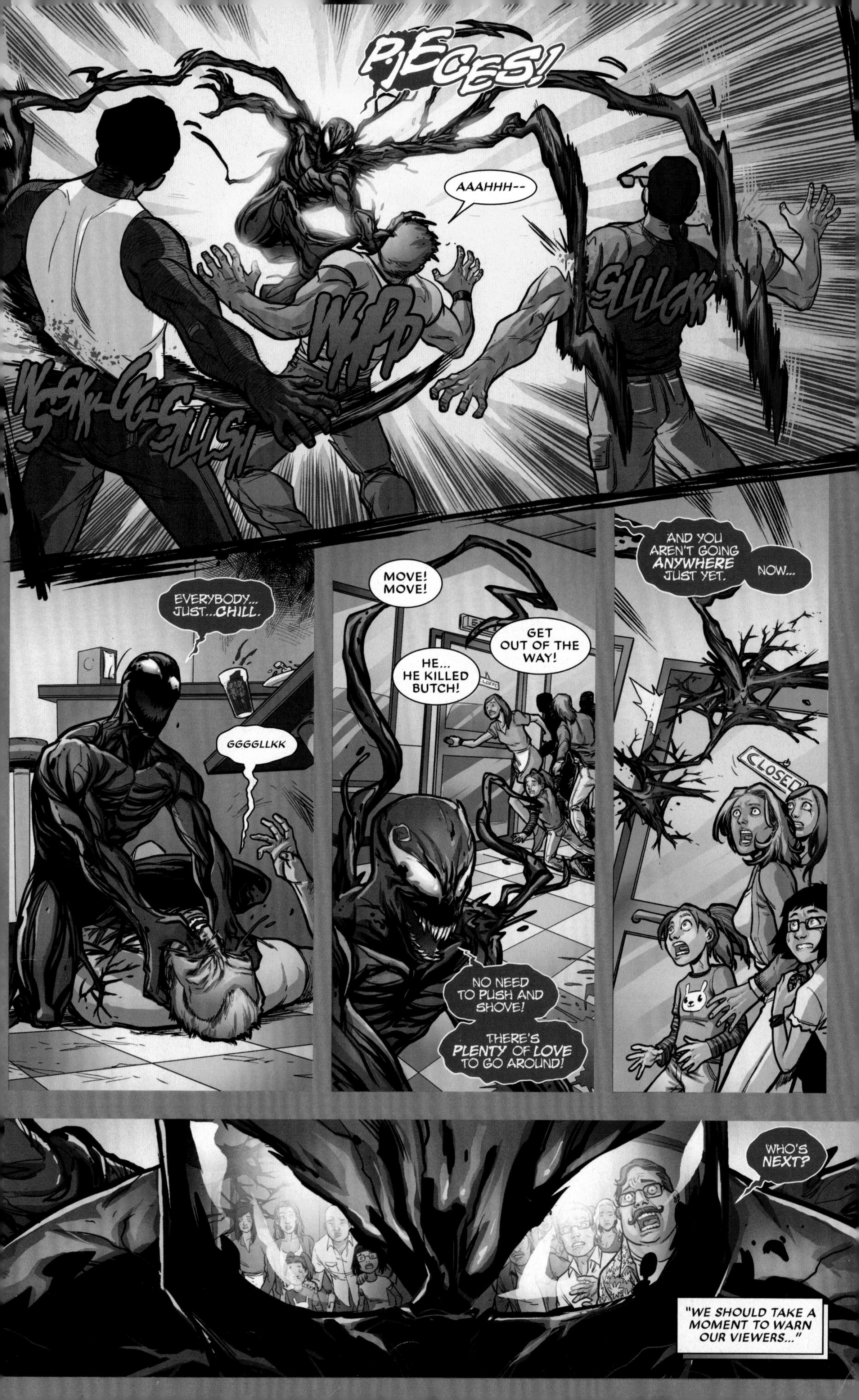
PIECES!
AAAHHH--
EVERYBODY... JUST...CHILL.
GGGGLLKK
MOVE! MOVE!
HE... HE KILLED BUTCH!
GET OUT OF THE WAY!
NO NEED TO PUSH AND SHOVE!
THERE'S PLENTY OF LOVE TO GO AROUND!
AND YOU AREN'T GOING ANYWHERE JUST YET.
NOW...
CLOSED
WHO'S NEXT?
"WE SHOULD TAKE A MOMENT TO WARN OUR VIEWERS..."

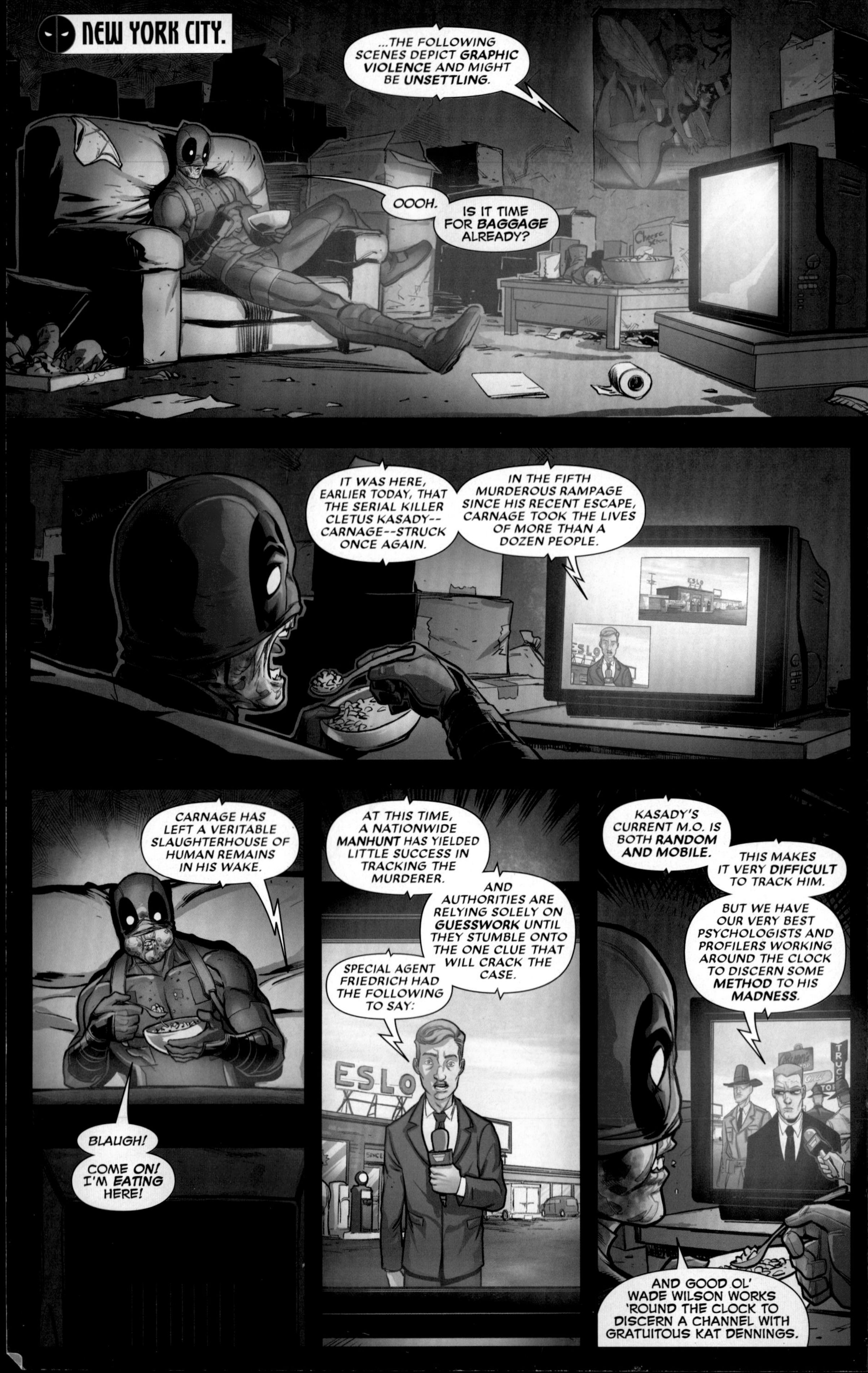
NEW YORK CITY.
...THE FOLLOWING SCENES DEPICT GRAPHIC VIOLENCE AND MIGHT BE UNSETTLING.
OOOH.
IS IT TIME FOR BAGGAGE ALREADY?
IT WAS HERE, EARLIER TODAY, THAT THE SERIAL KILLER CLETUS KASADY--CARNAGE--STRUCK ONCE AGAIN.
IN THE FIFTH MURDEROUS RAMPAGE SINCE HIS RECENT ESCAPE, CARNAGE TOOK THE LIVES OF MORE THAN A DOZEN PEOPLE.
CARNAGE HAS LEFT A VERITABLE SLAUGHTERHOUSE OF HUMAN REMAINS IN HIS WAKE.
BLAUGH!
COME ON! I'M EATING HERE!
AT THIS TIME, A NATIONWIDE MANHUNT HAS YIELDED LITTLE SUCCESS IN TRACKING THE MURDERER.
AND AUTHORITIES ARE RELYING SOLELY ON GUESSWORK UNTIL THEY STUMBLE ONTO THE ONE CLUE THAT WILL CRACK THE CASE.
SPECIAL AGENT FRIEDRICH HAD THE FOLLOWING TO SAY:
ESLO
KASADY'S CURRENT M.O. IS BOTH RANDOM AND MOBILE.
THIS MAKES IT VERY DIFFICULT TO TRACK HIM.
BUT WE HAVE OUR VERY BEST PSYCHOLOGISTS AND PROFILERS WORKING AROUND THE CLOCK TO DISCERN SOME METHOD TO HIS MADNESS.
AND GOOD OL' WADE WILSON WORKS 'ROUND THE CLOCK TO DISCERN A CHANNEL WITH GRATUITOUS KAT DENNINGS.

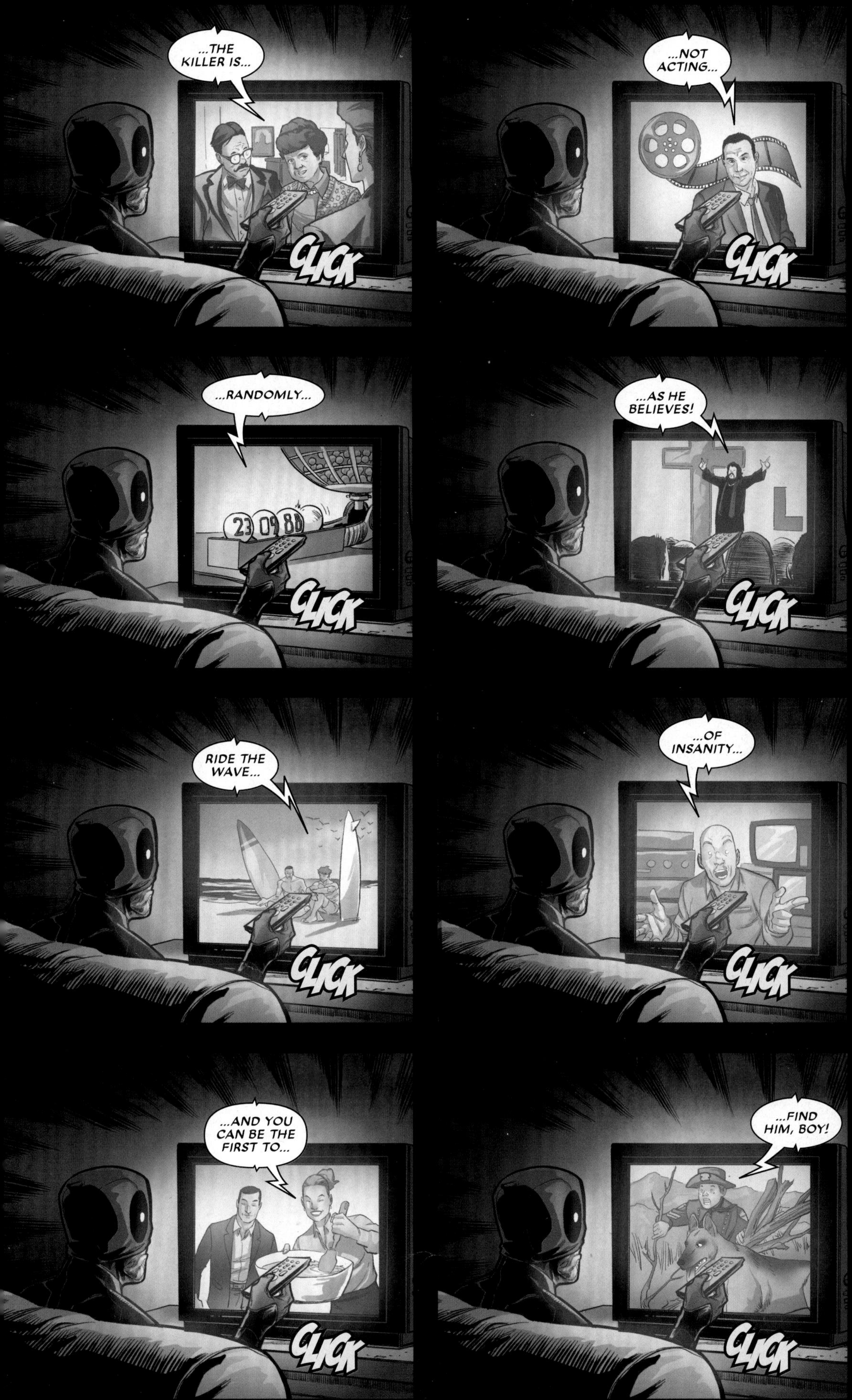
...THE KILLER IS...
CLICK
...NOT ACTING...
CLICK
...RANDOMLY...
23 09 88
CLICK
...AS HE BELIEVES!
CLICK
RIDE THE WAVE...
CLICK
...OF INSANITY...
CLICK
...AND YOU CAN BE THE FIRST TO...
CLICK
...FIND HIM, BOY!
CLICK

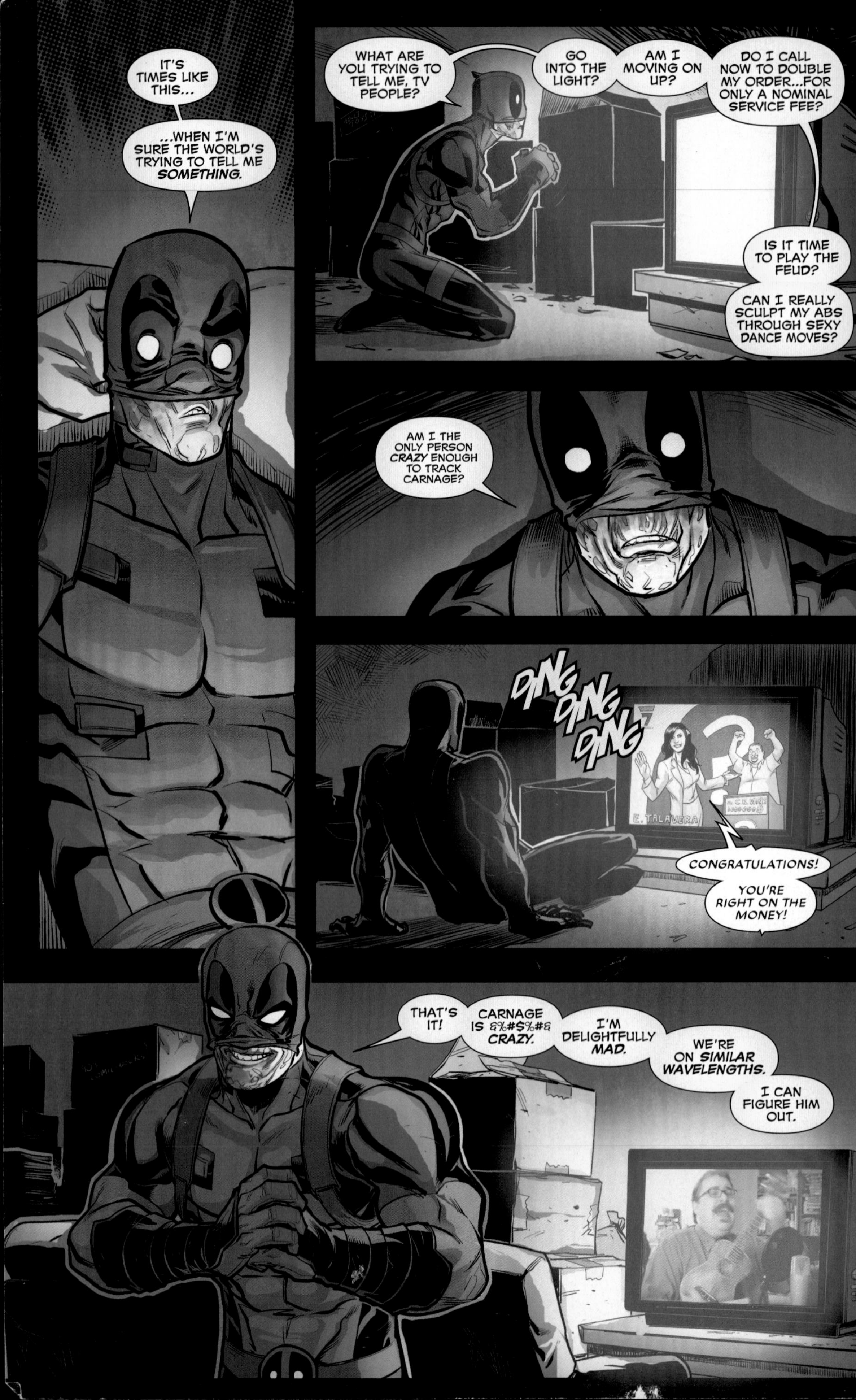
IT'S TIMES LIKE THIS...
...WHEN I'M SURE THE WORLD'S TRYING TO TELL ME SOMETHING.
WHAT ARE YOU TRYING TO TELL ME, TV PEOPLE?
GO INTO THE LIGHT?
AM I MOVING ON UP?
DO I CALL NOW TO DOUBLE MY ORDER...FOR ONLY A NOMINAL SERVICE FEE?
IS IT TIME TO PLAY THE FEUD?
CAN I REALLY SCULPT MY ABS THROUGH SEXY DANCE MOVES?
AM I THE ONLY PERSON CRAZY ENOUGH TO TRACK CARNAGE?
DING DING DING
E. TALAVERA
CONGRATULATIONS!
YOU'RE RIGHT ON THE MONEY!
THAT'S IT!
CARNAGE IS &%#$%#& CRAZY.
I'M DELIGHTFULLY MAD.
WE'RE ON SIMILAR WAVELENGTHS.
I CAN FIGURE HIM OUT.

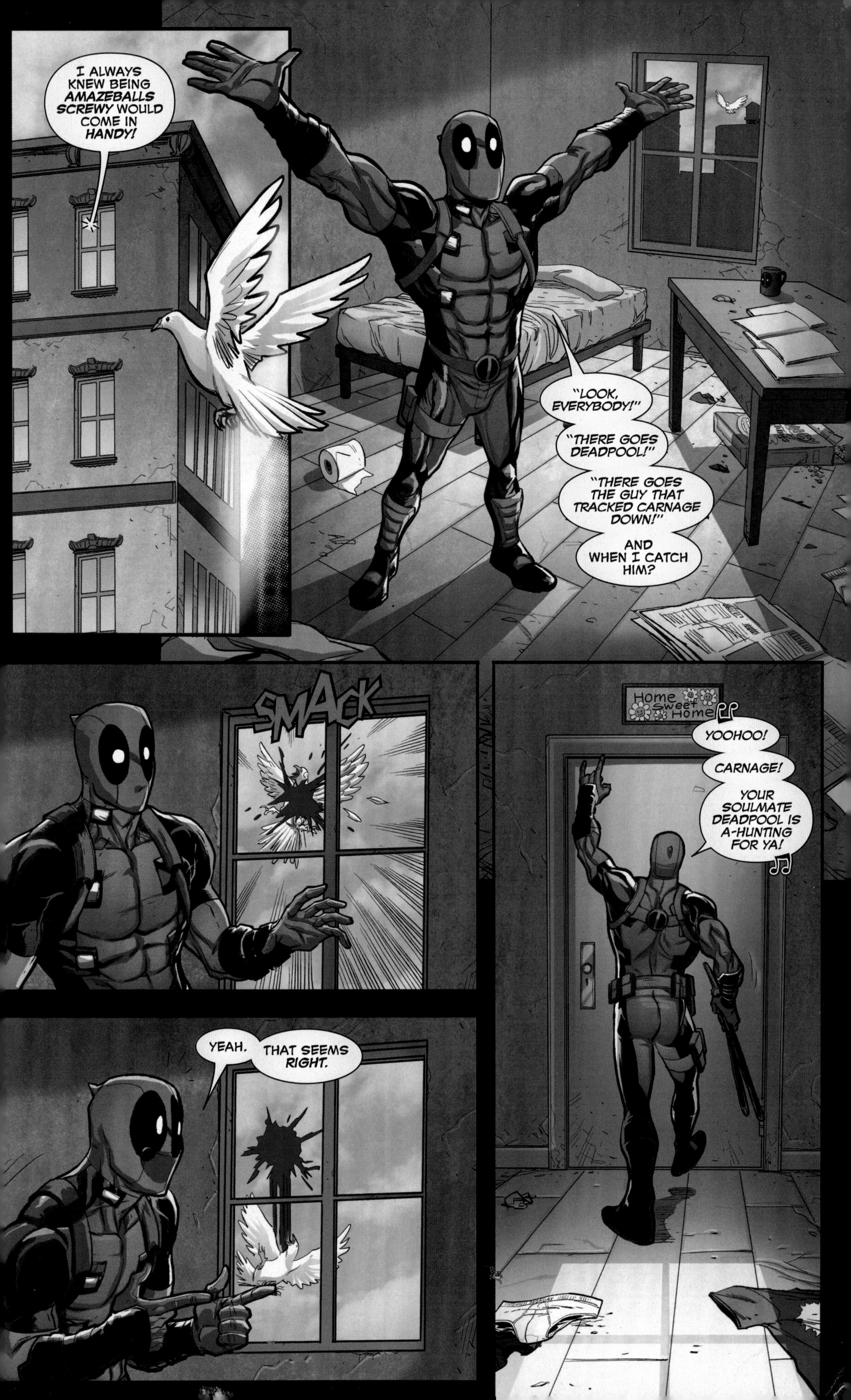
I ALWAYS KNEW BEING AMAZEBALLS SCREWY WOULD COME IN HANDY!
"LOOK, EVERYBODY!"
"THERE GOES DEADPOOL!"
"THERE GOES THE GUY THAT TRACKED CARNAGE DOWN!"
AND WHEN I CATCH HIM?
SMACK
YEAH.
THAT SEEMS RIGHT.
Home Sweet Home
YOOHOO!
CARNAGE!
YOUR SOULMATE DEADPOOL IS A-HUNTING FOR YA!

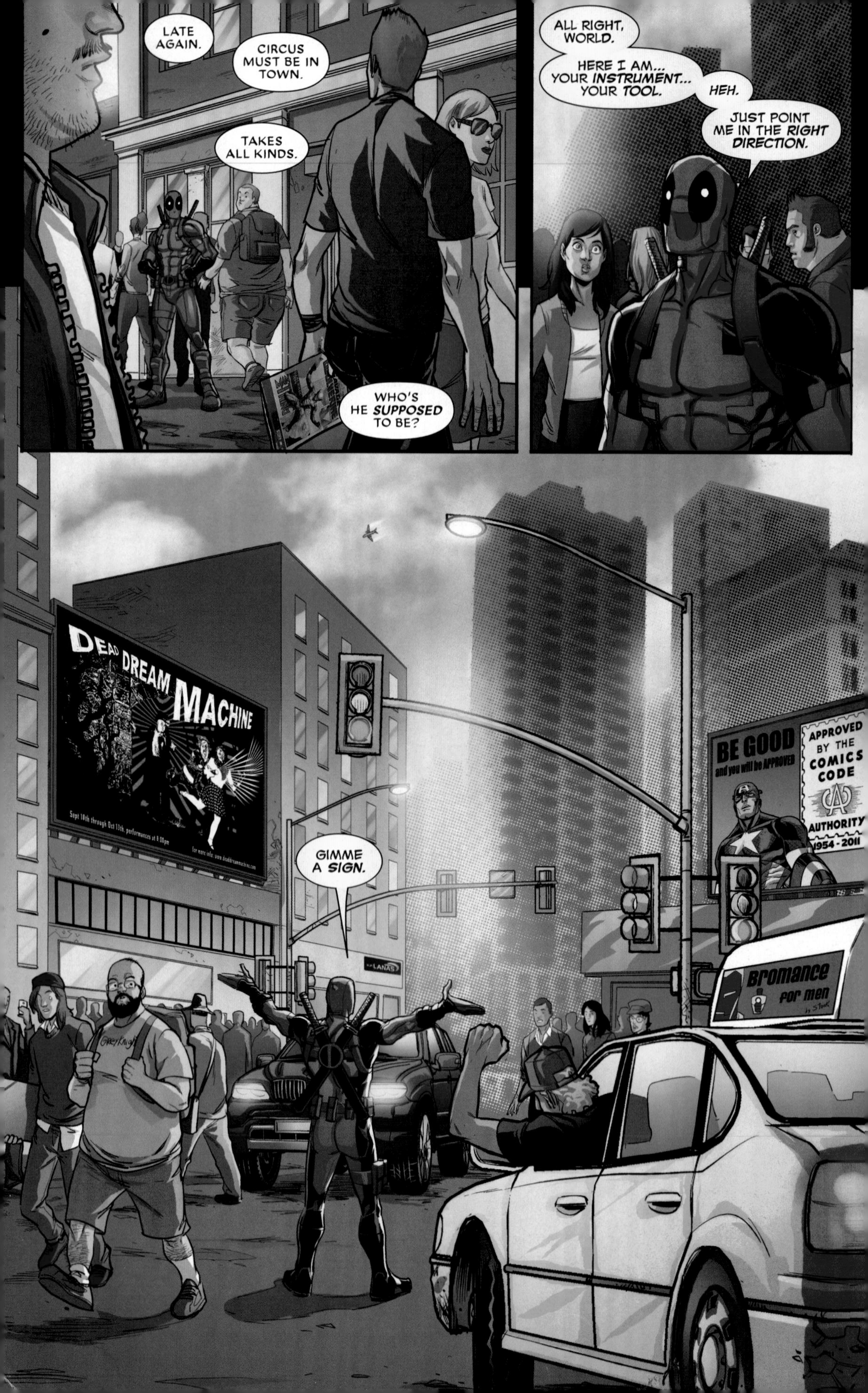
LATE AGAIN.
CIRCUS MUST BE IN TOWN.
TAKES ALL KINDS.
WHO'S HE *SUPPOSED* TO BE?
ALL RIGHT, WORLD.
HERE I AM... YOUR *INSTRUMENT*... YOUR *TOOL*.
HEH.
JUST POINT ME IN THE *RIGHT DIRECTION*.
DEAD DREAM MACHINE
BE GOOD
and you will be APPROVED
APPROVED BY THE COMICS CODE AUTHORITY 1954 - 2011
GIMME A *SIGN*.
Bromance for men

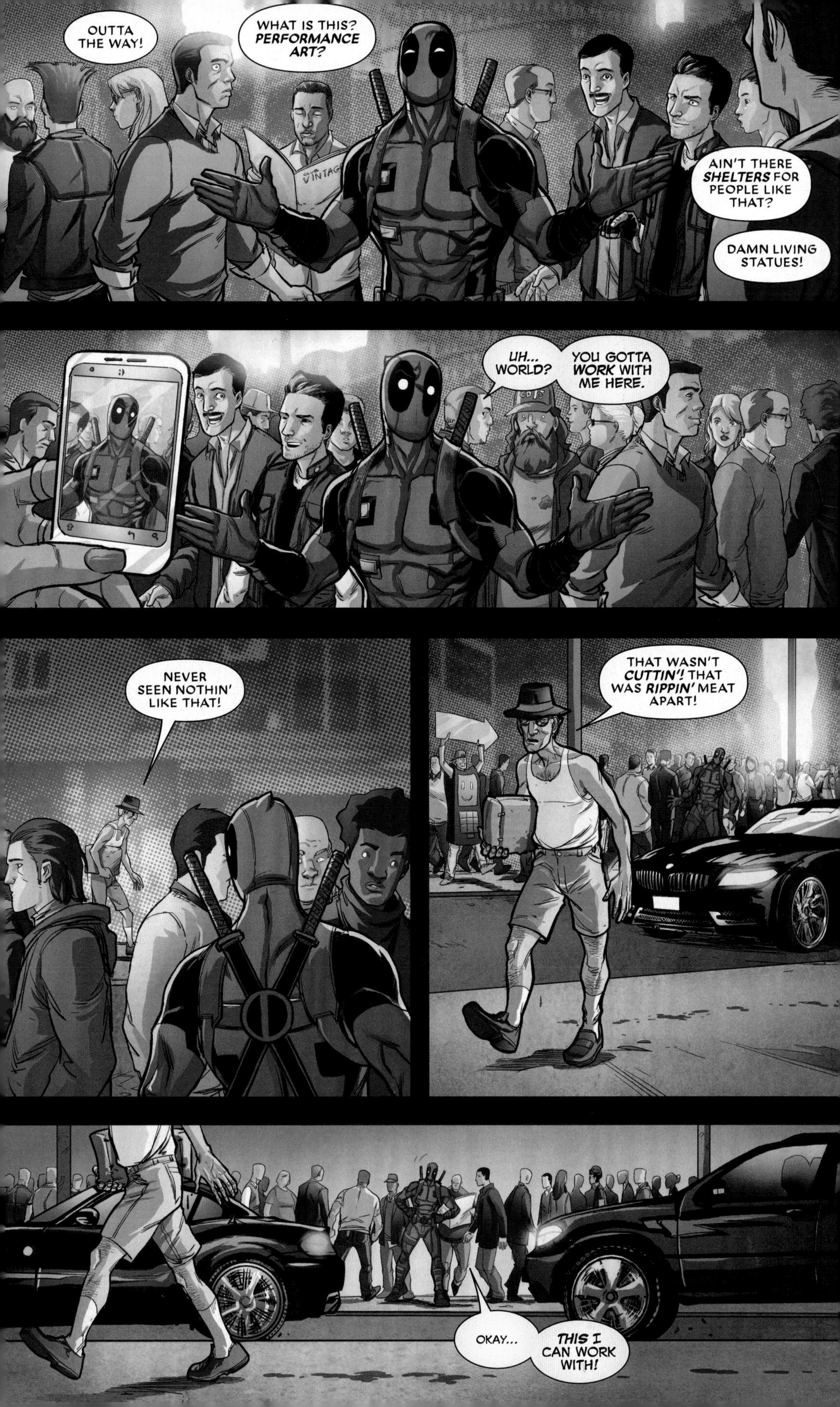
OUTTA THE WAY!
WHAT IS THIS? PERFORMANCE ART?
AIN'T THERE SHELTERS FOR PEOPLE LIKE THAT?
DAMN LIVING STATUES!
UH... WORLD?
YOU GOTTA WORK WITH ME HERE.
NEVER SEEN NOTHIN' LIKE THAT!
THAT WASN'T CUTTIN'! THAT WAS RIPPIN' MEAT APART!
OKAY...
THIS I CAN WORK WITH!

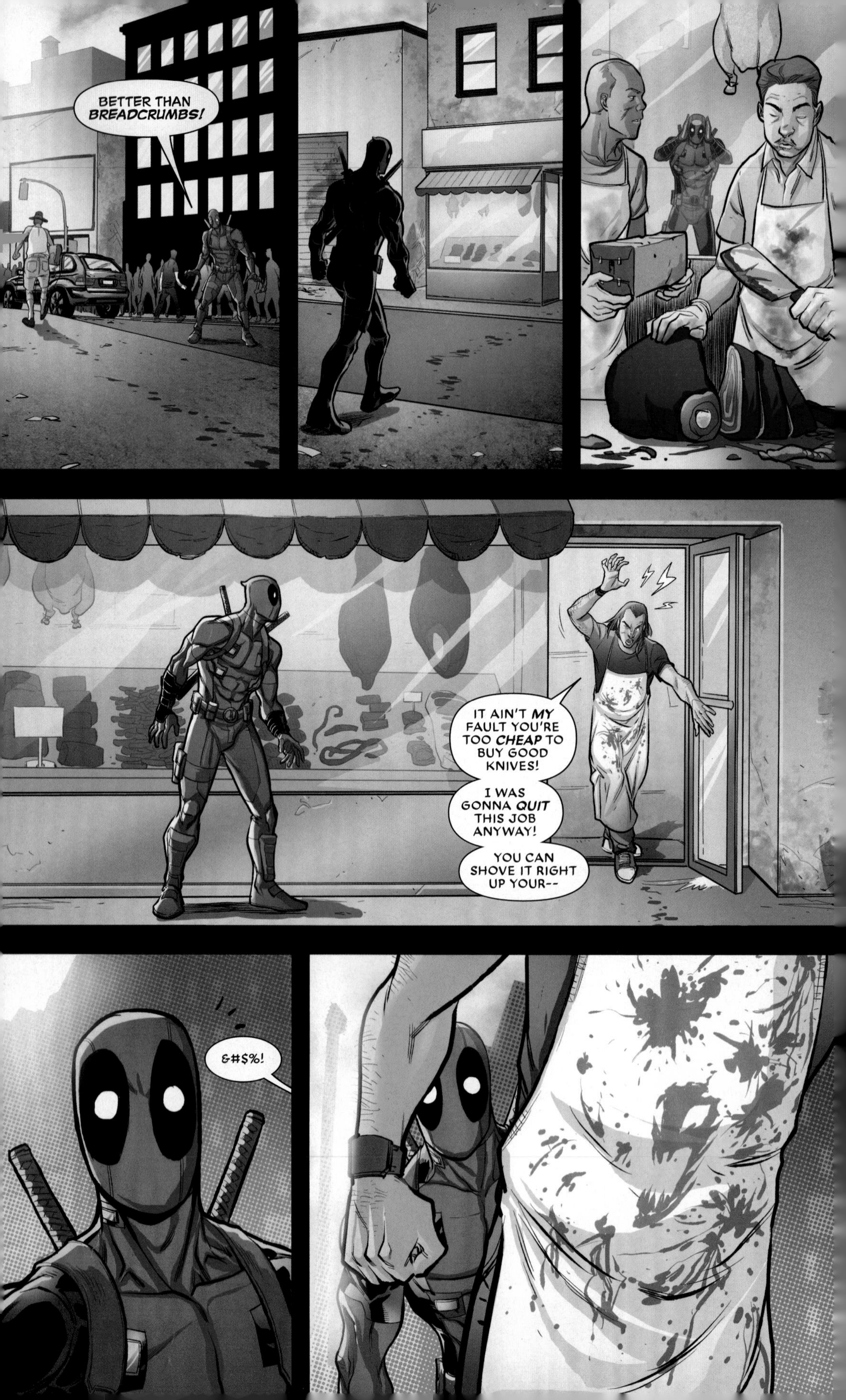
BETTER THAN BREADCRUMBS!
IT AIN'T MY FAULT YOU'RE TOO CHEAP TO BUY GOOD KNIVES!
I WAS GONNA QUIT THIS JOB ANYWAY!
YOU CAN SHOVE IT RIGHT UP YOUR--
&#$%!

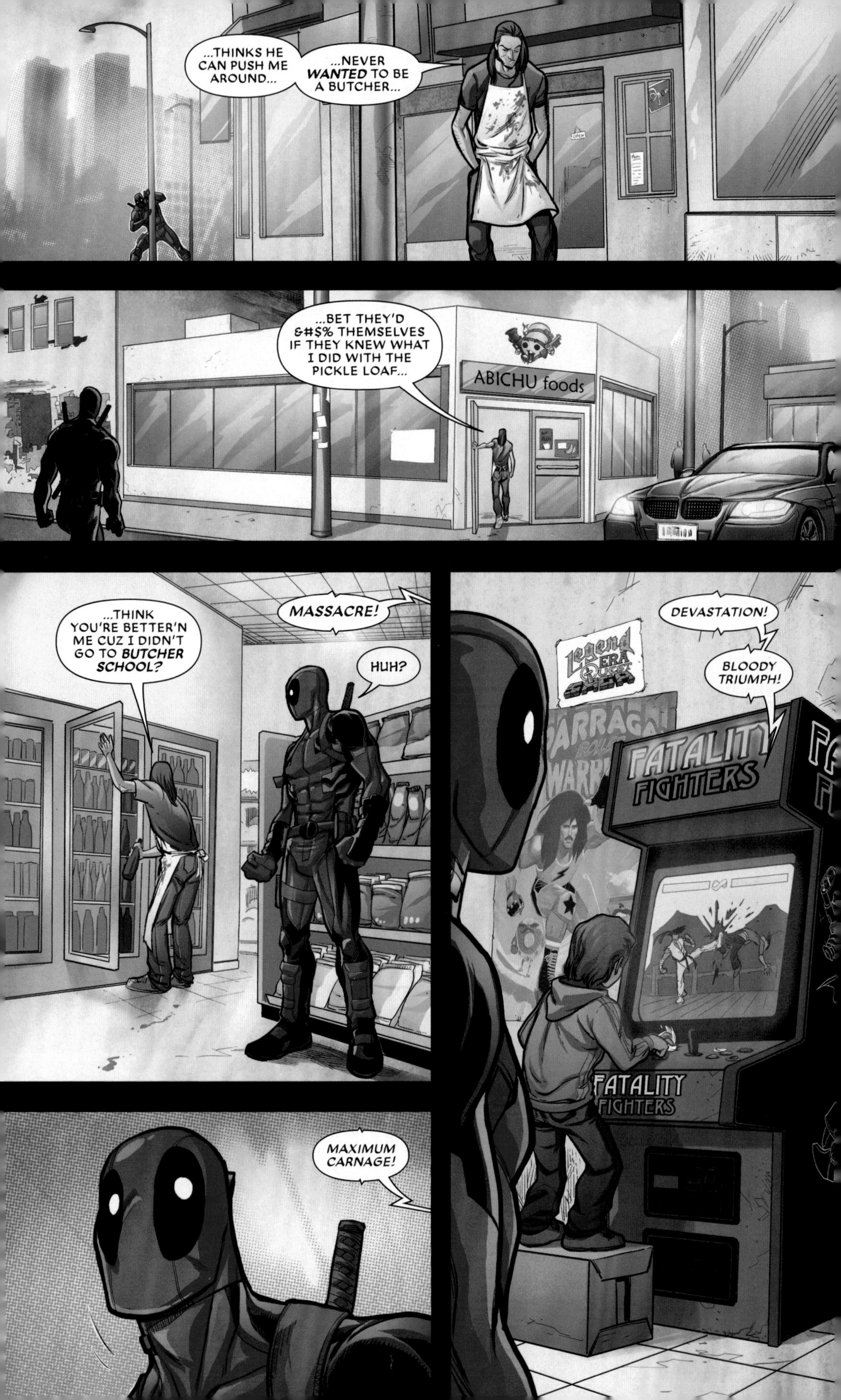

...THINKS HE CAN PUSH ME AROUND...
...NEVER *WANTED* TO BE A BUTCHER...
...BET THEY'D &#$% THEMSELVES IF THEY KNEW WHAT I DID WITH THE PICKLE LOAF...
ABICHU foods
...THINK YOU'RE BETTER'N ME CUZ I DIDN'T GO TO *BUTCHER SCHOOL?*
MASSACRE!
HUH?
DEVASTATION!
BLOODY TRIUMPH!
FATALITY FIGHTERS
FATALITY FIGHTERS
MAXIMUM CARNAGE!

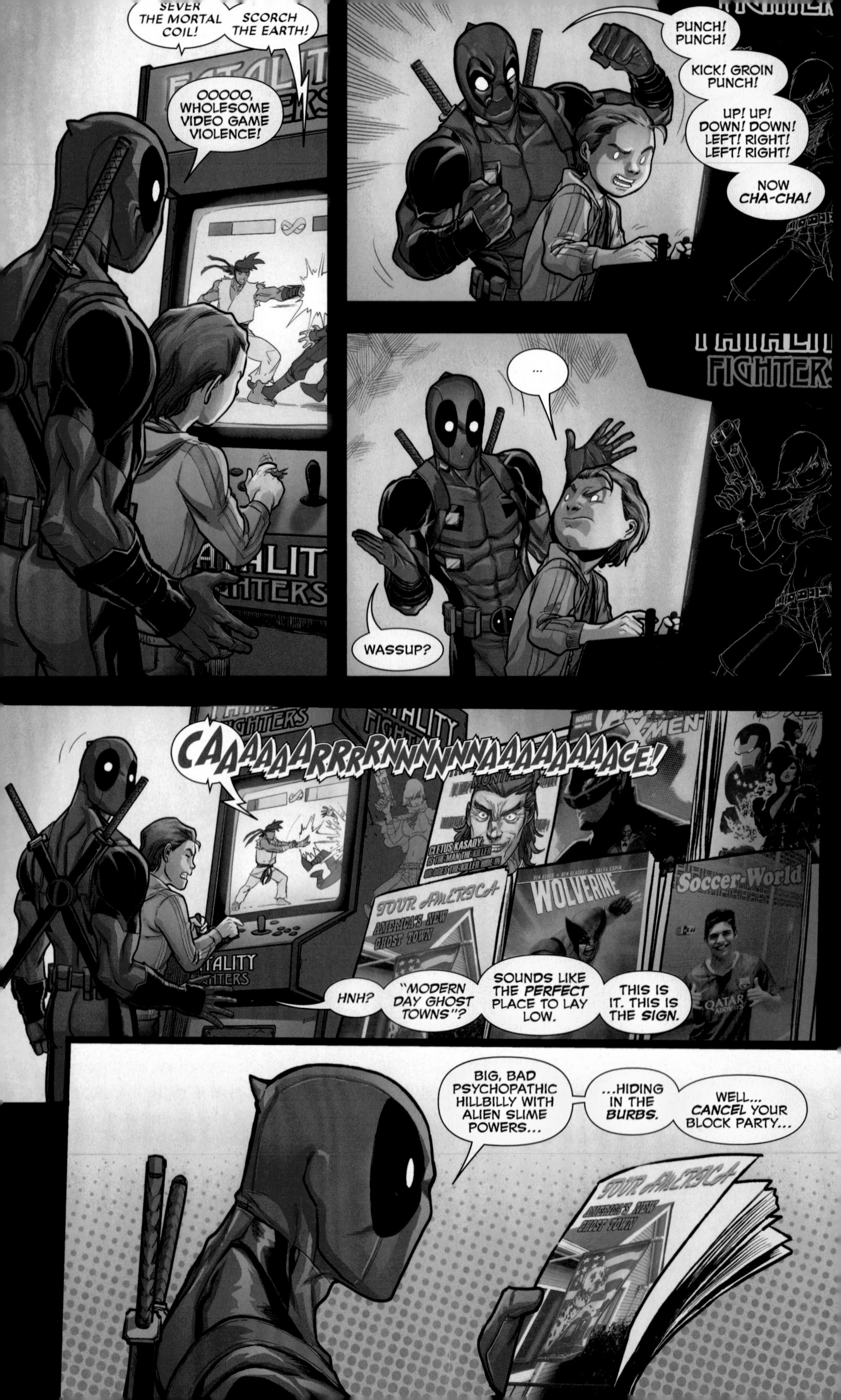
SEVER THE MORTAL COIL!
SCORCH THE EARTH!
FATALITY FIGHTERS
OOOOO, WHOLESOME VIDEO GAME VIOLENCE!
FATALITY FIGHTERS
PUNCH! PUNCH!
KICK! GROIN PUNCH!
UP! UP! DOWN! DOWN! LEFT! RIGHT! LEFT! RIGHT!
NOW CHA-CHA!
FATALITY FIGHTERS
...
WASSUP?
CAAAAAARRRRNNNNNNAAAAAAAAAGE!
FATALITY FIGHTERS
CLETUS KASADY: IS THE MAN THE KILLER OR DOES THE KILLER HIDE IN
YOUR AMERICA
AMERICA'S NEW GHOST TOWN
WOLVERINE
Soccer-World
HNH?
"MODERN DAY GHOST TOWNS"?
SOUNDS LIKE THE PERFECT PLACE TO LAY LOW.
THIS IS IT. THIS IS THE SIGN.
BIG, BAD PSYCHOPATHIC HILLBILLY WITH ALIEN SLIME POWERS...
...HIDING IN THE BURBS.
WELL... CANCEL YOUR BLOCK PARTY...
YOUR AMERICA
AMERICA'S NEW GHOST TOWN

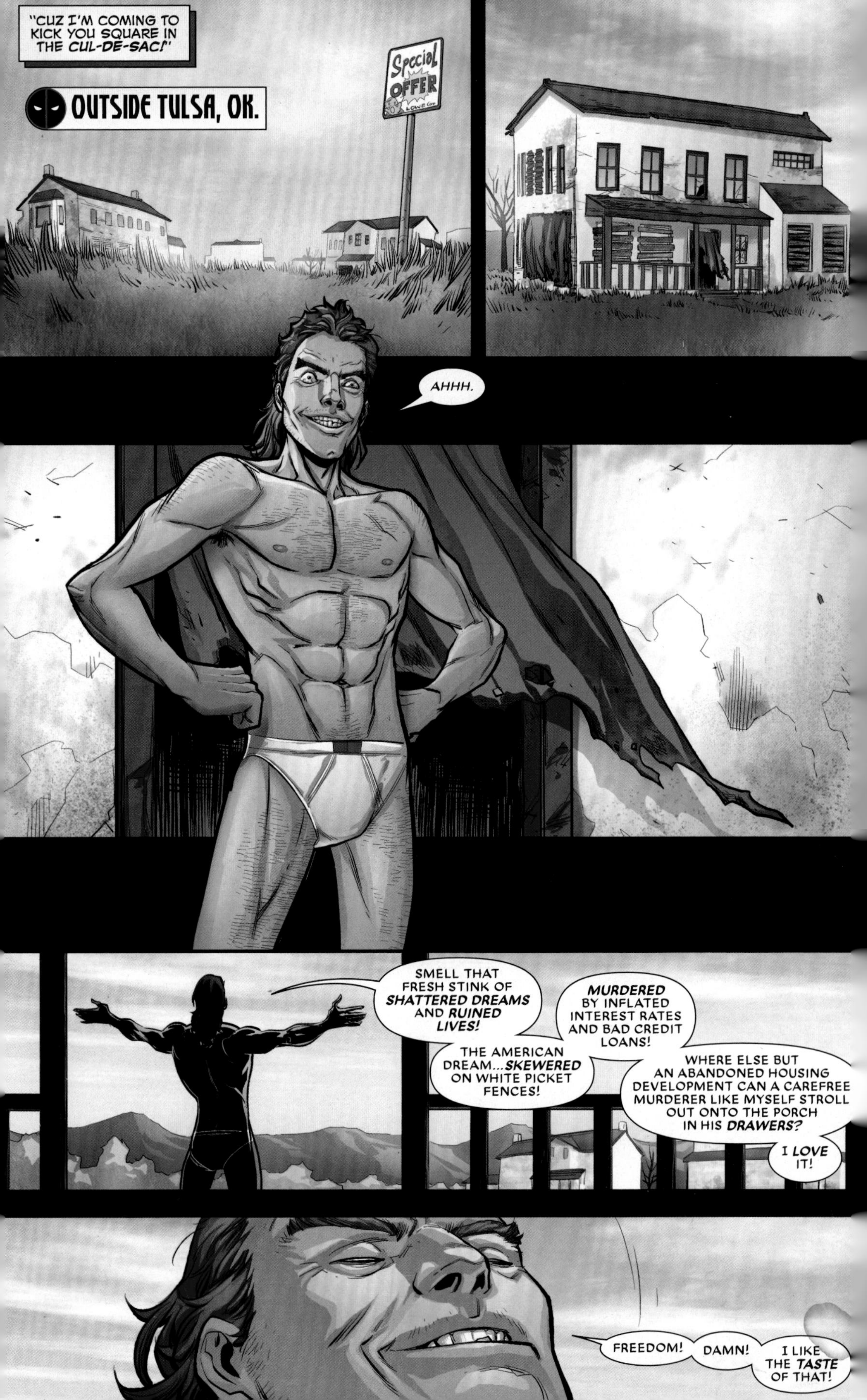
"CUZ I'M COMING TO KICK YOU SQUARE IN THE CUL-DE-SAC!"
OUTSIDE TULSA, OK.
Special OFFER
AHHH.
SMELL THAT FRESH STINK OF SHATTERED DREAMS AND RUINED LIVES!
THE AMERICAN DREAM...SKEWERED ON WHITE PICKET FENCES!
MURDERED BY INFLATED INTEREST RATES AND BAD CREDIT LOANS!
WHERE ELSE BUT AN ABANDONED HOUSING DEVELOPMENT CAN A CAREFREE MURDERER LIKE MYSELF STROLL OUT ONTO THE PORCH IN HIS DRAWERS?
I LOVE IT!
FREEDOM!
DAMN!
I LIKE THE TASTE OF THAT!

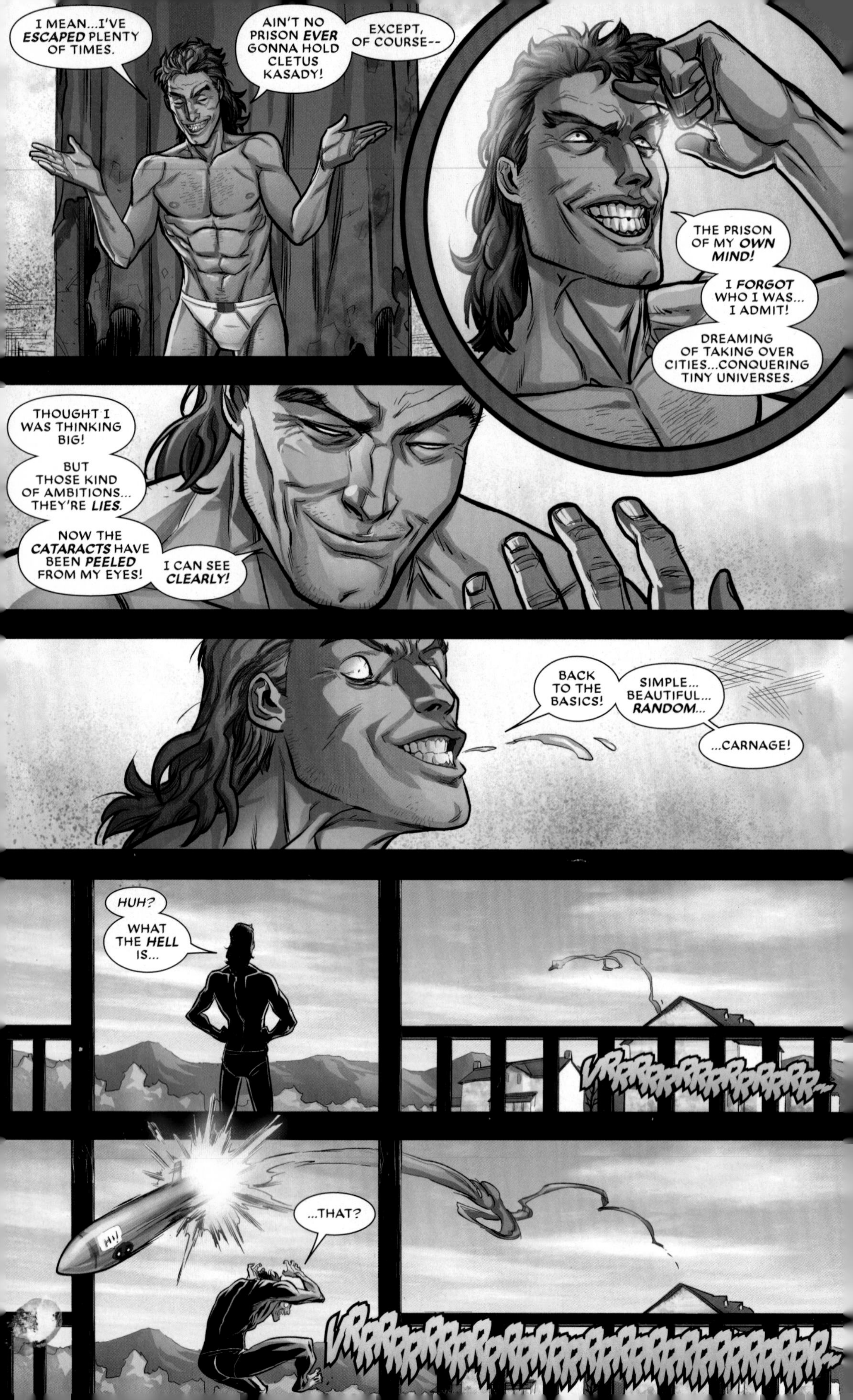
I MEAN...I'VE *ESCAPED* PLENTY OF TIMES.
AIN'T NO PRISON *EVER* GONNA HOLD CLETUS KASADY!
EXCEPT, OF COURSE--
THE PRISON OF MY *OWN MIND!*
I *FORGOT* WHO I WAS... I ADMIT!
DREAMING OF TAKING OVER CITIES...CONQUERING TINY UNIVERSES.
THOUGHT I WAS THINKING BIG!
BUT THOSE KIND OF AMBITIONS... THEY'RE *LIES*.
NOW THE *CATARACTS* HAVE BEEN *PEELED* FROM MY EYES!
I CAN SEE *CLEARLY!*
BACK TO THE BASICS!
SIMPLE... BEAUTIFUL... *RANDOM*...
...CARNAGE!
HUH?
WHAT THE *HELL* IS...
VRRRRRRRRRRRRRRRR--
...THAT?
HI!
VRRRRRRRRRRRRRRRRRRRRRRRRRRRRRRR--

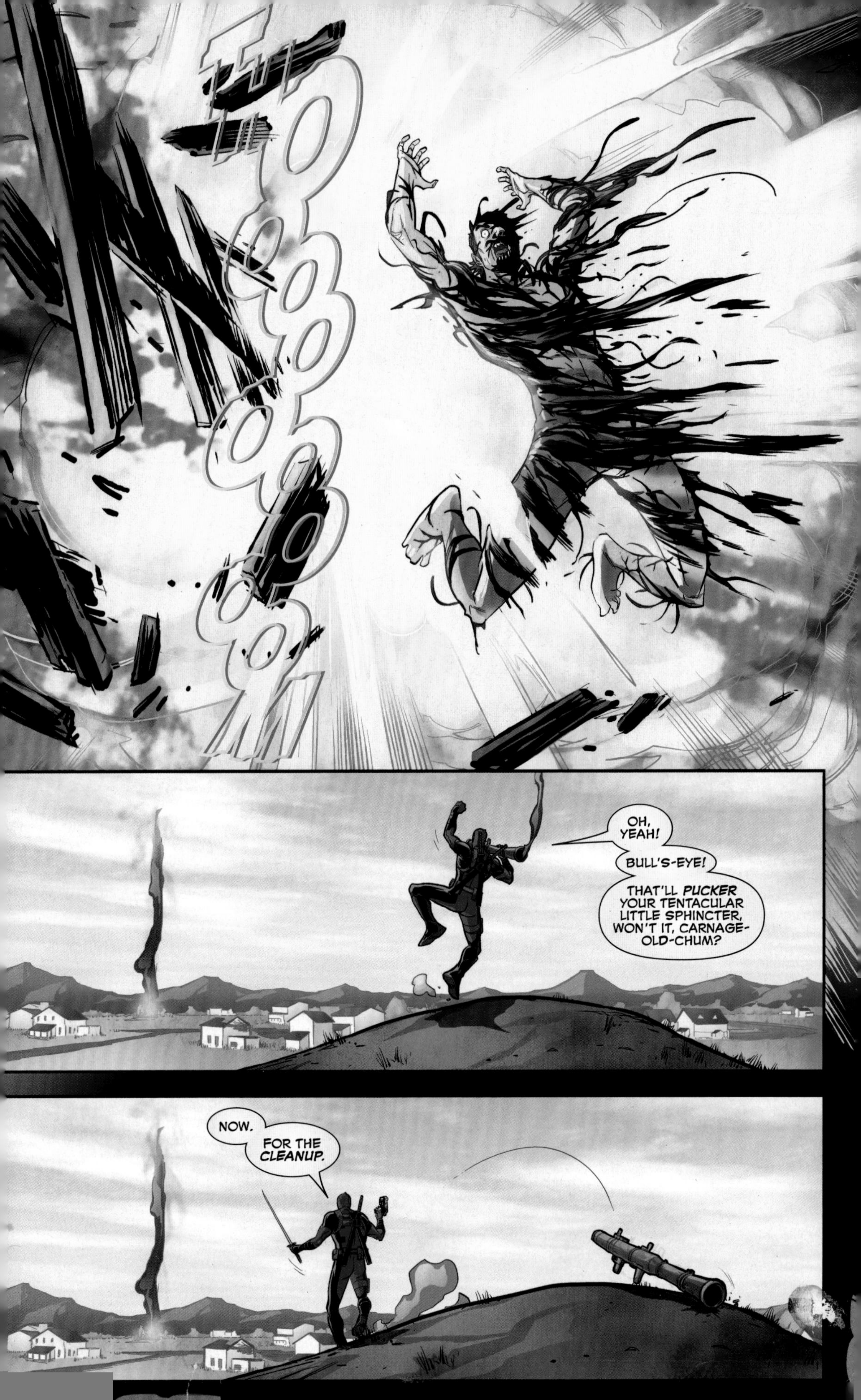
OH, YEAH!
BULL'S-EYE!
THAT'LL *PUCKER* YOUR TENTACULAR LITTLE SPHINCTER, WON'T IT, CARNAGE-OLD-CHUM?
NOW.
FOR THE *CLEANUP*.

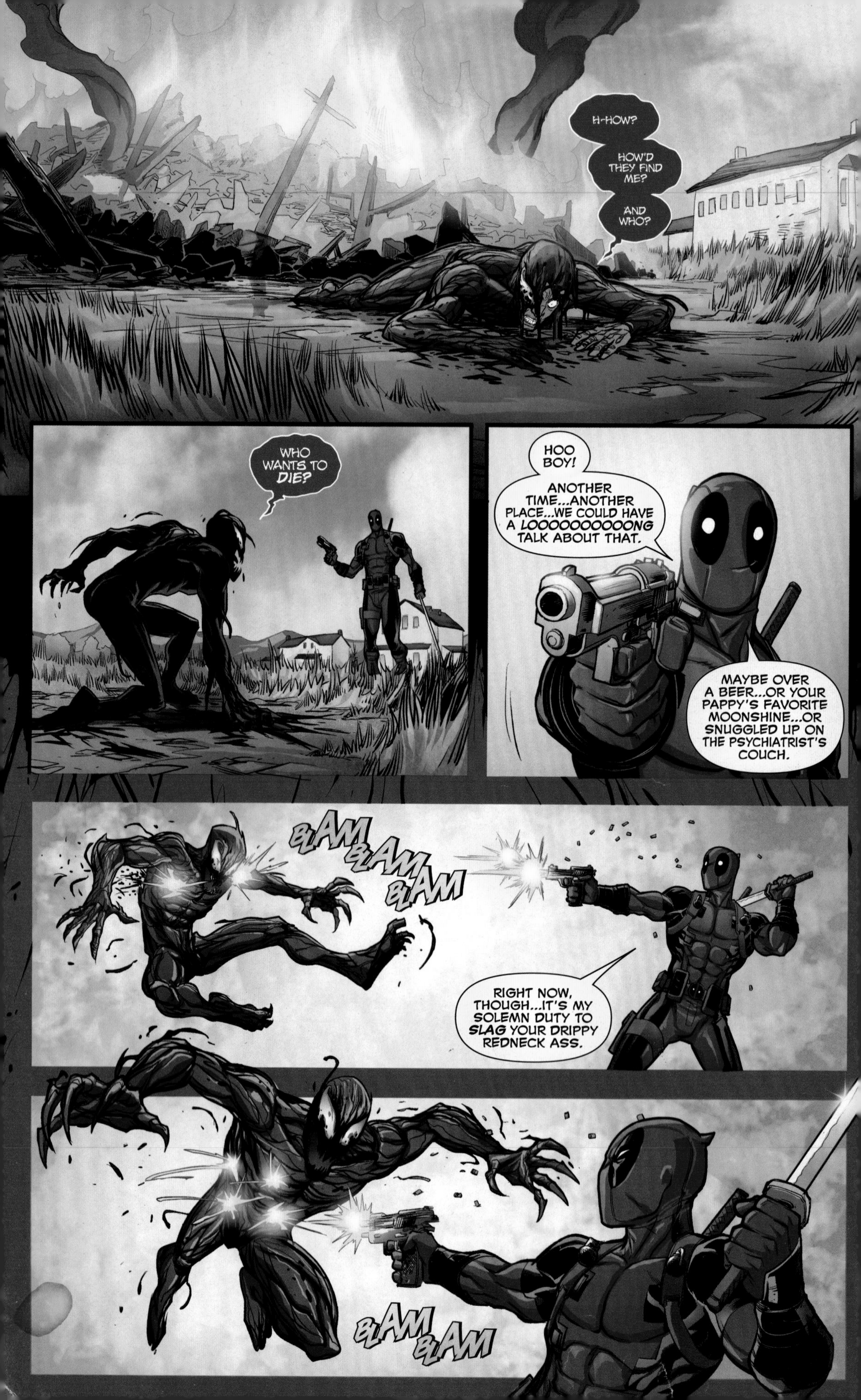
H-HOW?
HOW'D THEY FIND ME?
AND WHO?
WHO WANTS TO DIE?
HOO BOY!
ANOTHER TIME...ANOTHER PLACE...WE COULD HAVE A LOOOOOOOOOONG TALK ABOUT THAT.
MAYBE OVER A BEER...OR YOUR PAPPY'S FAVORITE MOONSHINE...OR SNUGGLED UP ON THE PSYCHIATRIST'S COUCH.
BLAM BLAM BLAM BLAM
RIGHT NOW, THOUGH...IT'S MY SOLEMN DUTY TO SLAG YOUR DRIPPY REDNECK ASS.
BLAM BLAM

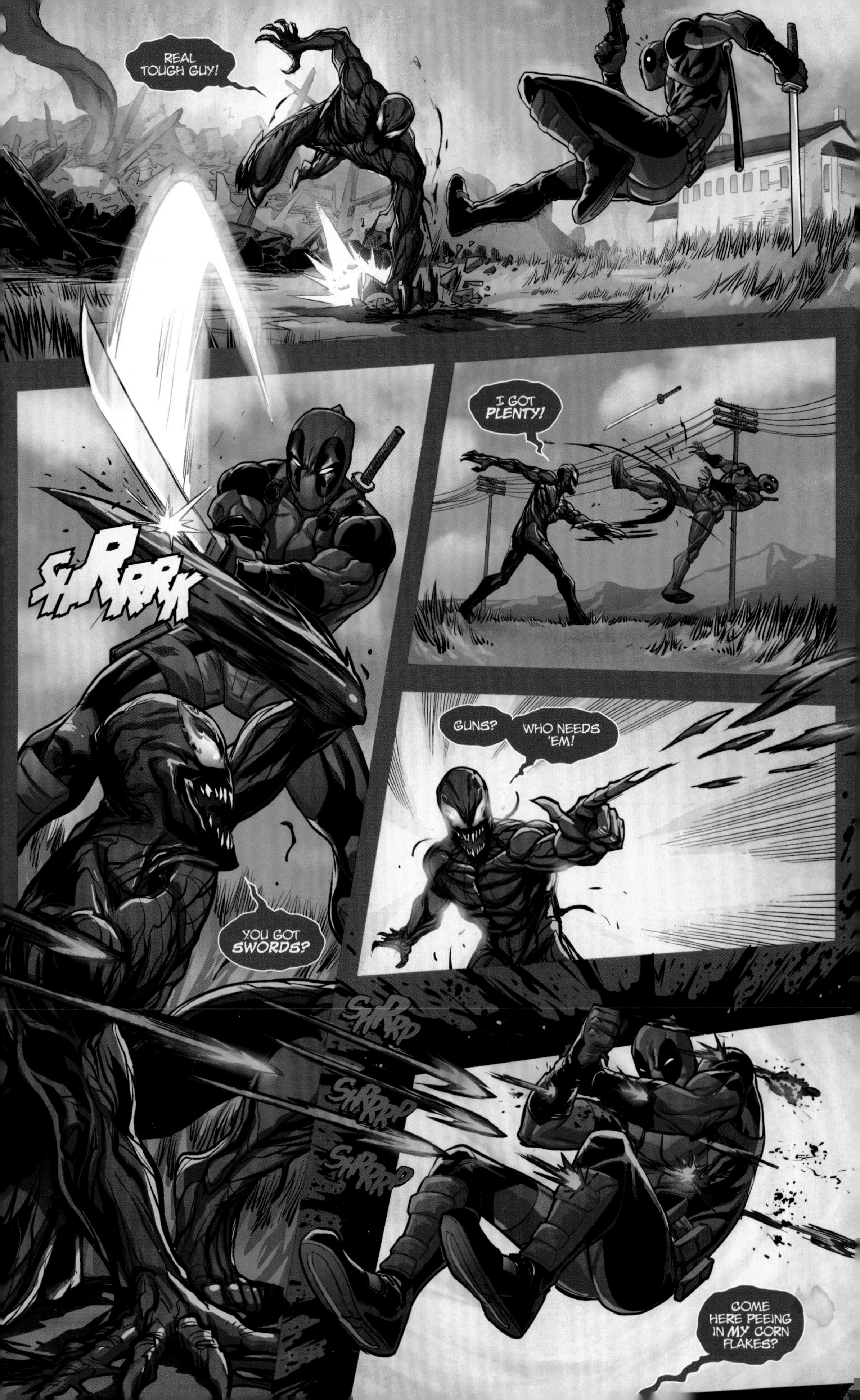
REAL TOUGH GUY!
SHRRRK
I GOT PLENTY!
YOU GOT SWORDS?
GUNS?
WHO NEEDS 'EM!
SHRRRP
SHRRRP
SHRRRP
COME HERE PEEING IN MY CORN FLAKES?

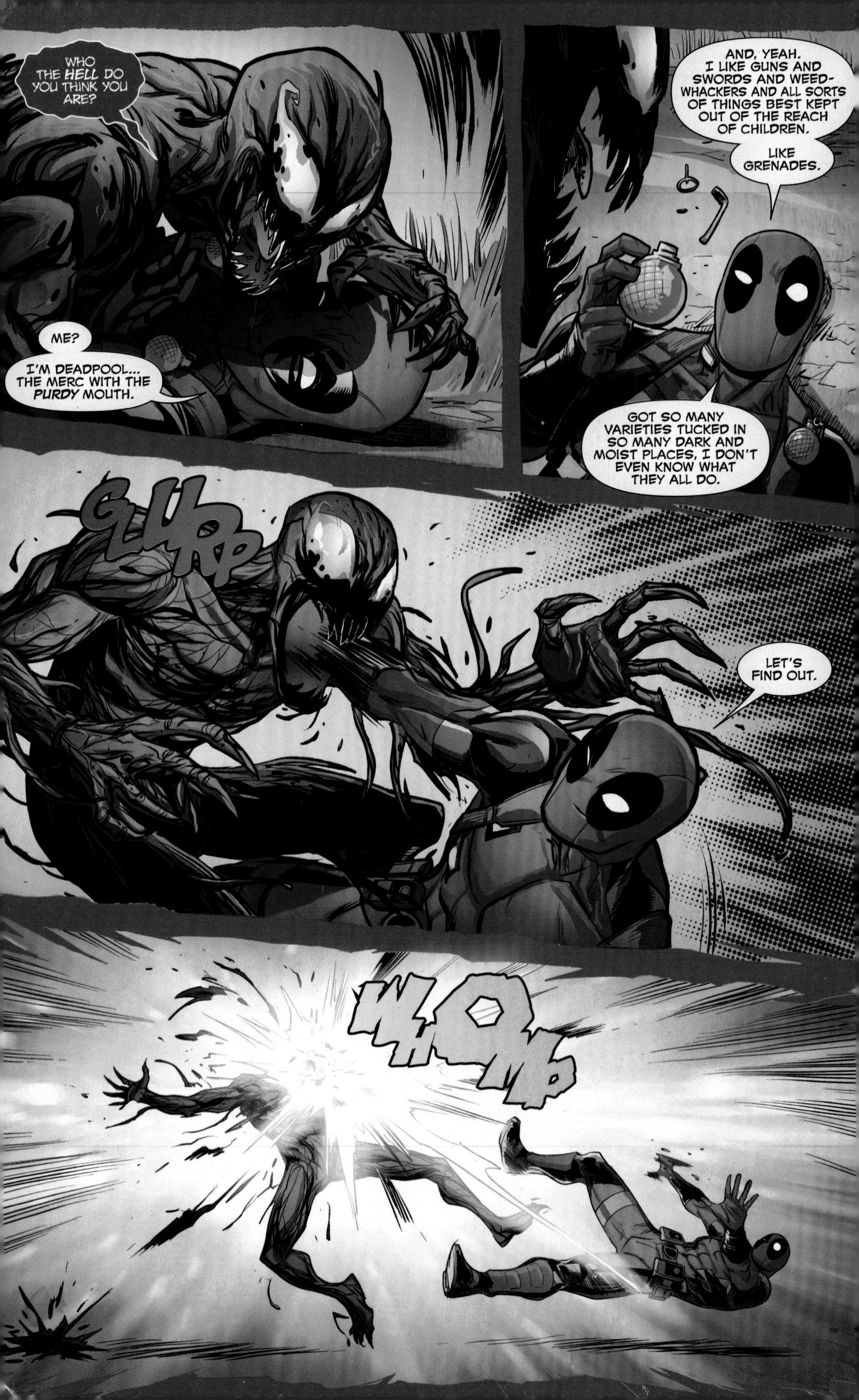
WHO THE HELL DO YOU THINK YOU ARE?
ME?
I'M DEADPOOL... THE MERC WITH THE PURDY MOUTH.
AND, YEAH. I LIKE GUNS AND SWORDS AND WEED-WHACKERS AND ALL SORTS OF THINGS BEST KEPT OUT OF THE REACH OF CHILDREN.
LIKE GRENADES.
GOT SO MANY VARIETIES TUCKED IN SO MANY DARK AND MOIST PLACES, I DON'T EVEN KNOW WHAT THEY ALL DO.
GLURP
LET'S FIND OUT.
WHOMB

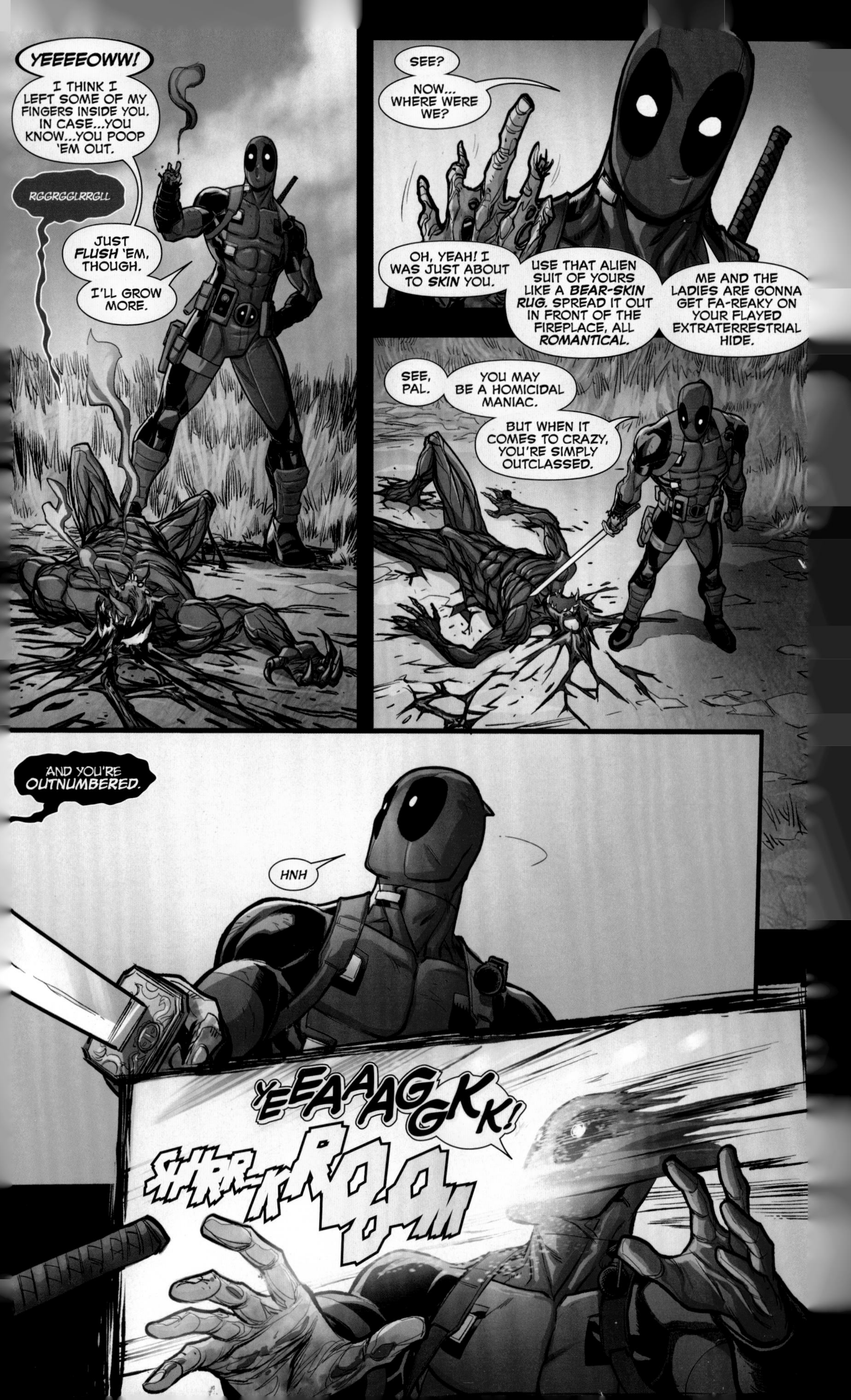
YEEEEOWW!
I THINK I LEFT SOME OF MY FINGERS INSIDE YOU. IN CASE...YOU KNOW...YOU POOP 'EM OUT.
RGGRGGLRRGLL
JUST FLUSH 'EM, THOUGH.
I'LL GROW MORE.
SEE?
NOW... WHERE WERE WE?
OH, YEAH! I WAS JUST ABOUT TO SKIN YOU.
USE THAT ALIEN SUIT OF YOURS LIKE A BEAR-SKIN RUG. SPREAD IT OUT IN FRONT OF THE FIREPLACE, ALL ROMANTICAL.
ME AND THE LADIES ARE GONNA GET FA-REAKY ON YOUR FLAYED EXTRATERRESTRIAL HIDE.
SEE, PAL.
YOU MAY BE A HOMICIDAL MANIAC.
BUT WHEN IT COMES TO CRAZY, YOU'RE SIMPLY OUTCLASSED.
AND YOU'RE OUTNUMBERED.
HNH
YEEAAAGGKKK!
SHRR-K-RA-BOOM

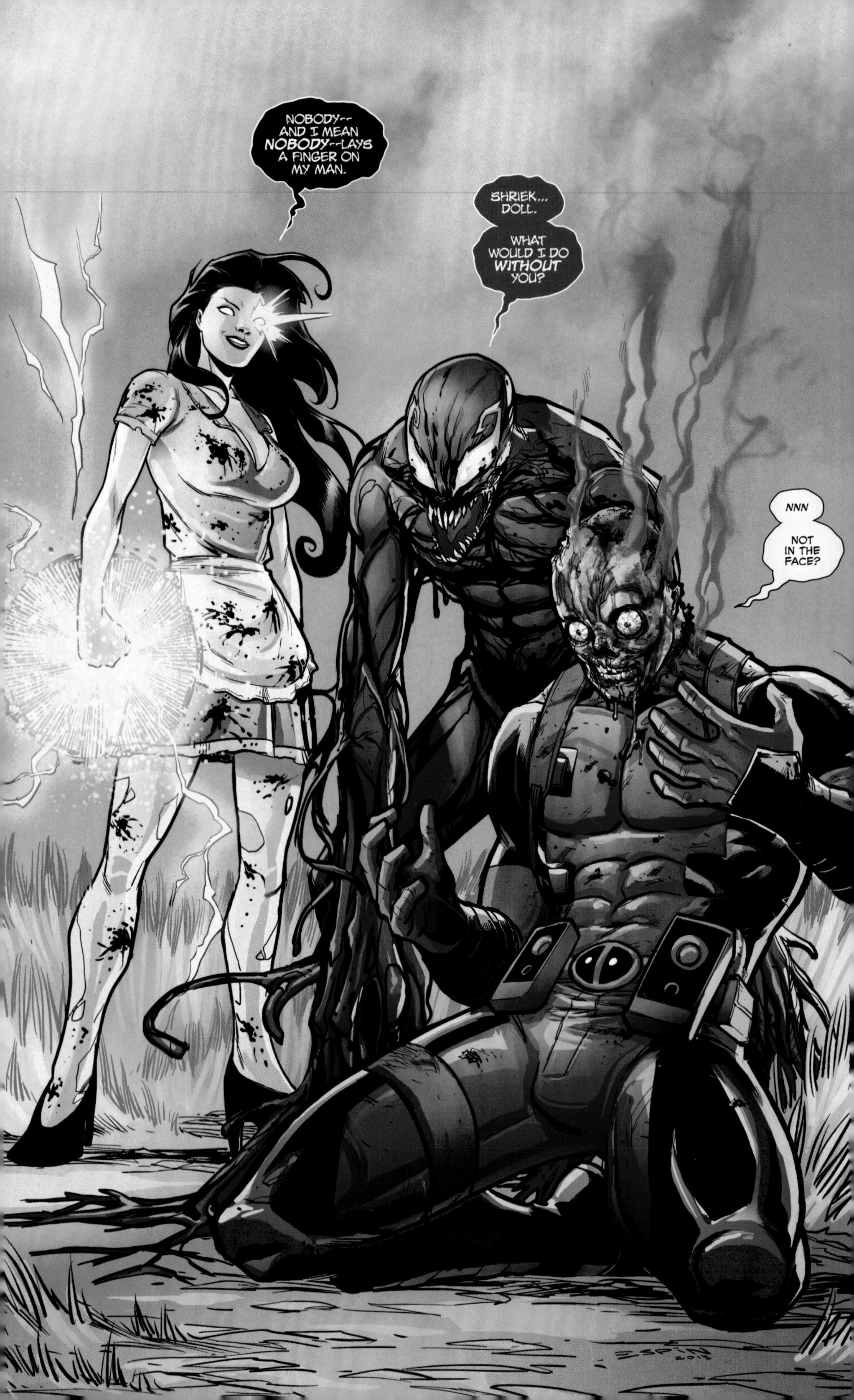
NOBODY-- AND I MEAN NOBODY--LAYS A FINGER ON MY MAN.
SHRIEK... DOLL.
WHAT WOULD I DO WITHOUT YOU?
NNN
NOT IN THE FACE?
ESPIN 2013

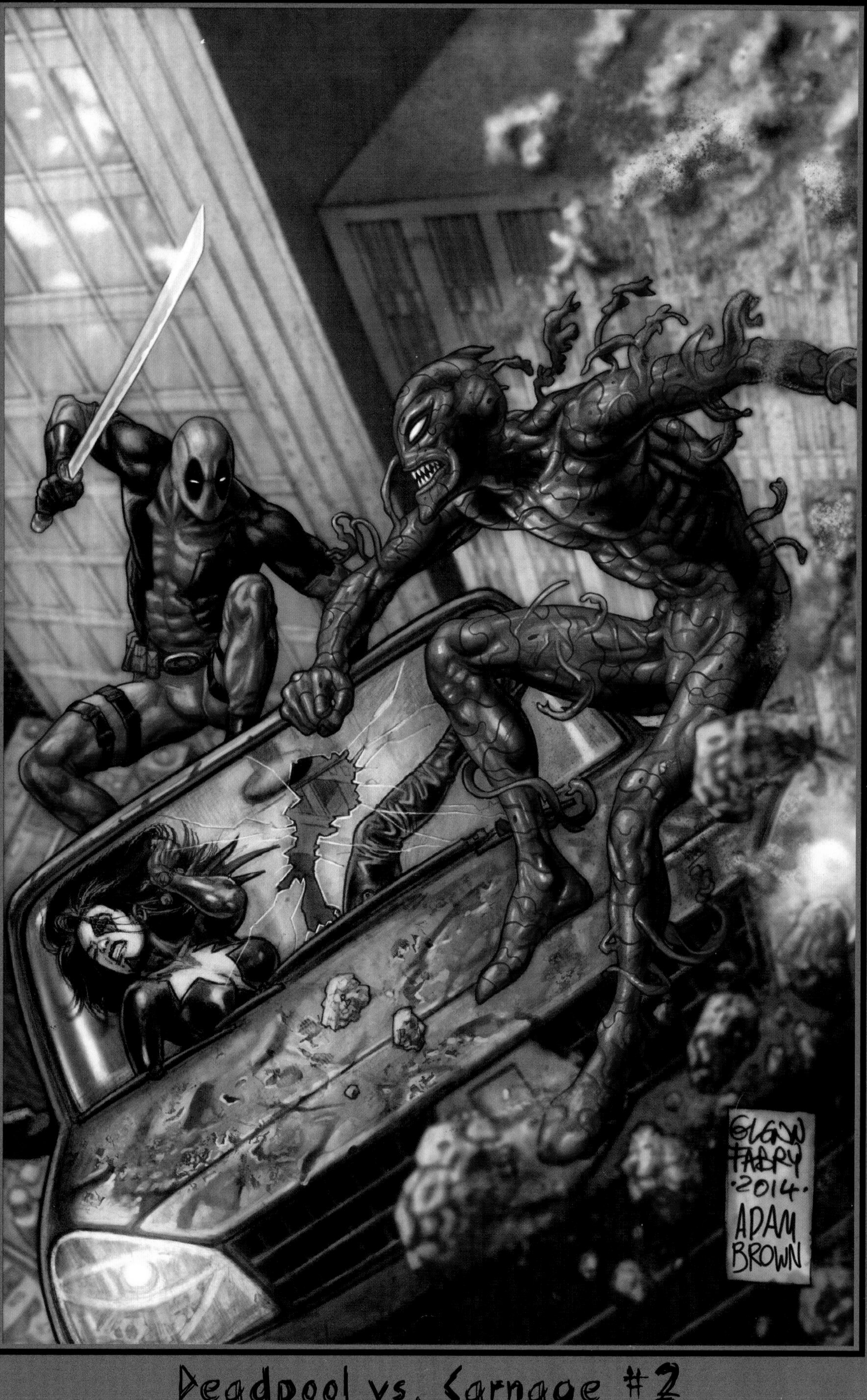
GLENN FABRY
·2014·
ADAM BROWN

Deadpool vs. Carnage #2

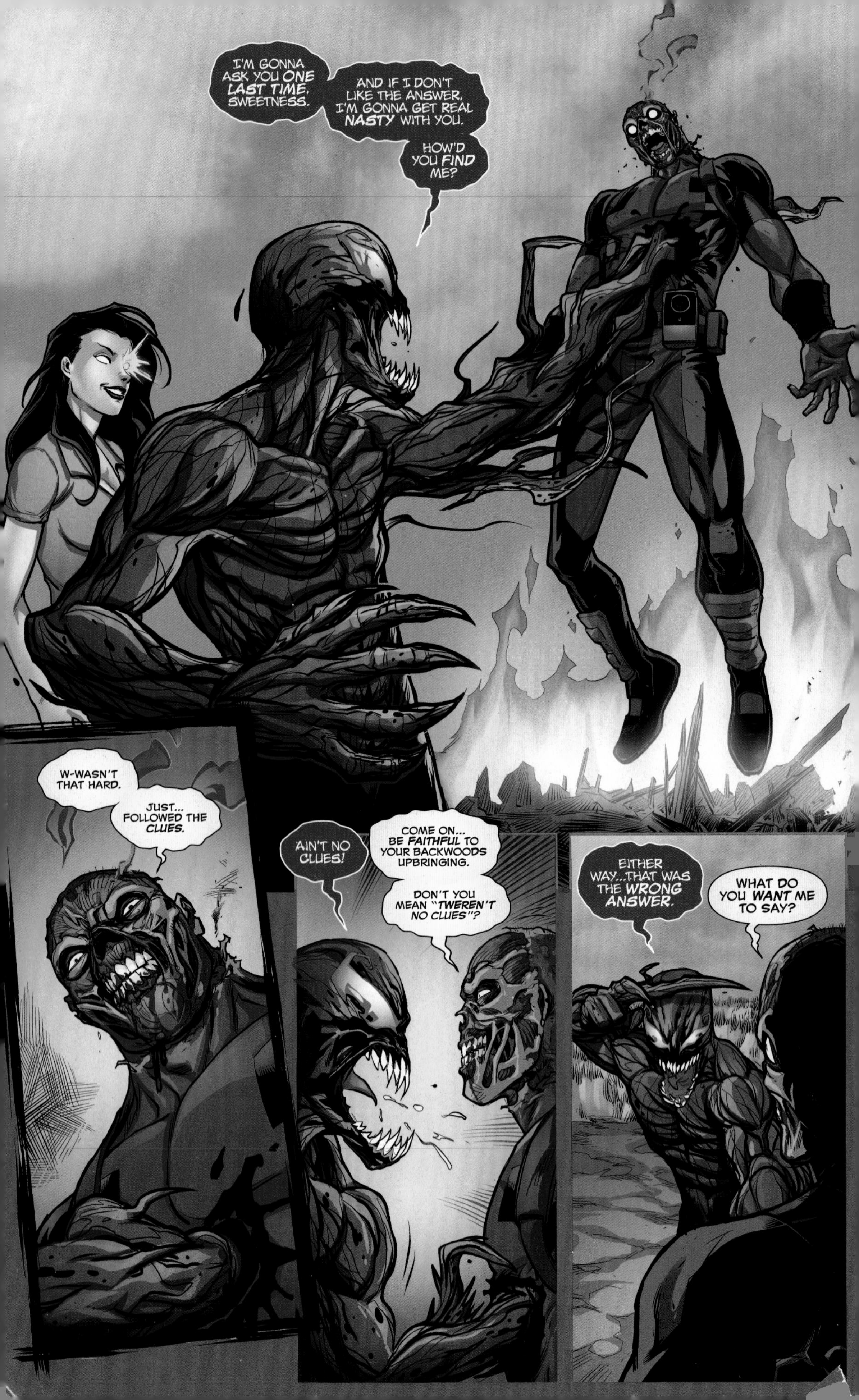
I'M GONNA ASK YOU ONE LAST TIME, SWEETNESS.
AND IF I DON'T LIKE THE ANSWER, I'M GONNA GET REAL NASTY WITH YOU.
HOW'D YOU FIND ME?
W-WASN'T THAT HARD.
JUST... FOLLOWED THE CLUES.
'AIN'T NO CLUES!
COME ON... BE FAITHFUL TO YOUR BACKWOODS UPBRINGING.
DON'T YOU MEAN "TWEREN'T NO CLUES"?
EITHER WAY...THAT WAS THE WRONG ANSWER.
WHAT DO YOU WANT ME TO SAY?

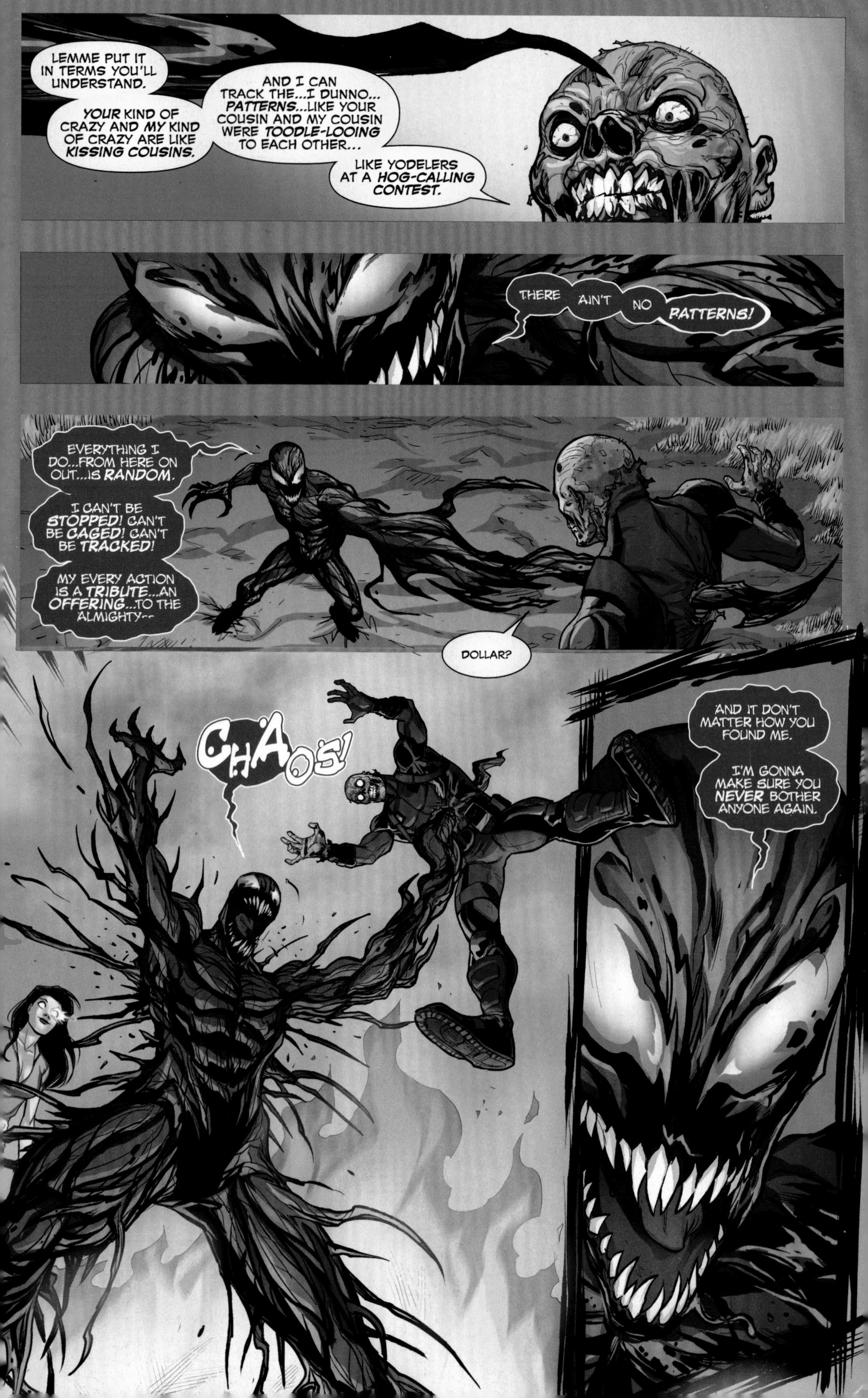
LEMME PUT IT IN TERMS YOU'LL UNDERSTAND.
YOUR KIND OF CRAZY AND MY KIND OF CRAZY ARE LIKE KISSING COUSINS.
AND I CAN TRACK THE...I DUNNO... PATTERNS...LIKE YOUR COUSIN AND MY COUSIN WERE TOODLE-LOOING TO EACH OTHER...
LIKE YODELERS AT A HOG-CALLING CONTEST.
THERE AIN'T NO PATTERNS!
EVERYTHING I DO...FROM HERE ON OUT...IS RANDOM.
I CAN'T BE STOPPED! CAN'T BE CAGED! CAN'T BE TRACKED!
MY EVERY ACTION IS A TRIBUTE...AN OFFERING...TO THE ALMIGHTY--
DOLLAR?
CHAOS!
AND IT DON'T MATTER HOW YOU FOUND ME.
I'M GONNA MAKE SURE YOU NEVER BOTHER ANYONE AGAIN.

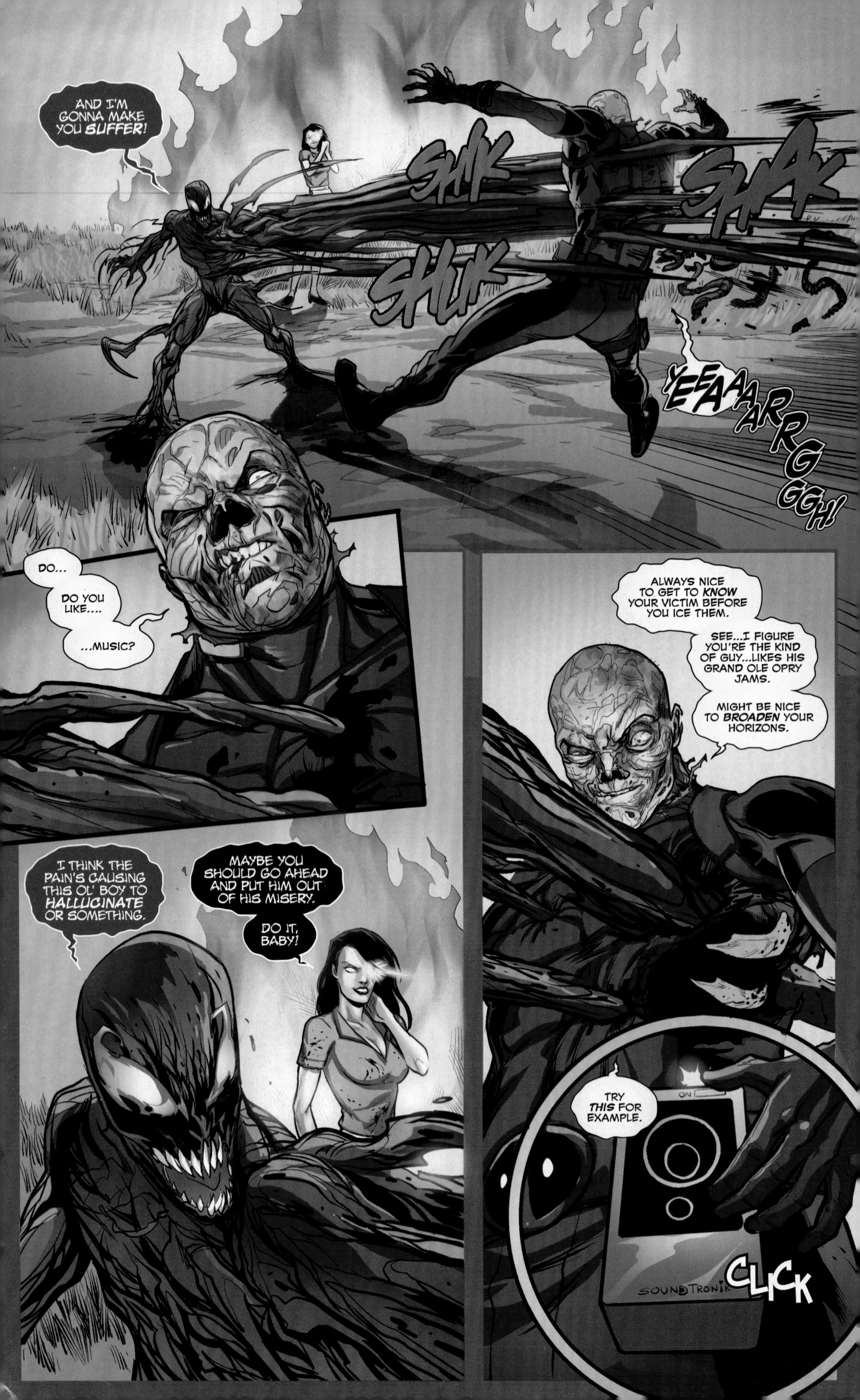
AND I'M GONNA MAKE YOU SUFFER!
SHIK
SHAK
SHUK
YEEAAAARRGGGH!
DO...
DO YOU LIKE....
...MUSIC?
ALWAYS NICE TO GET TO KNOW YOUR VICTIM BEFORE YOU ICE THEM.
SEE...I FIGURE YOU'RE THE KIND OF GUY...LIKES HIS GRAND OLE OPRY JAMS.
MIGHT BE NICE TO BROADEN YOUR HORIZONS.
I THINK THE PAIN'S CAUSING THIS OL' BOY TO HALLUCINATE OR SOMETHING.
MAYBE YOU SHOULD GO AHEAD AND PUT HIM OUT OF HIS MISERY.
DO IT, BABY!
TRY THIS FOR EXAMPLE.
ON
SOUNDTRONIK
CLICK

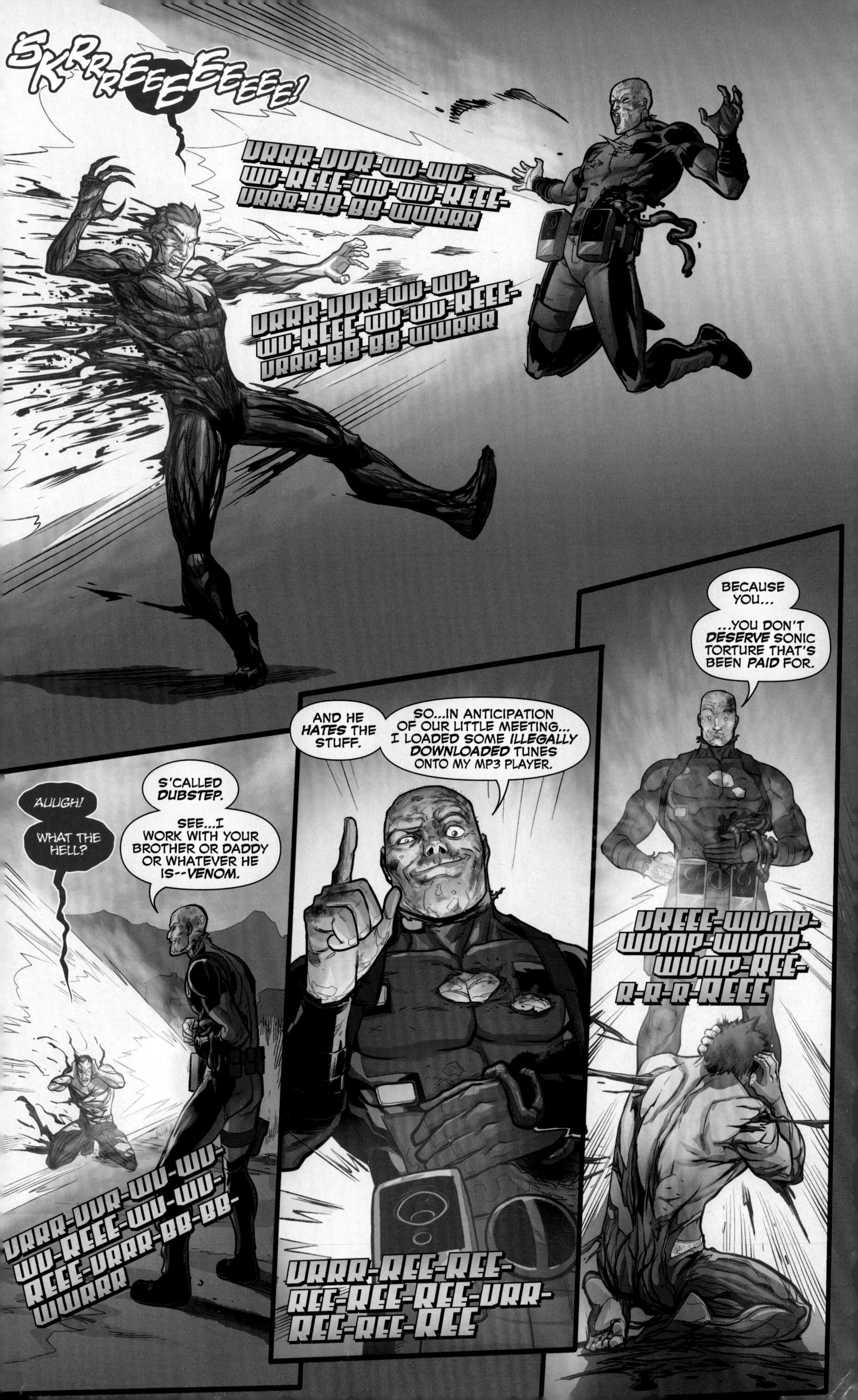
SKRRREEEEEEEEEE!
VRRR-VVR-WV-WV-WV-REEE-WV-WV-REEE-VRRR-BB-BB-WWRRR
VRRR-VVR-WV-WV-WV-REEE-WV-WV-REEE-VRRR-BB-BB-WWRRR
AUUGH!
WHAT THE HELL?
S'CALLED DUBSTEP.
SEE...I WORK WITH YOUR BROTHER OR DADDY OR WHATEVER HE IS--VENOM.
VRRR-VVR-WV-WV-WV-REEE-WV-WV-REEE-VRRR-BB-BB-WWRRR
AND HE HATES THE STUFF.
SO...IN ANTICIPATION OF OUR LITTLE MEETING... I LOADED SOME ILLEGALLY DOWNLOADED TUNES ONTO MY MP3 PLAYER.
VRRR-REE-REE-REE-REE-REE-VRR-REE-REE-REE
BECAUSE YOU...
...YOU DON'T DESERVE SONIC TORTURE THAT'S BEEN PAID FOR.
VREEE-WUMP-WUMP-WUMP-WUMP-REE-R-R-R-REEE

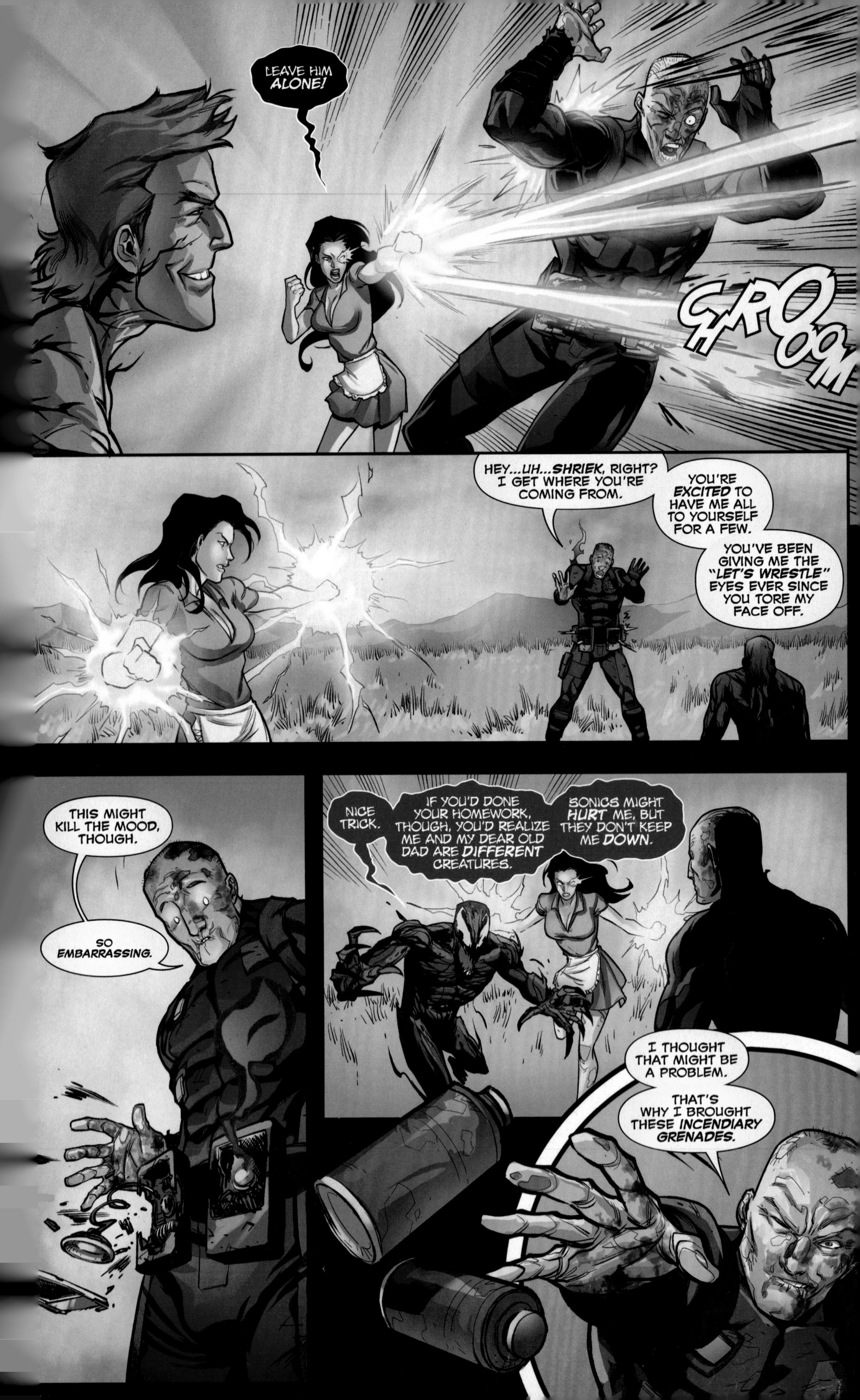
LEAVE HIM ALONE!
CHROOOOM
HEY...UH...SHRIEK, RIGHT? I GET WHERE YOU'RE COMING FROM.
YOU'RE EXCITED TO HAVE ME ALL TO YOURSELF FOR A FEW.
YOU'VE BEEN GIVING ME THE "LET'S WRESTLE" EYES EVER SINCE YOU TORE MY FACE OFF.
THIS MIGHT KILL THE MOOD, THOUGH.
SO EMBARRASSING.
NICE TRICK.
IF YOU'D DONE YOUR HOMEWORK, THOUGH, YOU'D REALIZE ME AND MY DEAR OLD DAD ARE DIFFERENT CREATURES.
SONICS MIGHT HURT ME, BUT THEY DON'T KEEP ME DOWN.
I THOUGHT THAT MIGHT BE A PROBLEM.
THAT'S WHY I BROUGHT THESE INCENDIARY GRENADES.

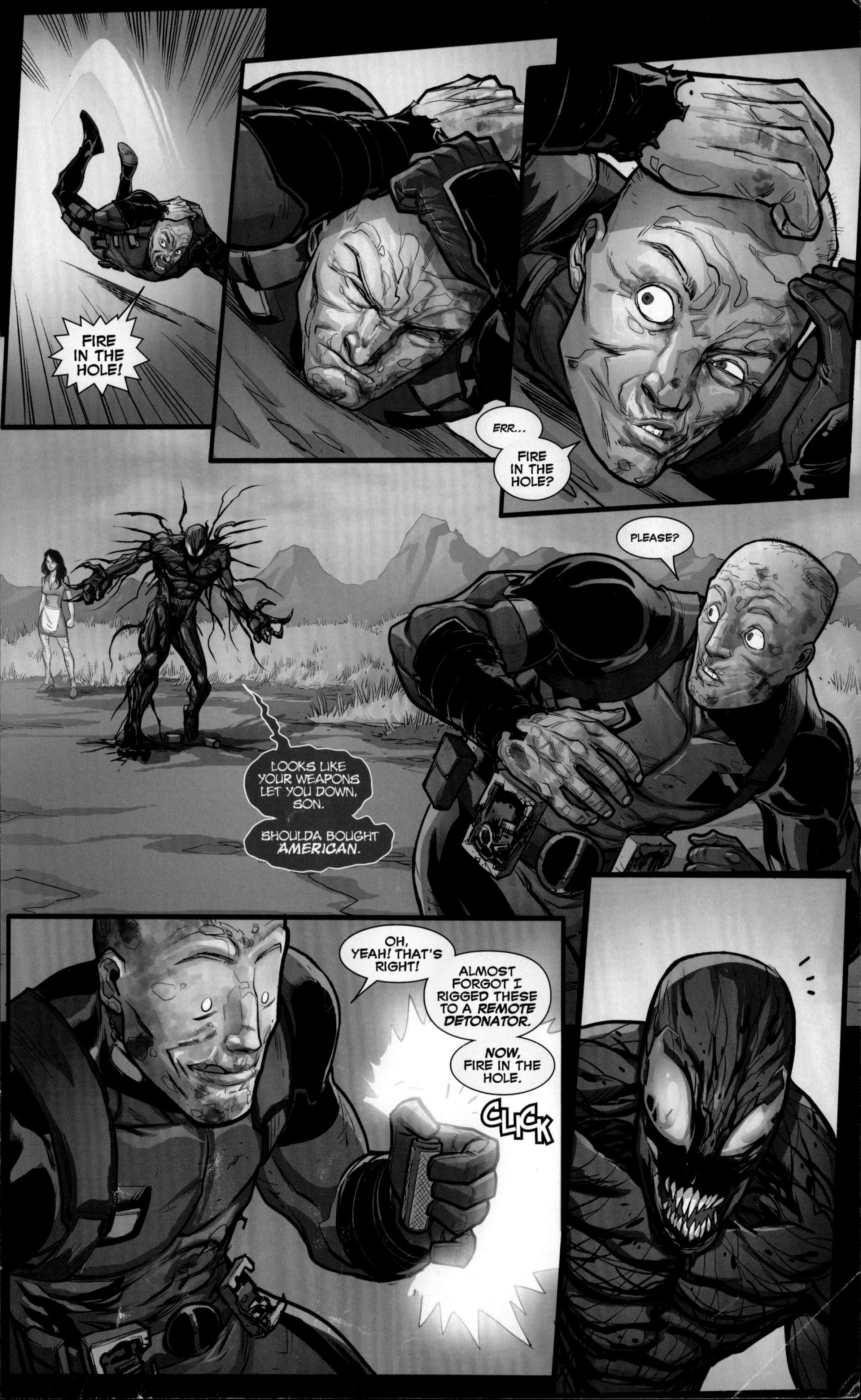

FIRE IN THE HOLE!
ERR...
FIRE IN THE HOLE?
PLEASE?
LOOKS LIKE YOUR WEAPONS LET YOU DOWN, SON.
SHOULDA BOUGHT AMERICAN.
OH, YEAH! THAT'S RIGHT!
ALMOST FORGOT I RIGGED THESE TO A REMOTE DETONATOR.
NOW, FIRE IN THE HOLE.
CLICK

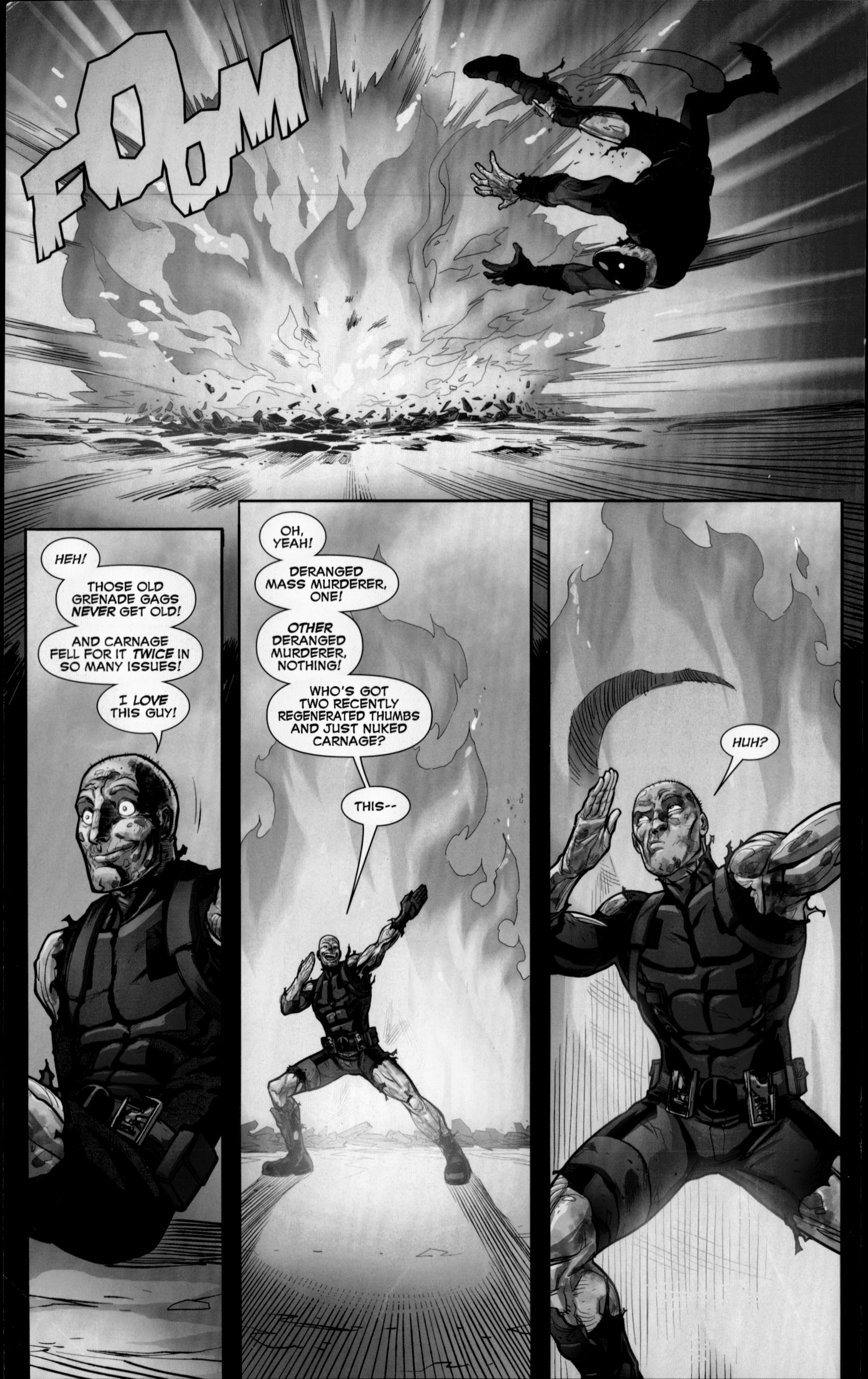
FOOM
HEH!
THOSE OLD GRENADE GAGS NEVER GET OLD!
AND CARNAGE FELL FOR IT TWICE IN SO MANY ISSUES!
I LOVE THIS GUY!
OH, YEAH!
DERANGED MASS MURDERER, ONE!
OTHER DERANGED MURDERER, NOTHING!
WHO'S GOT TWO RECENTLY REGENERATED THUMBS AND JUST NUKED CARNAGE?
THIS--
HUH?

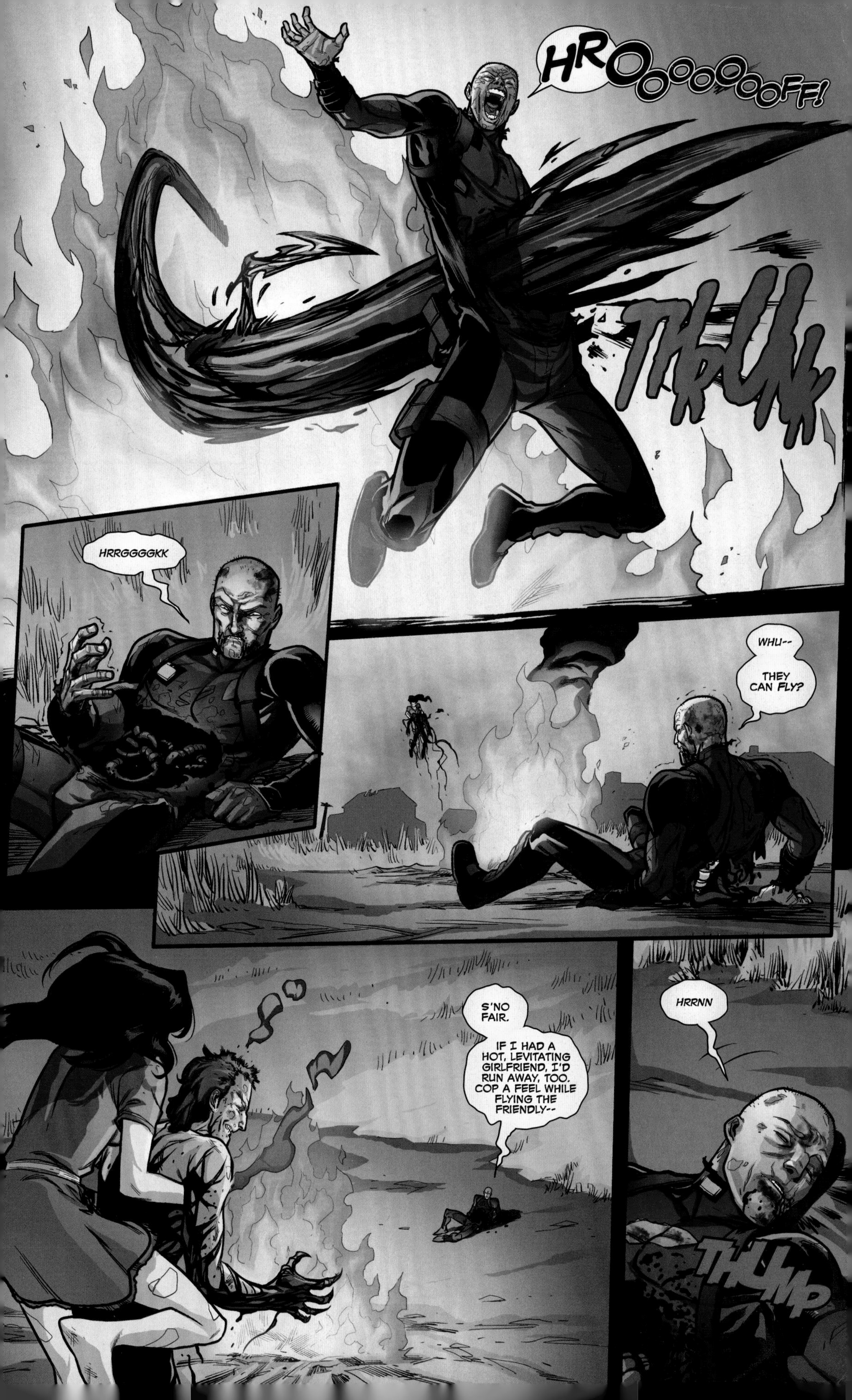
HROOOOOOOOFF!
THHUNK
HRRGGGGKK
WHU--
THEY CAN FLY?
S'NO FAIR.
IF I HAD A HOT, LEVITATING GIRLFRIEND, I'D RUN AWAY, TOO. COP A FEEL WHILE FLYING THE FRIENDLY--
HRRNN
THUMP

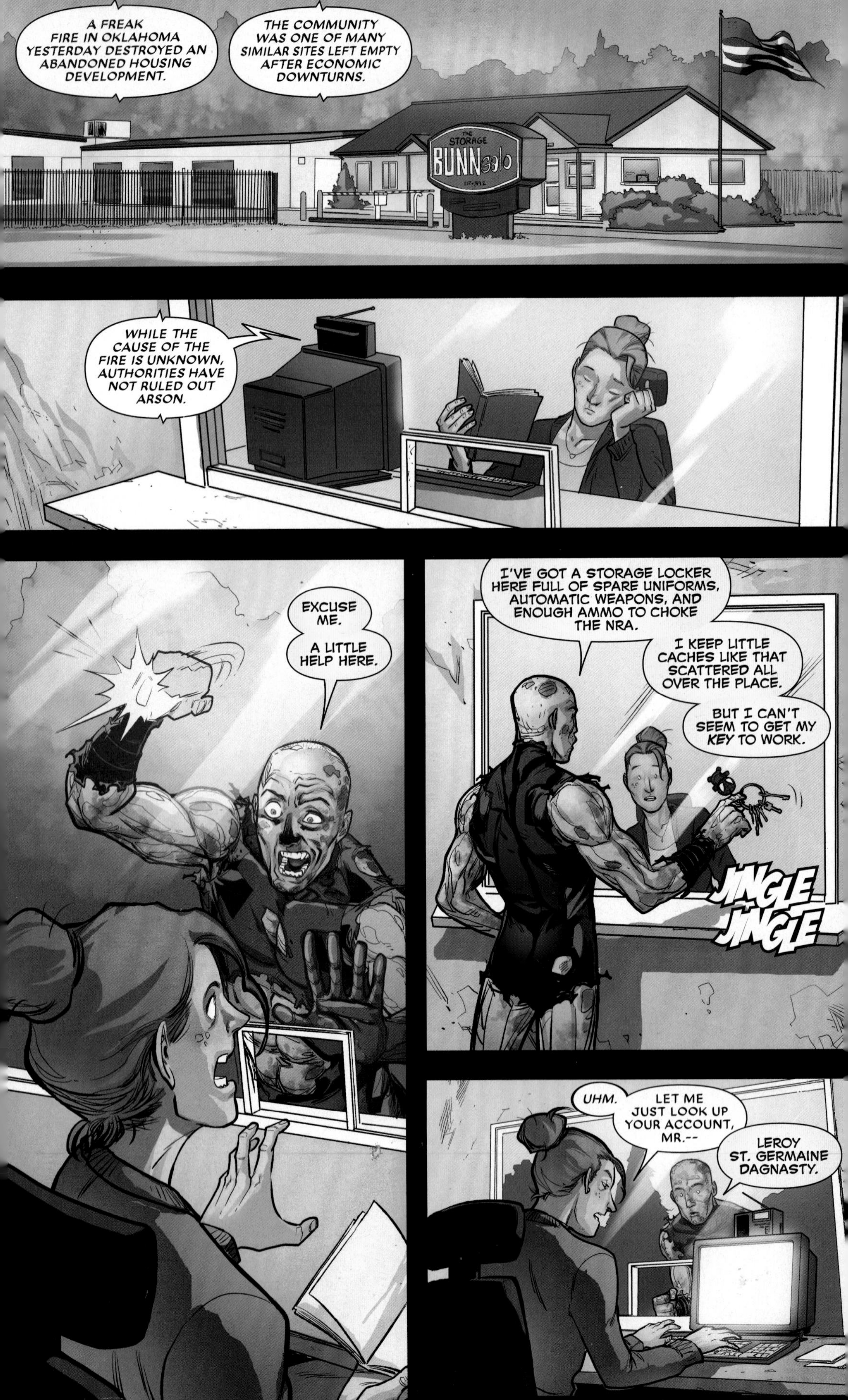

A FREAK FIRE IN OKLAHOMA YESTERDAY DESTROYED AN ABANDONED HOUSING DEVELOPMENT.
THE COMMUNITY WAS ONE OF MANY SIMILAR SITES LEFT EMPTY AFTER ECONOMIC DOWNTURNS.
the STORAGE BUNNgalo
WHILE THE CAUSE OF THE FIRE IS UNKNOWN, AUTHORITIES HAVE NOT RULED OUT ARSON.
EXCUSE ME.
A LITTLE HELP HERE.
I'VE GOT A STORAGE LOCKER HERE FULL OF SPARE UNIFORMS, AUTOMATIC WEAPONS, AND ENOUGH AMMO TO CHOKE THE NRA.
I KEEP LITTLE CACHES LIKE THAT SCATTERED ALL OVER THE PLACE.
BUT I CAN'T SEEM TO GET MY *KEY* TO WORK.
JINGLE JINGLE
UHM.
LET ME JUST LOOK UP YOUR ACCOUNT, MR.--
LEROY ST. GERMAINE DAGNASTY.

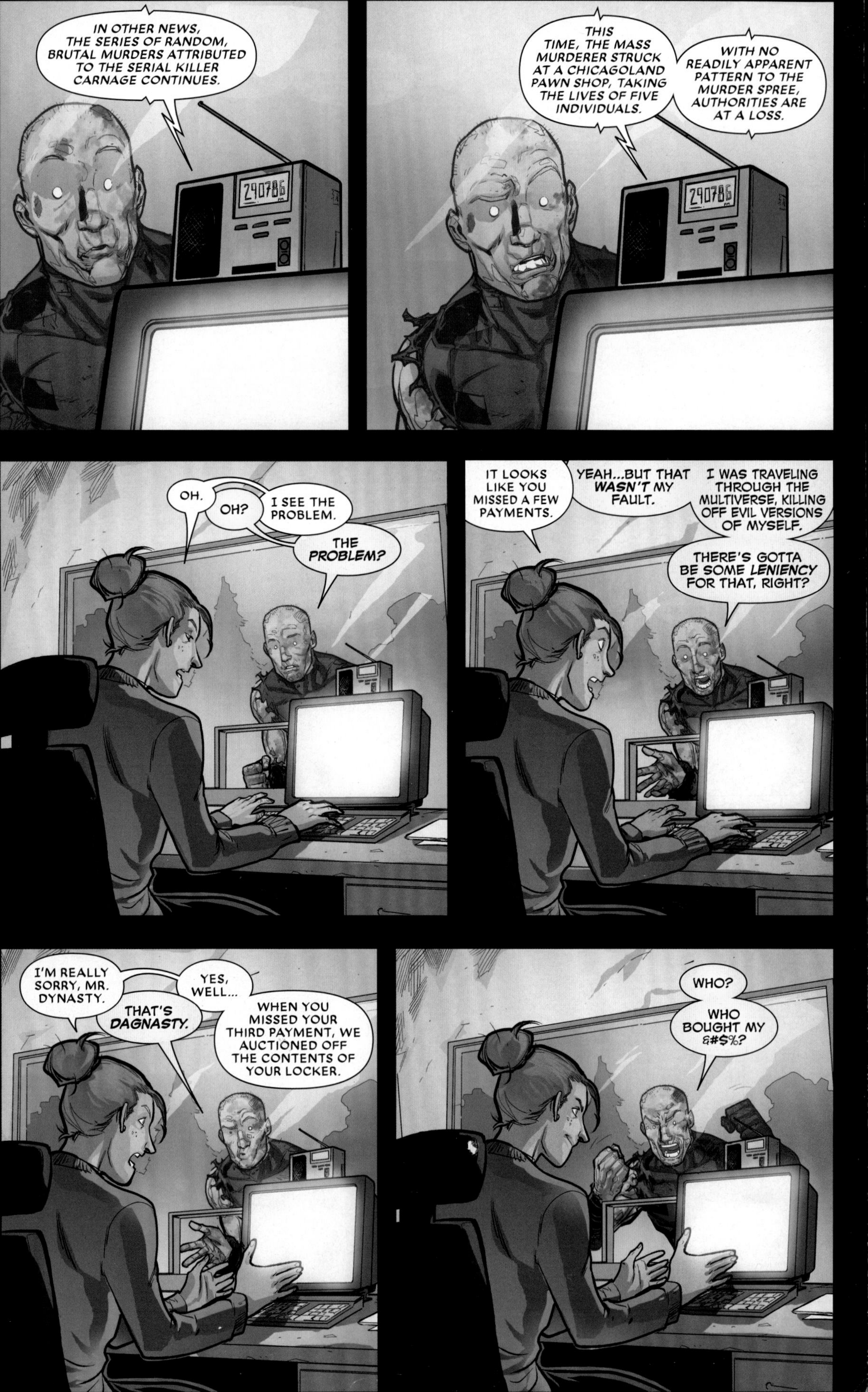
IN OTHER NEWS, THE SERIES OF RANDOM, BRUTAL MURDERS ATTRIBUTED TO THE SERIAL KILLER CARNAGE CONTINUES.
THIS TIME, THE MASS MURDERER STRUCK AT A CHICAGOLAND PAWN SHOP, TAKING THE LIVES OF FIVE INDIVIDUALS.
WITH NO READILY APPARENT PATTERN TO THE MURDER SPREE, AUTHORITIES ARE AT A LOSS.
OH.
OH?
I SEE THE PROBLEM.
THE *PROBLEM?*
IT LOOKS LIKE YOU MISSED A FEW PAYMENTS.
YEAH...BUT THAT *WASN'T* MY FAULT.
I WAS TRAVELING THROUGH THE MULTIVERSE, KILLING OFF EVIL VERSIONS OF MYSELF.
THERE'S GOTTA BE SOME *LENIENCY* FOR THAT, RIGHT?
I'M REALLY SORRY, MR. DYNASTY.
THAT'S *DAGNASTY.*
YES, WELL...
WHEN YOU MISSED YOUR THIRD PAYMENT, WE AUCTIONED OFF THE CONTENTS OF YOUR LOCKER.
WHO?
WHO BOUGHT MY &#$%?

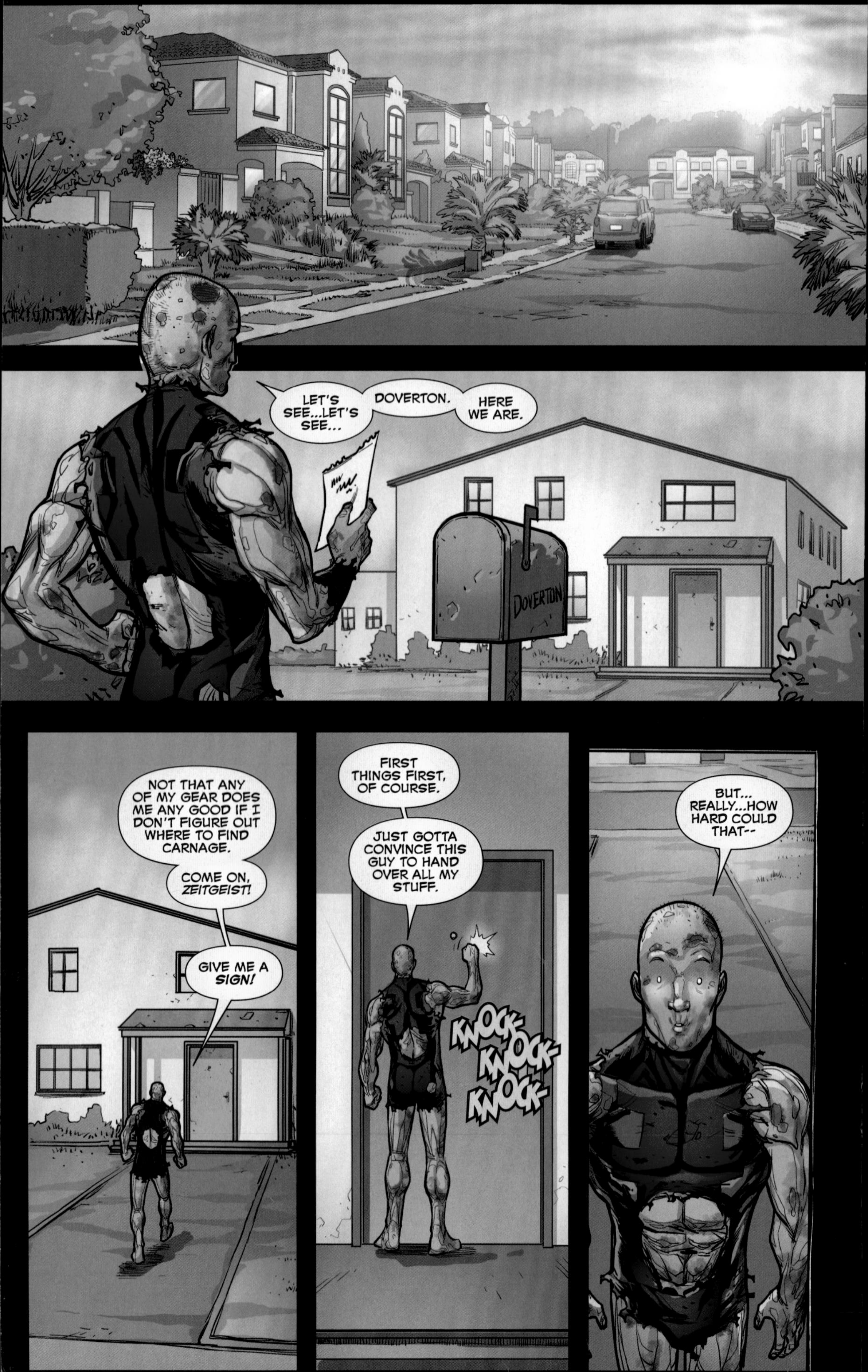
LET'S SEE...LET'S SEE...
DOVERTON.
HERE WE ARE.
DOVERTON
NOT THAT ANY OF MY GEAR DOES ME ANY GOOD IF I DON'T FIGURE OUT WHERE TO FIND CARNAGE.
COME ON, ZEITGEIST!
GIVE ME A SIGN!
FIRST THINGS FIRST, OF COURSE.
JUST GOTTA CONVINCE THIS GUY TO HAND OVER ALL MY STUFF.
KNOCK KNOCK KNOCK
BUT... REALLY...HOW HARD COULD THAT--

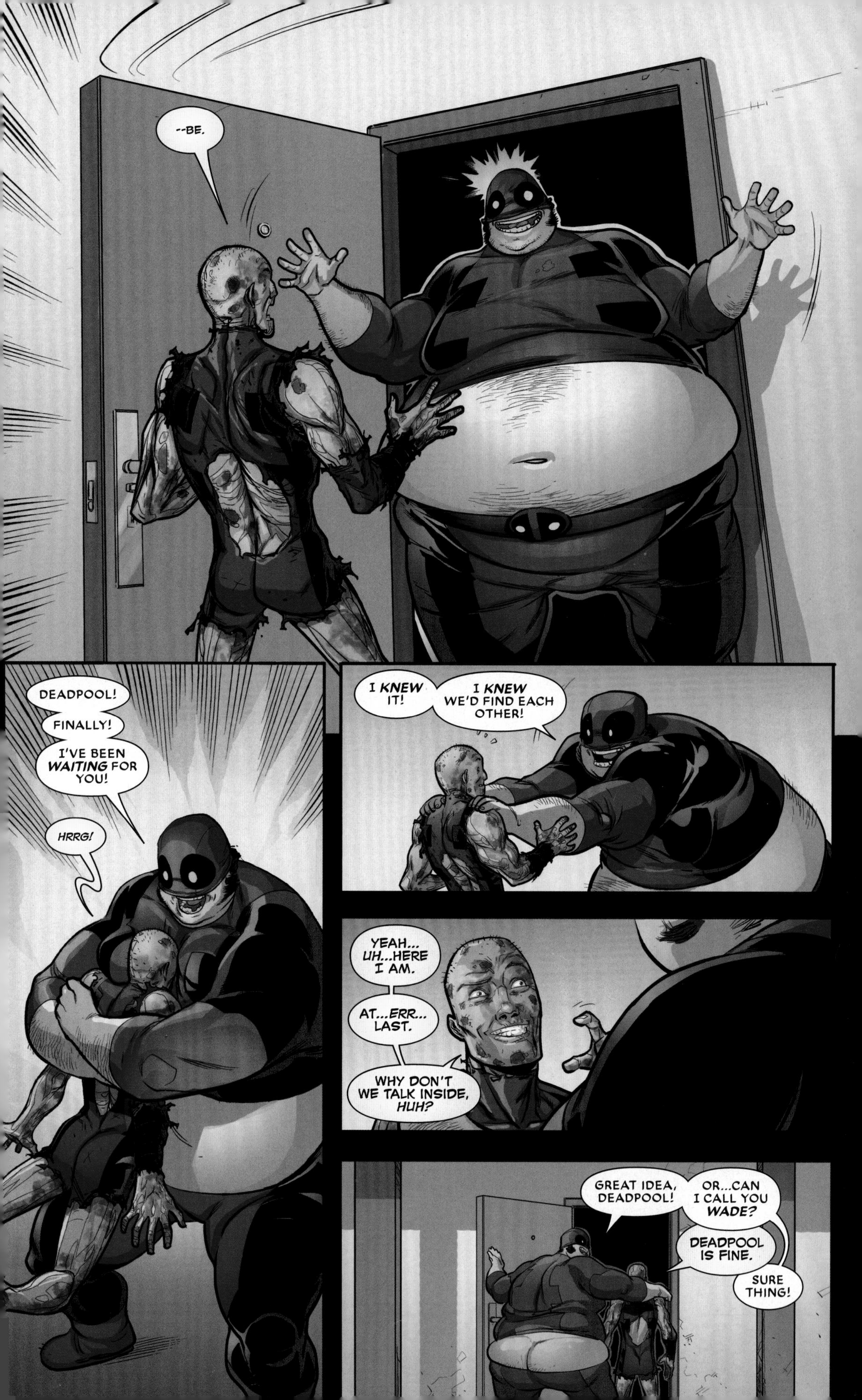
--BE.
DEADPOOL!
FINALLY!
I'VE BEEN *WAITING* FOR YOU!
HRRG!
I *KNEW* IT!
I *KNEW* WE'D FIND EACH OTHER!
YEAH... *UH*...HERE I AM.
AT...ERR... LAST.
WHY DON'T WE TALK INSIDE, *HUH?*
GREAT IDEA, DEADPOOL!
OR...CAN I CALL YOU *WADE?*
DEADPOOL IS FINE.
SURE THING!

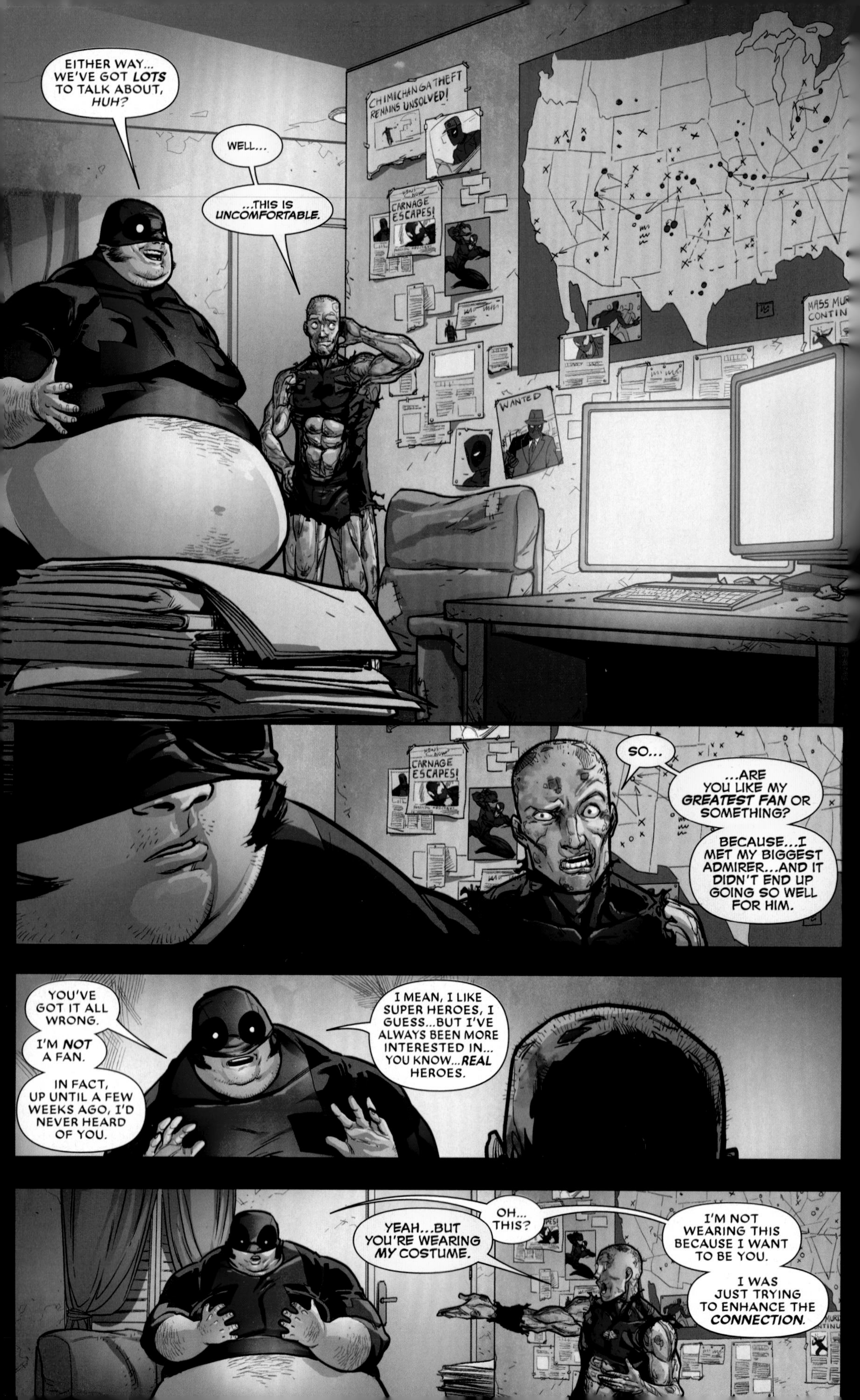
EITHER WAY... WE'VE GOT LOTS TO TALK ABOUT, HUH?
WELL...
...THIS IS UNCOMFORTABLE.
CHIMICHANGA THEFT REMAINS UNSOLVED!
CARNAGE ESCAPES!
WANTED
MASS MUR CONTIN
SO...
...ARE YOU LIKE MY GREATEST FAN OR SOMETHING?
BECAUSE...I MET MY BIGGEST ADMIRER...AND IT DIDN'T END UP GOING SO WELL FOR HIM.
YOU'VE GOT IT ALL WRONG.
I'M NOT A FAN.
IN FACT, UP UNTIL A FEW WEEKS AGO, I'D NEVER HEARD OF YOU.
I MEAN, I LIKE SUPER HEROES, I GUESS...BUT I'VE ALWAYS BEEN MORE INTERESTED IN... YOU KNOW...REAL HEROES.
YEAH...BUT YOU'RE WEARING MY COSTUME.
OH... THIS?
I'M NOT WEARING THIS BECAUSE I WANT TO BE YOU.
I WAS JUST TRYING TO ENHANCE THE CONNECTION.

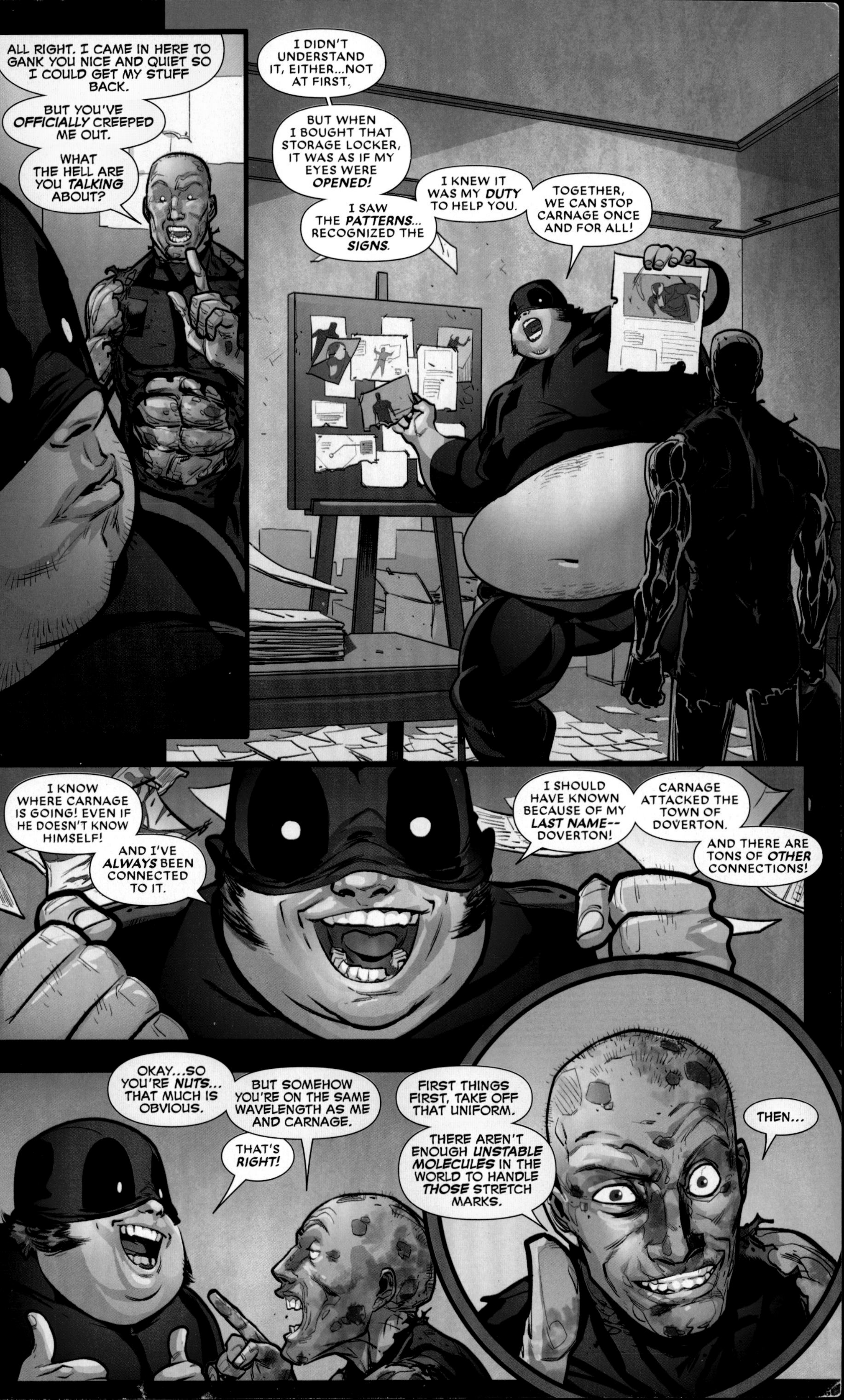

ALL RIGHT. I CAME IN HERE TO GANK YOU NICE AND QUIET SO I COULD GET MY STUFF BACK.
BUT YOU'VE *OFFICIALLY* CREEPED ME OUT.
WHAT THE HELL ARE YOU *TALKING* ABOUT?
I DIDN'T UNDERSTAND IT, EITHER...NOT AT FIRST.
BUT WHEN I BOUGHT THAT STORAGE LOCKER, IT WAS AS IF MY EYES WERE *OPENED!*
I SAW THE *PATTERNS*... RECOGNIZED THE *SIGNS*.
I KNEW IT WAS MY *DUTY* TO HELP YOU.
TOGETHER, WE CAN STOP CARNAGE ONCE AND FOR ALL!
I KNOW WHERE CARNAGE IS GOING! EVEN IF HE DOESN'T KNOW HIMSELF!
AND I'VE *ALWAYS* BEEN CONNECTED TO IT.
I SHOULD HAVE KNOWN BECAUSE OF MY *LAST NAME--* DOVERTON!
CARNAGE ATTACKED THE TOWN OF DOVERTON.
AND THERE ARE TONS OF *OTHER* CONNECTIONS!
OKAY...SO YOU'RE *NUTS*... THAT MUCH IS OBVIOUS.
BUT SOMEHOW YOU'RE ON THE SAME WAVELENGTH AS ME AND CARNAGE.
THAT'S *RIGHT!*
FIRST THINGS FIRST, TAKE OFF THAT UNIFORM.
THERE AREN'T ENOUGH *UNSTABLE MOLECULES* IN THE WORLD TO HANDLE *THOSE* STRETCH MARKS.
THEN...

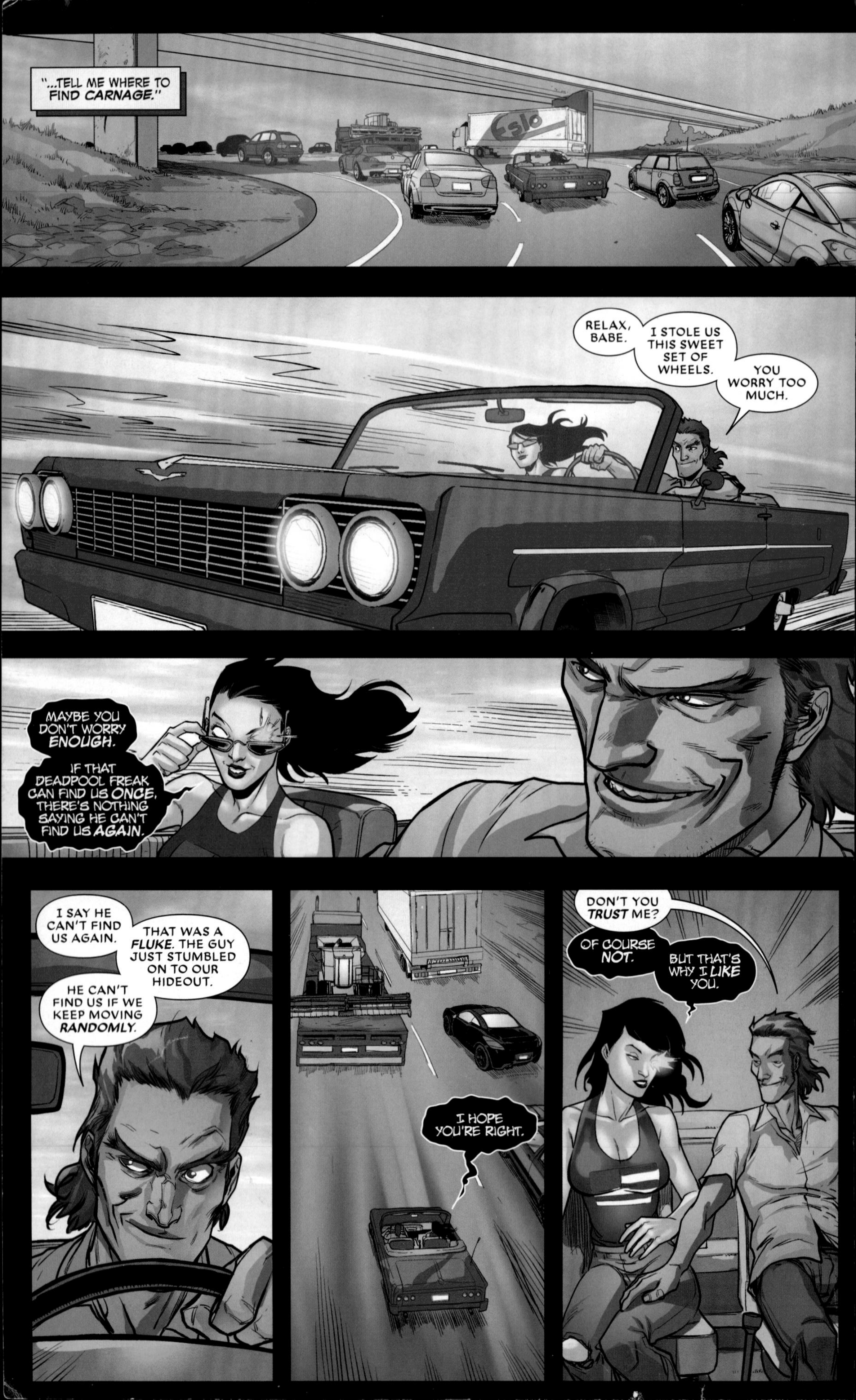
"...TELL ME WHERE TO FIND CARNAGE."
Eslo
RELAX, BABE.
I STOLE US THIS SWEET SET OF WHEELS.
YOU WORRY TOO MUCH.
MAYBE YOU DON'T WORRY ENOUGH.
IF THAT DEADPOOL FREAK CAN FIND US ONCE, THERE'S NOTHING SAYING HE CAN'T FIND US AGAIN.
I SAY HE CAN'T FIND US AGAIN.
THAT WAS A FLUKE. THE GUY JUST STUMBLED ON TO OUR HIDEOUT.
HE CAN'T FIND US IF WE KEEP MOVING RANDOMLY.
I HOPE YOU'RE RIGHT.
DON'T YOU TRUST ME?
OF COURSE NOT.
BUT THAT'S WHY I LIKE YOU.

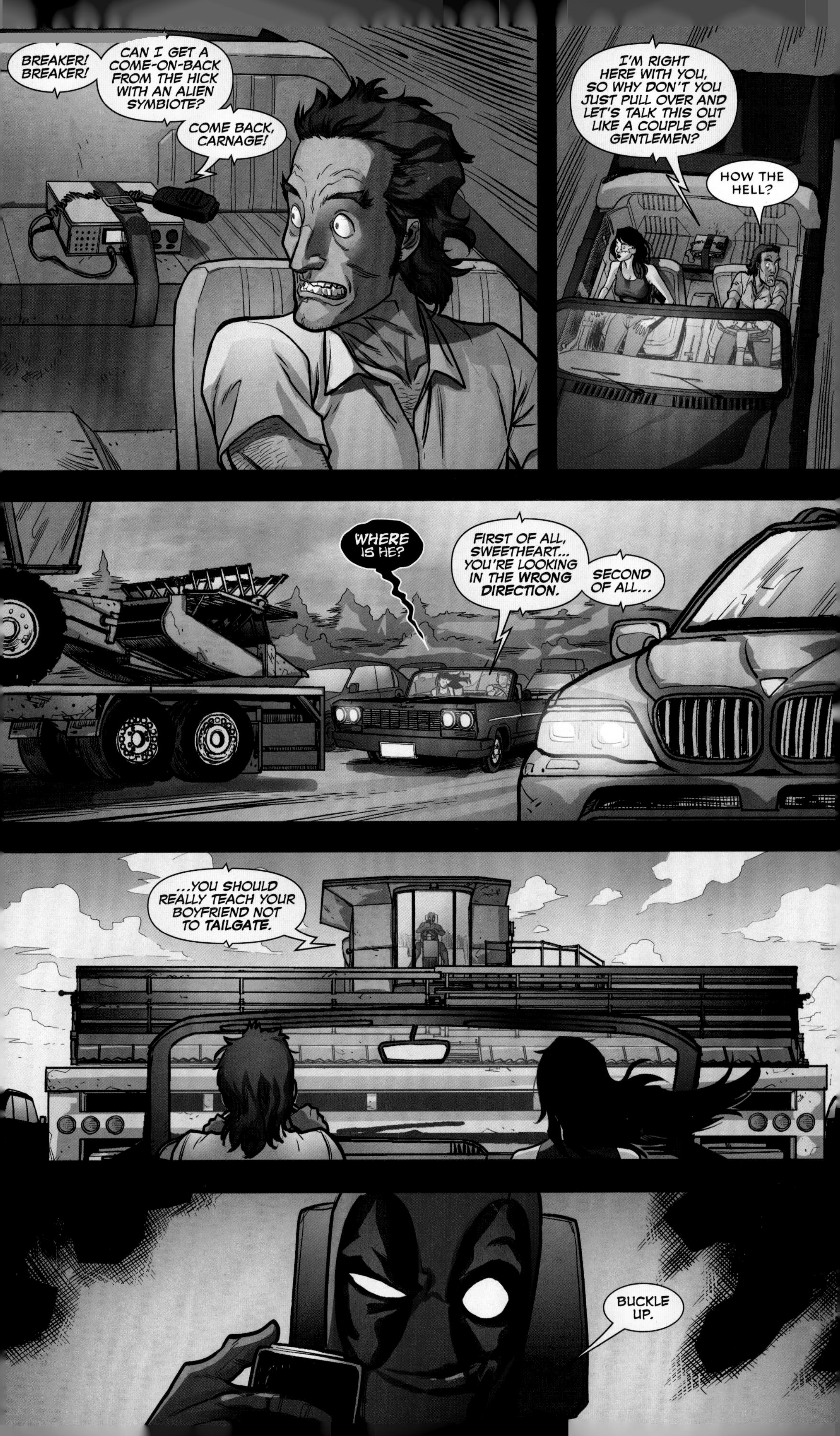
BREAKER! BREAKER!
CAN I GET A COME-ON-BACK FROM THE HICK WITH AN ALIEN SYMBIOTE?
COME BACK, CARNAGE!
I'M RIGHT HERE WITH YOU, SO WHY DON'T YOU JUST PULL OVER AND LET'S TALK THIS OUT LIKE A COUPLE OF GENTLEMEN?
HOW THE HELL?
WHERE IS HE?
FIRST OF ALL, SWEETHEART... YOU'RE LOOKING IN THE WRONG DIRECTION.
SECOND OF ALL...
...YOU SHOULD REALLY TEACH YOUR BOYFRIEND NOT TO TAILGATE.
BUCKLE UP.

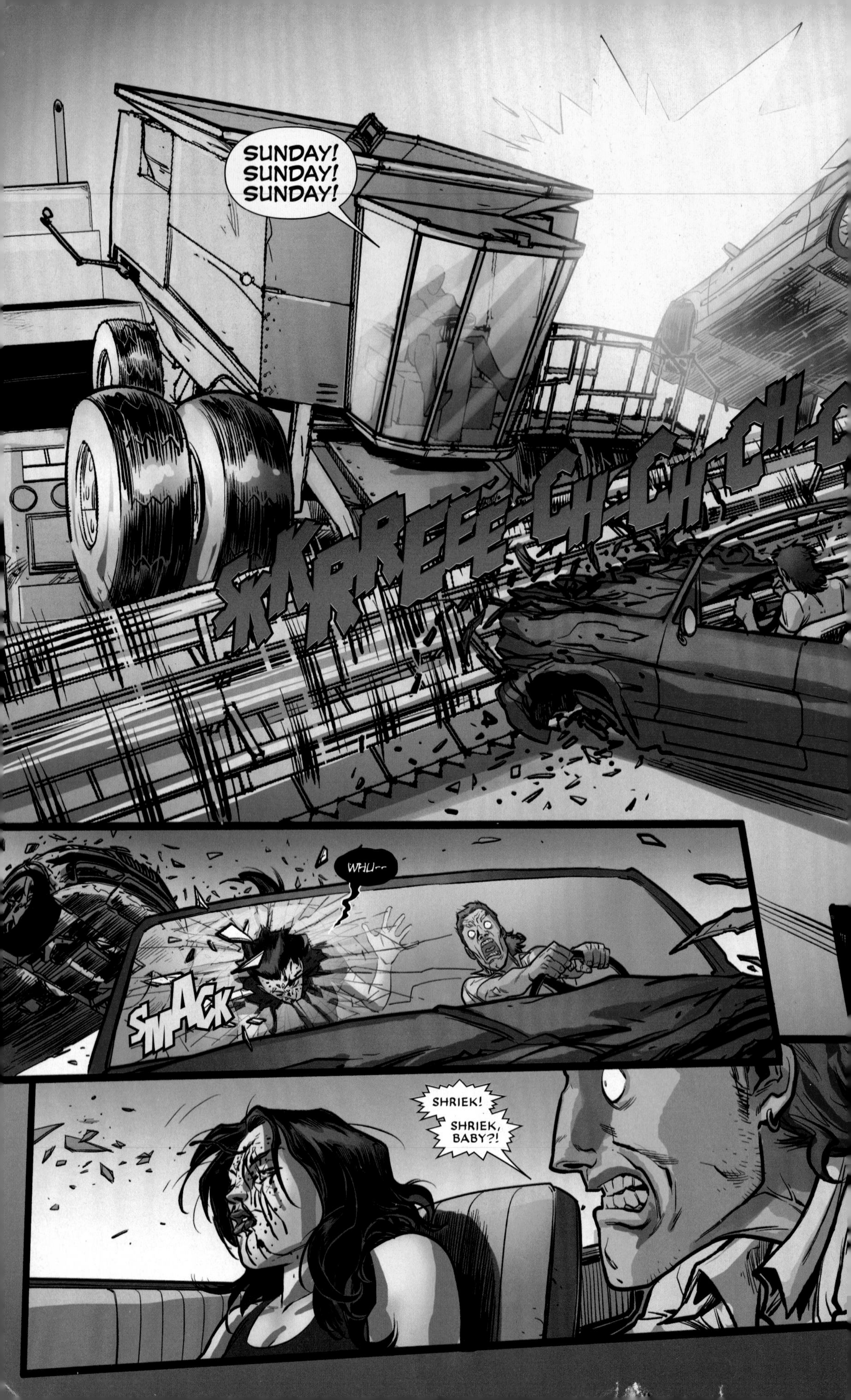
SUNDAY!
SUNDAY!
SUNDAY!
SKRREEE-CH-CH-CH-CH
WHU--
SMACK
SHRIEK!
SHRIEK, BABY?!

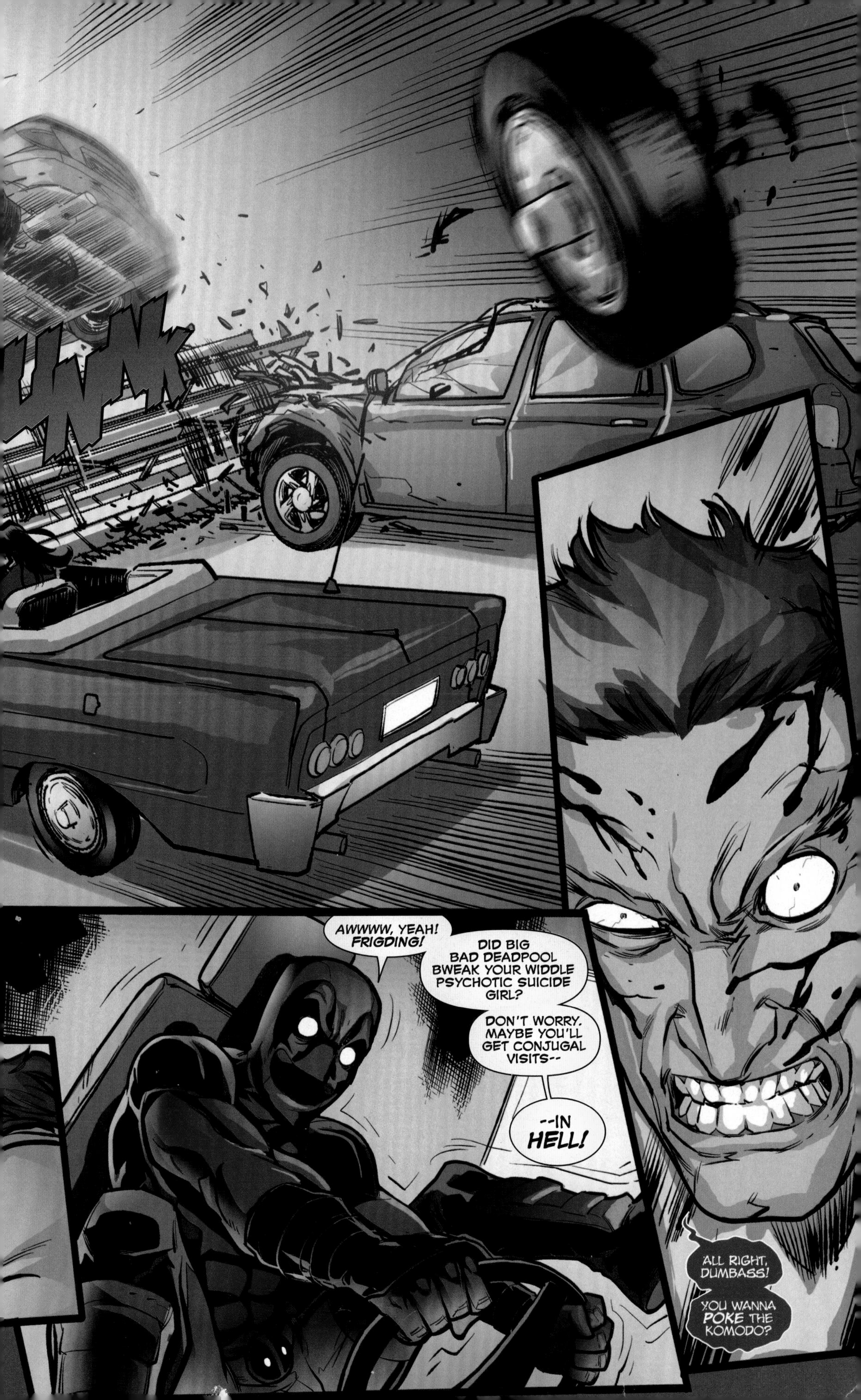

UNK
AWWWW, YEAH! FRIGDING!
DID BIG BAD DEADPOOL BWEAK YOUR WIDDLE PSYCHOTIC SUICIDE GIRL?
DON'T WORRY. MAYBE YOU'LL GET CONJUGAL VISITS--
--IN HELL!
ALL RIGHT, DUMBASS!
YOU WANNA POKE THE KOMODO?

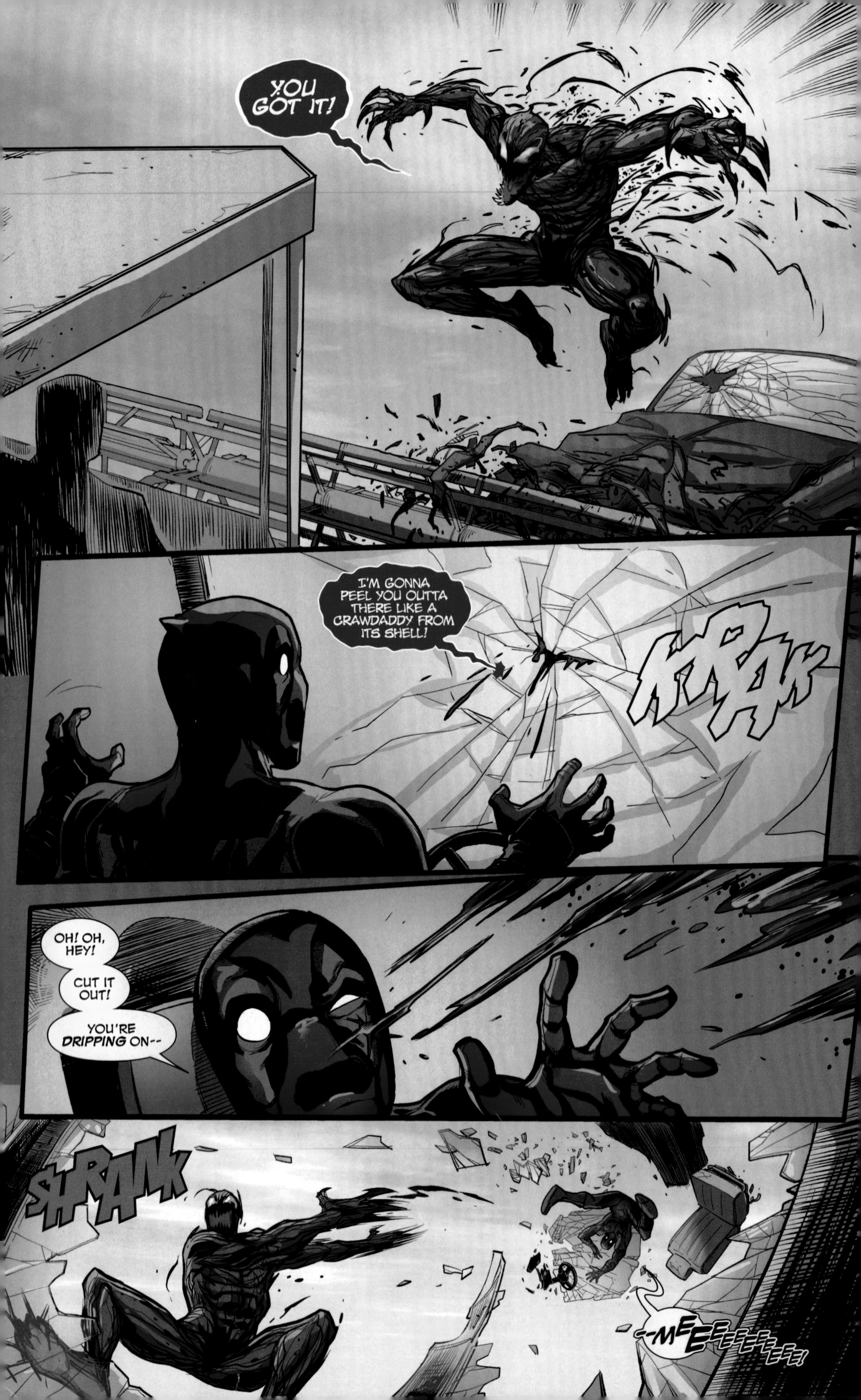
YOU GOT IT!
I'M GONNA PEEL YOU OUTTA THERE LIKE A CRAWDADDY FROM ITS SHELL!
KRAK
OH! OH, HEY!
CUT IT OUT!
YOU'RE DRIPPING ON--
SHRANK
--MEEEEEEEEEEE!

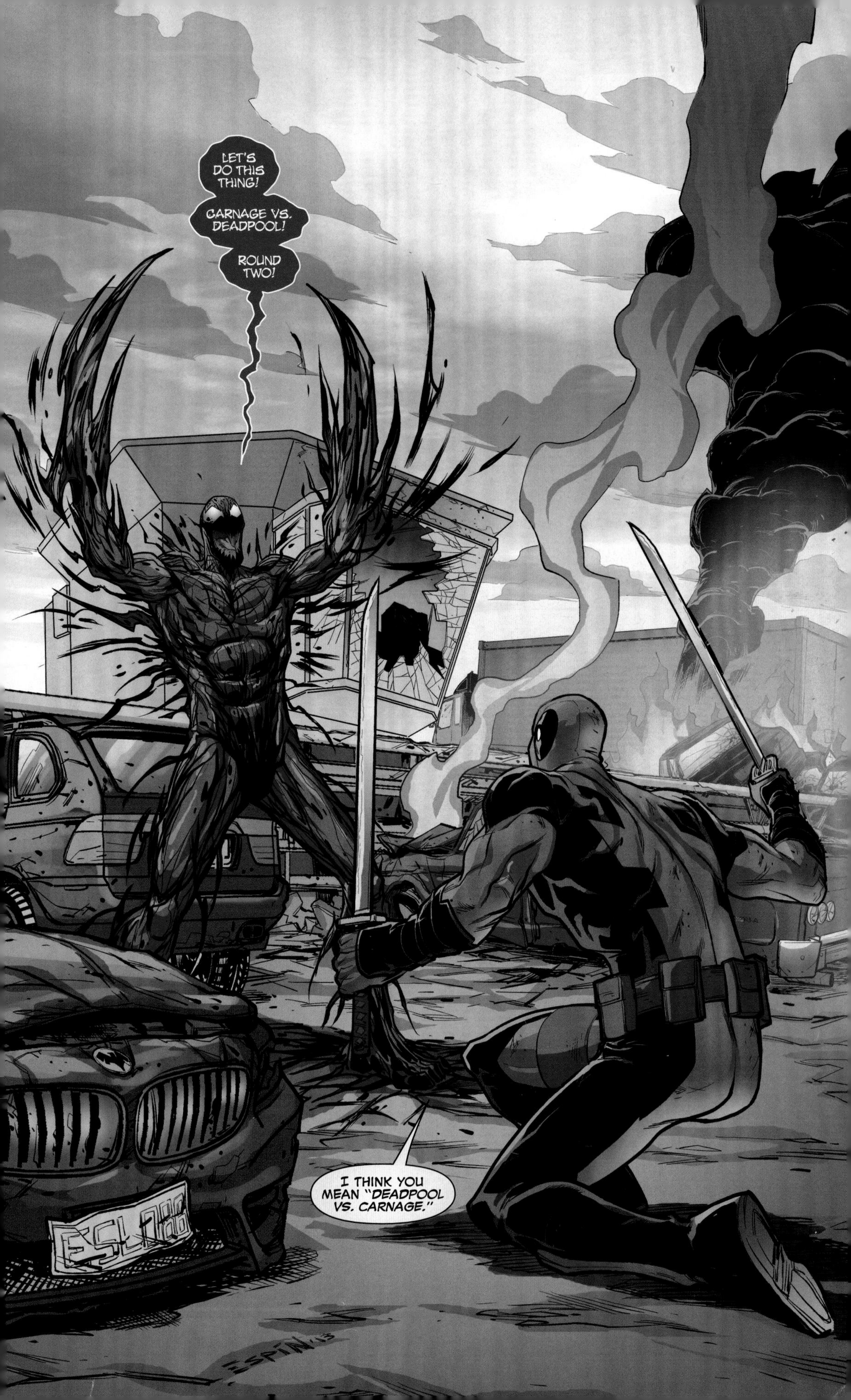
LET'S DO THIS THING!
CARNAGE VS. DEADPOOL!
ROUND TWO!
I THINK YOU MEAN "DEADPOOL VS. CARNAGE."

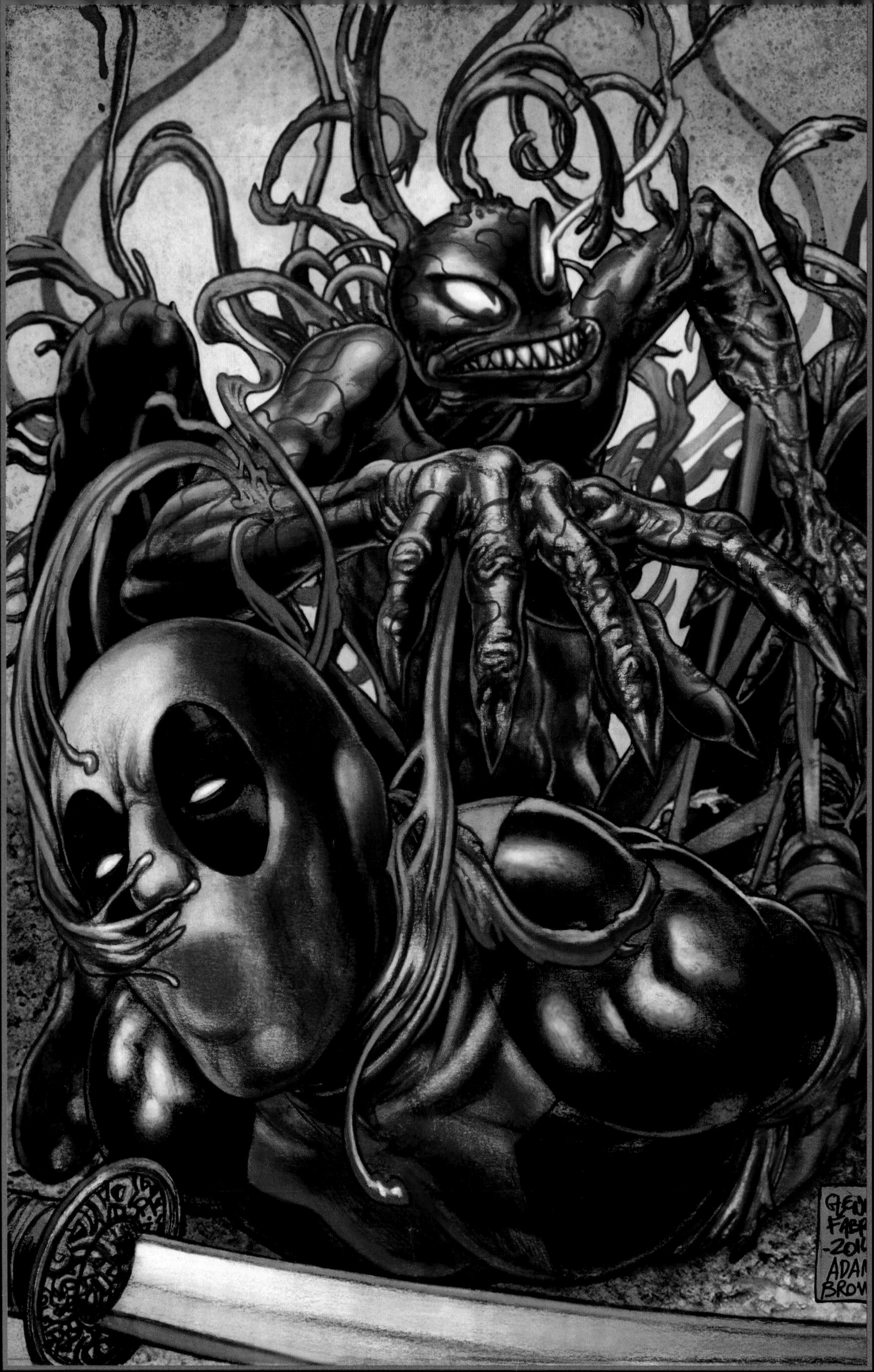

Deadpool vs. Carnage #3

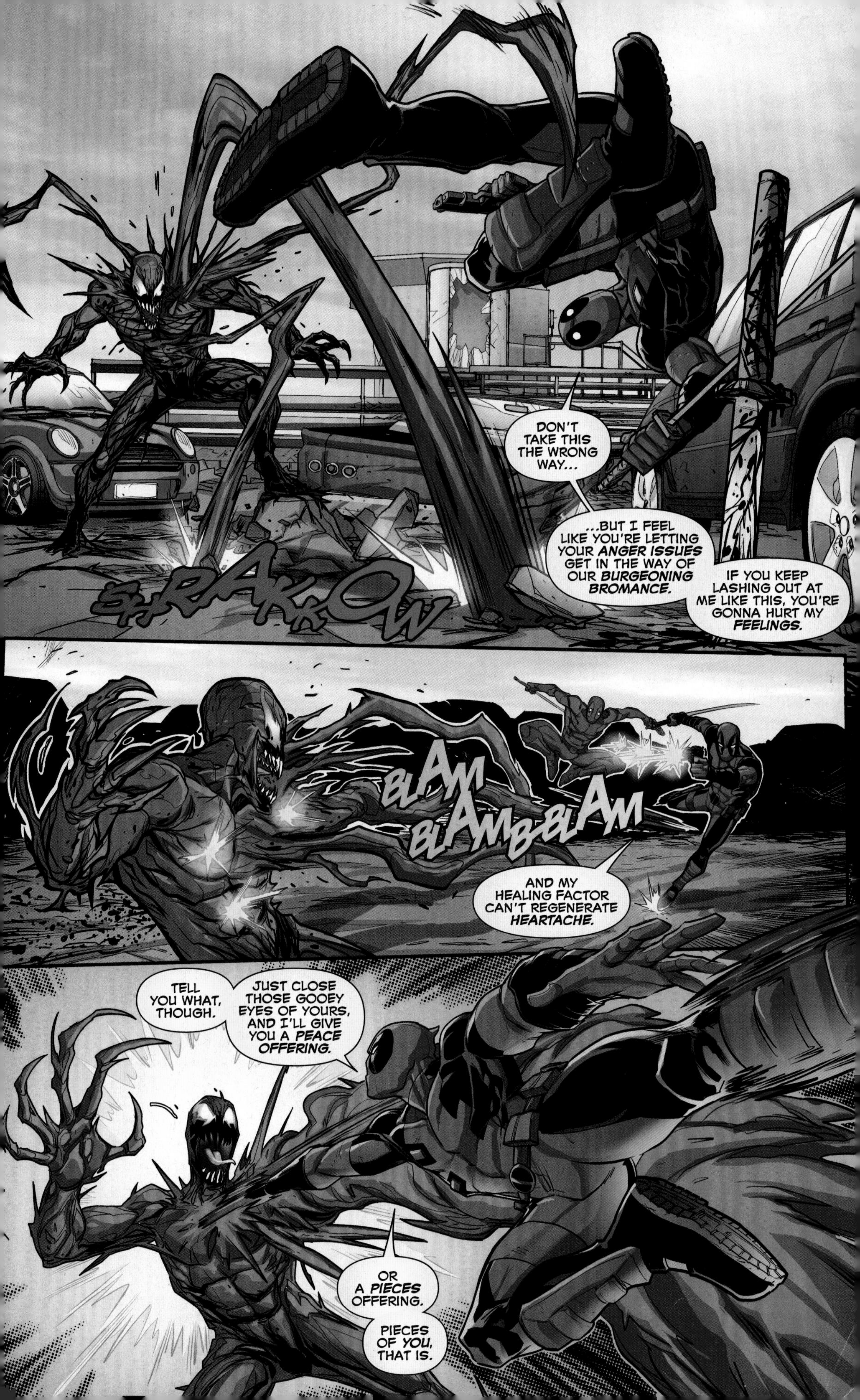
SHRAKKOW
DON'T TAKE THIS THE WRONG WAY...
...BUT I FEEL LIKE YOU'RE LETTING YOUR ANGER ISSUES GET IN THE WAY OF OUR BURGEONING BROMANCE.
IF YOU KEEP LASHING OUT AT ME LIKE THIS, YOU'RE GONNA HURT MY FEELINGS.
BLAM BLAM BLAM BLAM
AND MY HEALING FACTOR CAN'T REGENERATE HEARTACHE.
TELL YOU WHAT, THOUGH.
JUST CLOSE THOSE GOOEY EYES OF YOURS, AND I'LL GIVE YOU A PEACE OFFERING.
OR A PIECES OFFERING.
PIECES OF YOU, THAT IS.

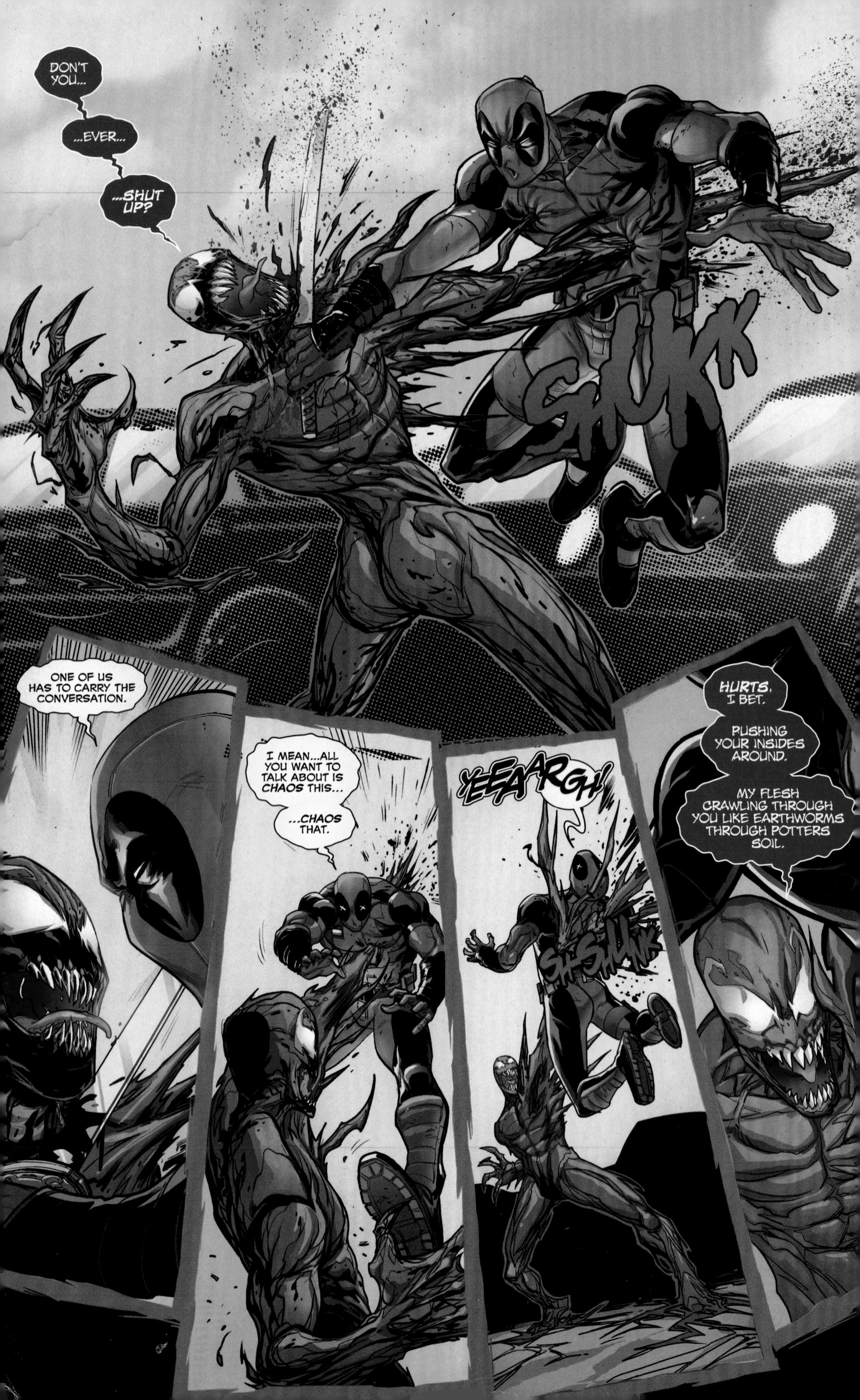
DON'T YOU...
...EVER...
...SHUT UP?
SHUKK
ONE OF US HAS TO CARRY THE CONVERSATION.
I MEAN...ALL YOU WANT TO TALK ABOUT IS CHAOS THIS...
...CHAOS THAT.
YEEAARGH!
SH-SHUNK
HURTS, I BET.
PUSHING YOUR INSIDES AROUND.
MY FLESH CRAWLING THROUGH YOU LIKE EARTHWORMS THROUGH POTTERS SOIL.

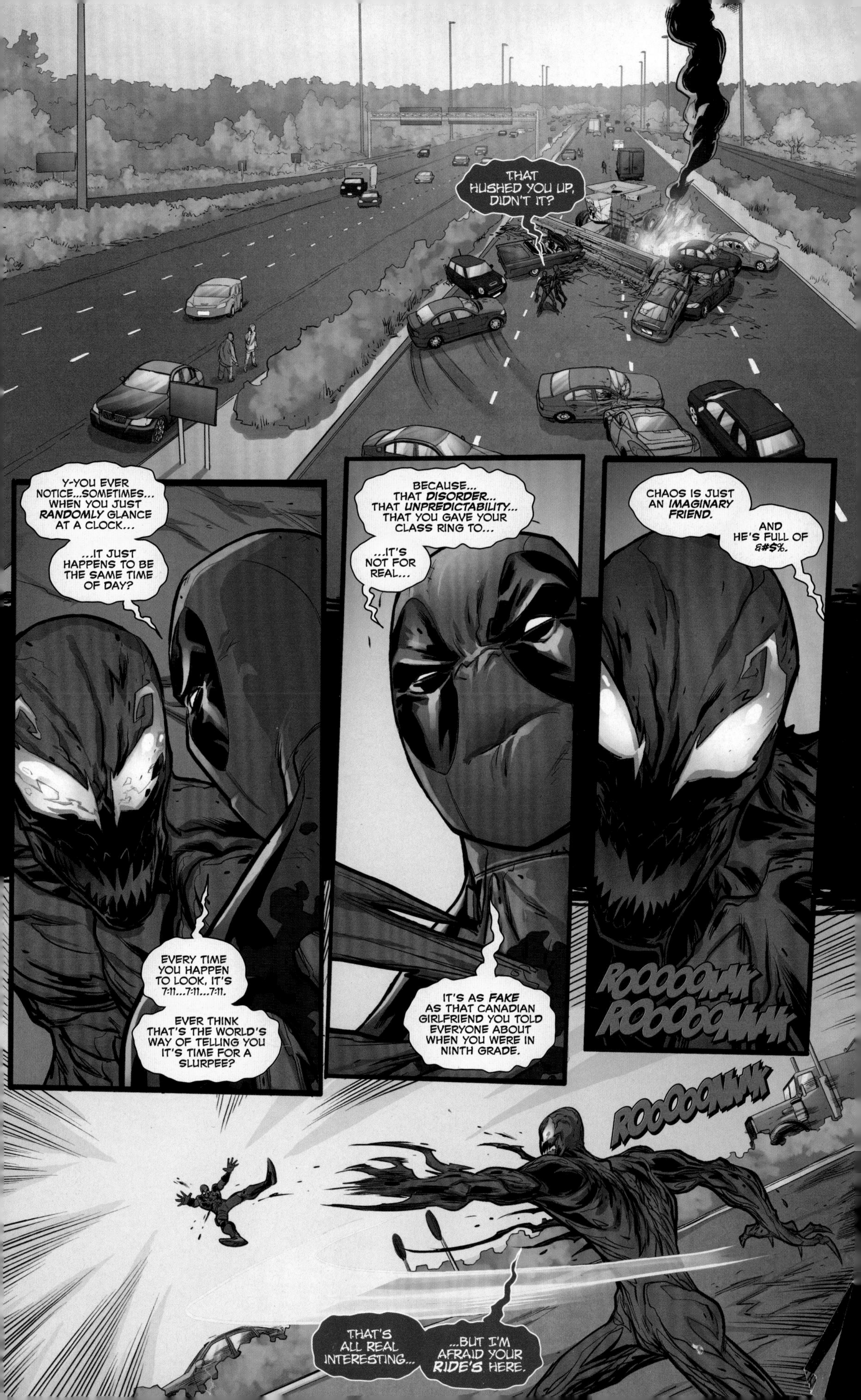

THAT HUSHED YOU UP, DIDN'T IT?
Y-YOU EVER NOTICE...SOMETIMES... WHEN YOU JUST RANDOMLY GLANCE AT A CLOCK...
...IT JUST HAPPENS TO BE THE SAME TIME OF DAY?
EVERY TIME YOU HAPPEN TO LOOK, IT'S 7:11...7:11...7:11.
EVER THINK THAT'S THE WORLD'S WAY OF TELLING YOU IT'S TIME FOR A SLURPEE?
BECAUSE... THAT DISORDER... THAT UNPREDICTABILITY... THAT YOU GAVE YOUR CLASS RING TO...
...IT'S NOT FOR REAL...
IT'S AS FAKE AS THAT CANADIAN GIRLFRIEND YOU TOLD EVERYONE ABOUT WHEN YOU WERE IN NINTH GRADE.
CHAOS IS JUST AN IMAGINARY FRIEND.
AND HE'S FULL OF &#$%.
ROOOOONNK
ROOOOONNK
ROOOOONNNK
THAT'S ALL REAL INTERESTING...
...BUT I'M AFRAID YOUR RIDE'S HERE.

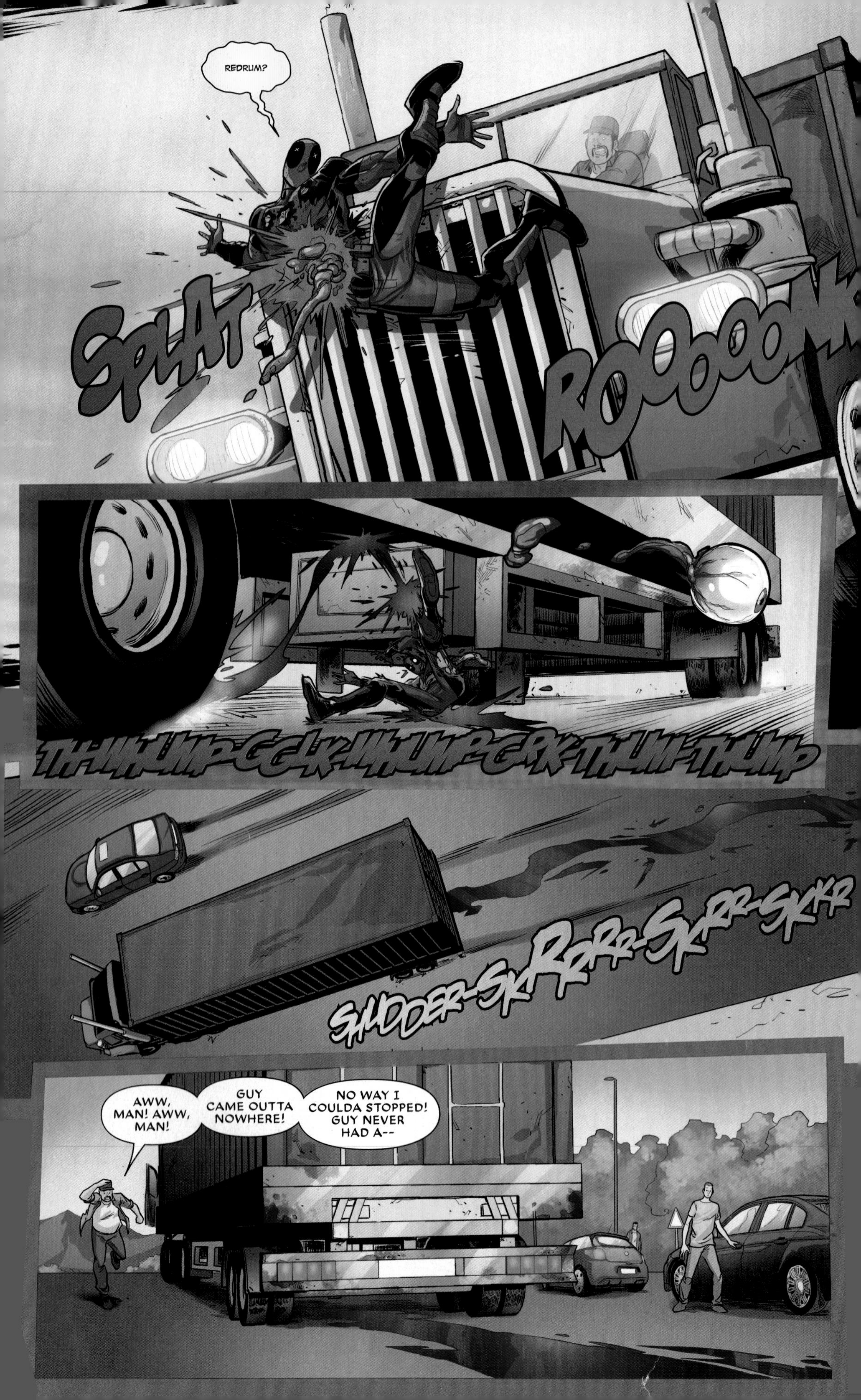
REDRUM?
SPLAT
ROOOOOONK
THWHUMP-GGLK-WHUMP-GRK-THUMP-THUMP
SHUDDER-SKRRRR-SKRR-SKKR
AWW, MAN! AWW, MAN!
GUY CAME OUTTA NOWHERE!
NO WAY I COULDA STOPPED! GUY NEVER HAD A--

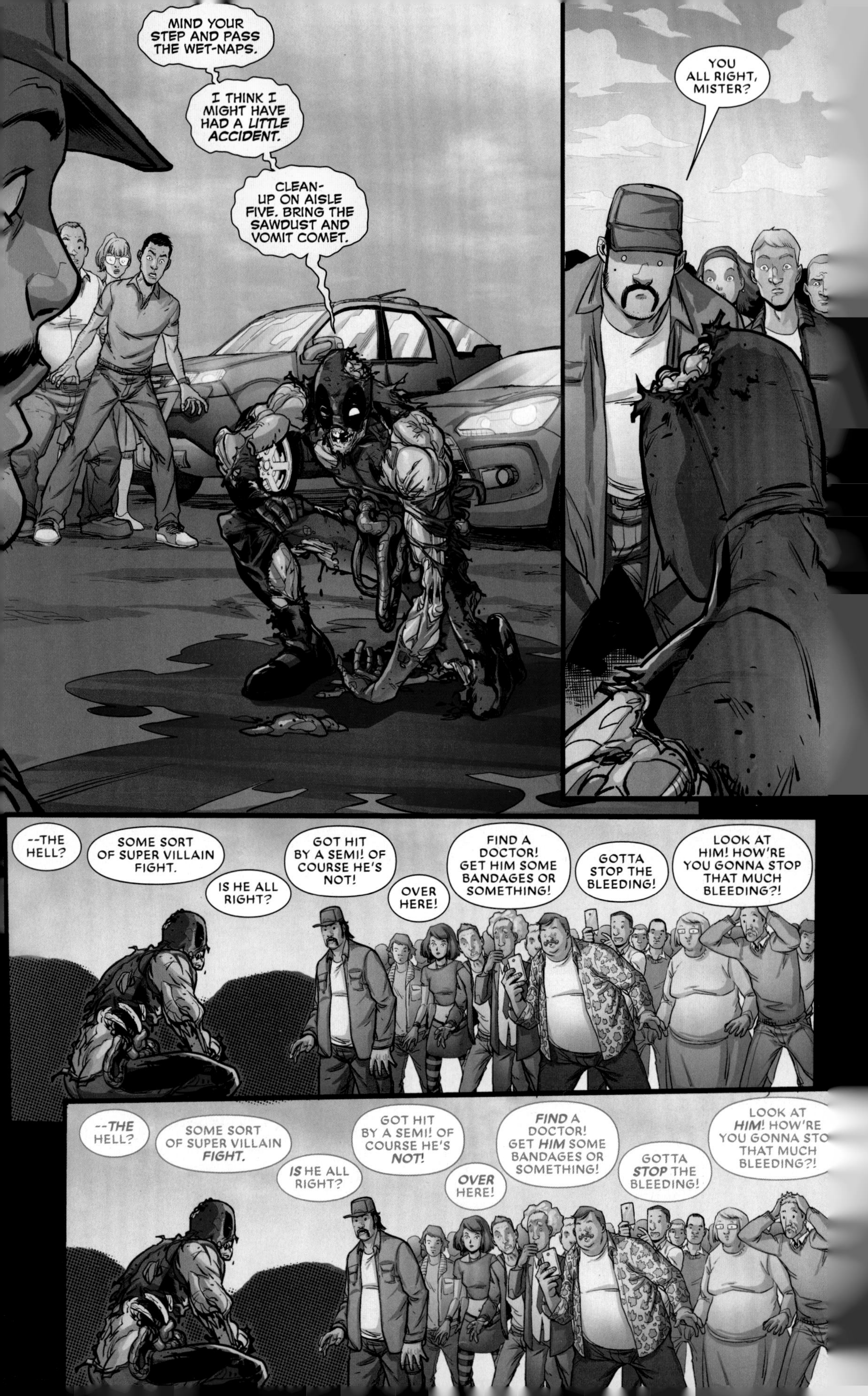
MIND YOUR STEP AND PASS THE WET-NAPS.
I THINK I MIGHT HAVE HAD A LITTLE ACCIDENT.
CLEAN-UP ON AISLE FIVE. BRING THE SAWDUST AND VOMIT COMET.
YOU ALL RIGHT, MISTER?
--THE HELL?
SOME SORT OF SUPER VILLAIN FIGHT.
IS HE ALL RIGHT?
GOT HIT BY A SEMI! OF COURSE HE'S NOT!
OVER HERE!
FIND A DOCTOR! GET HIM SOME BANDAGES OR SOMETHING!
GOTTA STOP THE BLEEDING!
LOOK AT HIM! HOW'RE YOU GONNA STOP THAT MUCH BLEEDING?!
--THE HELL?
SOME SORT OF SUPER VILLAIN FIGHT.
IS HE ALL RIGHT?
GOT HIT BY A SEMI! OF COURSE HE'S NOT!
OVER HERE!
FIND A DOCTOR! GET HIM SOME BANDAGES OR SOMETHING!
GOTTA STOP THE BLEEDING!
LOOK AT HIM! HOW'RE YOU GONNA STO
THAT MUCH BLEEDING?!

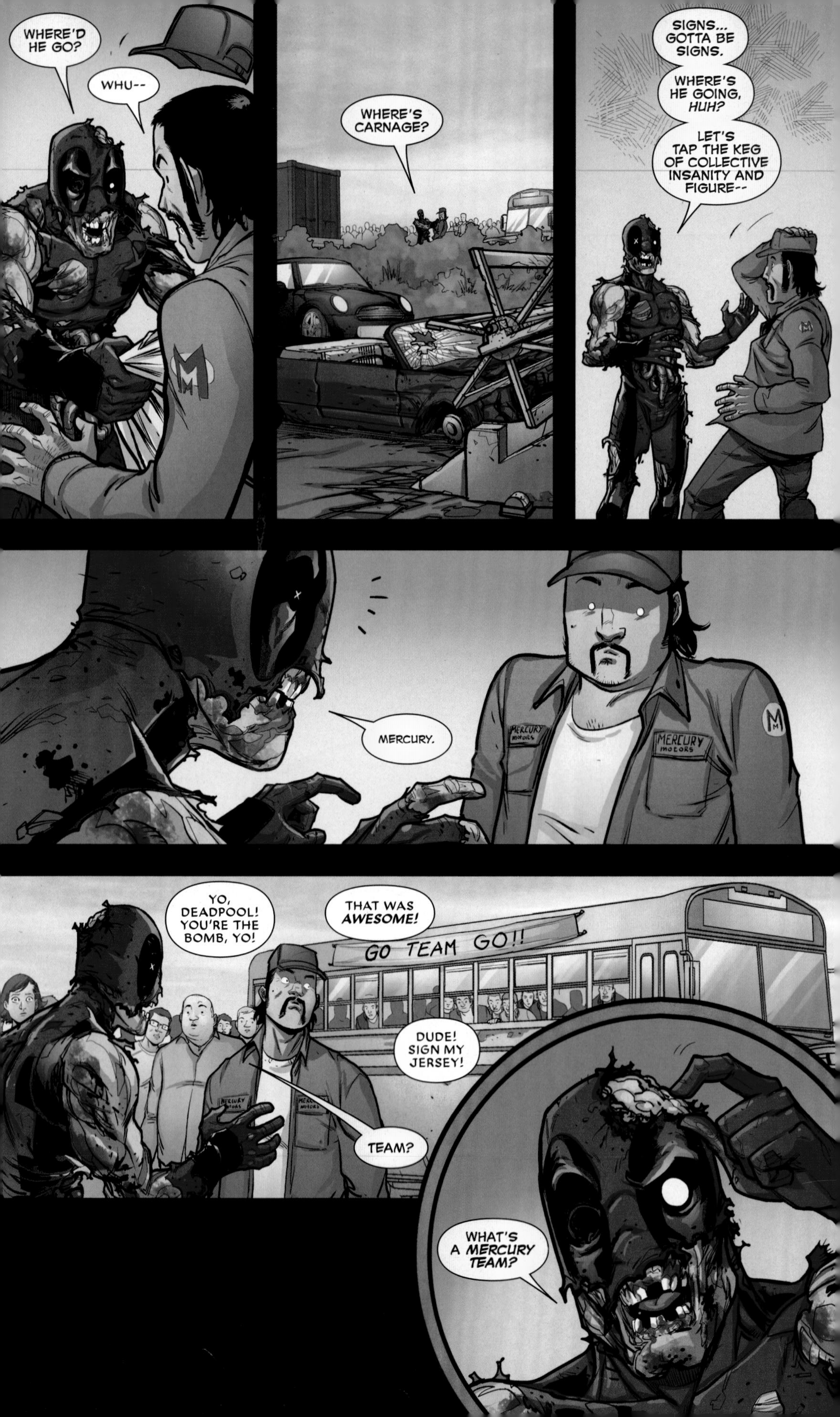
WHERE'D HE GO?
WHU--
WHERE'S CARNAGE?
SIGNS... GOTTA BE SIGNS.
WHERE'S HE GOING, *HUH?*
LET'S TAP THE KEG OF COLLECTIVE INSANITY AND FIGURE--
MERCURY MOTORS
MERCURY.
YO, DEADPOOL! YOU'RE THE BOMB, YO!
THAT WAS **AWESOME!**
GO TEAM GO!!
DUDE! SIGN MY JERSEY!
TEAM?
WHAT'S A *MERCURY TEAM?*

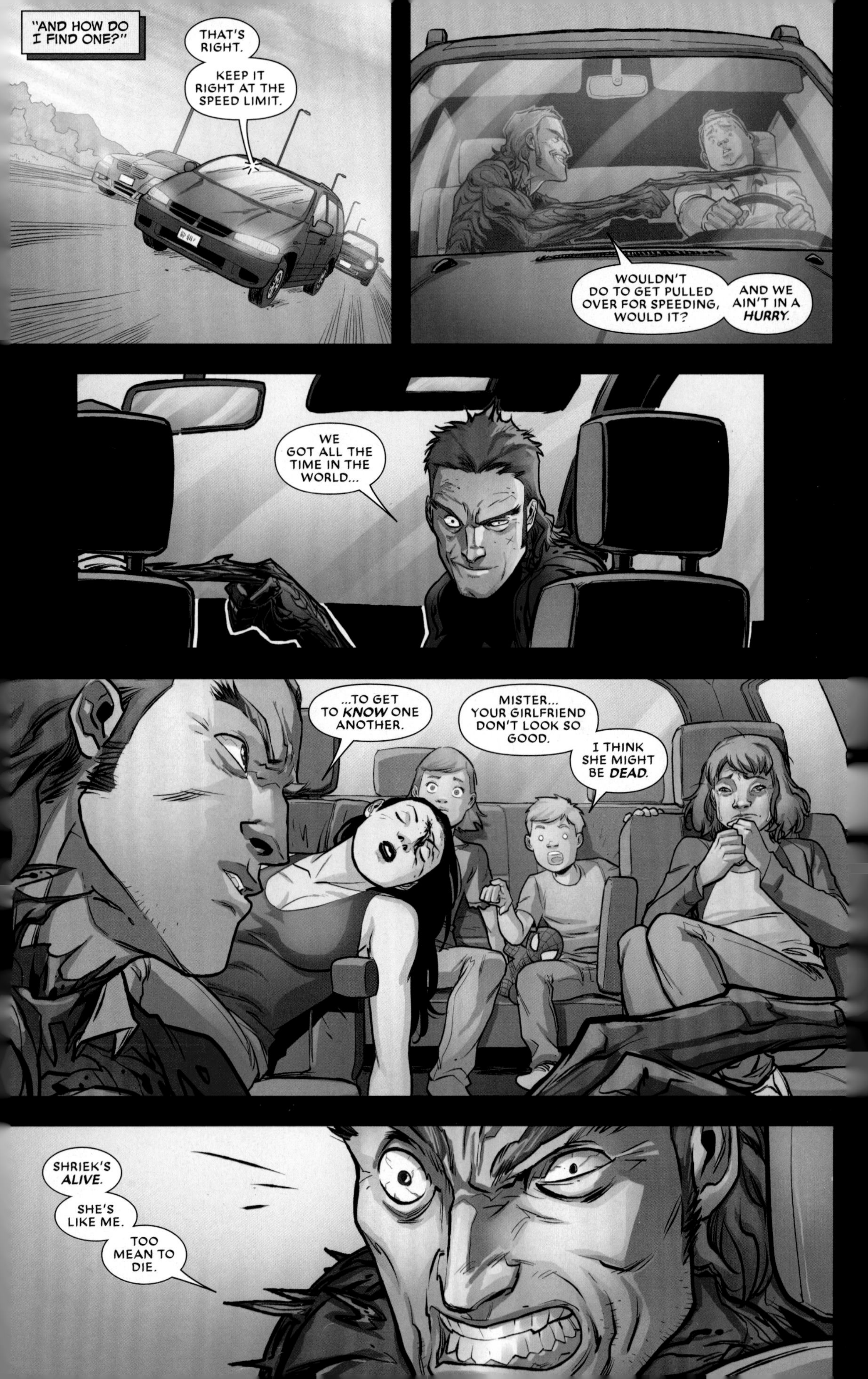
"AND HOW DO I FIND ONE?"
THAT'S RIGHT.
KEEP IT RIGHT AT THE SPEED LIMIT.
WOULDN'T DO TO GET PULLED OVER FOR SPEEDING, WOULD IT?
AND WE AIN'T IN A *HURRY*.
WE GOT ALL THE TIME IN THE WORLD...
...TO GET TO *KNOW* ONE ANOTHER.
MISTER... YOUR GIRLFRIEND DON'T LOOK SO GOOD.
I THINK SHE MIGHT BE *DEAD*.
SHRIEK'S *ALIVE*.
SHE'S LIKE ME.
TOO MEAN TO DIE.

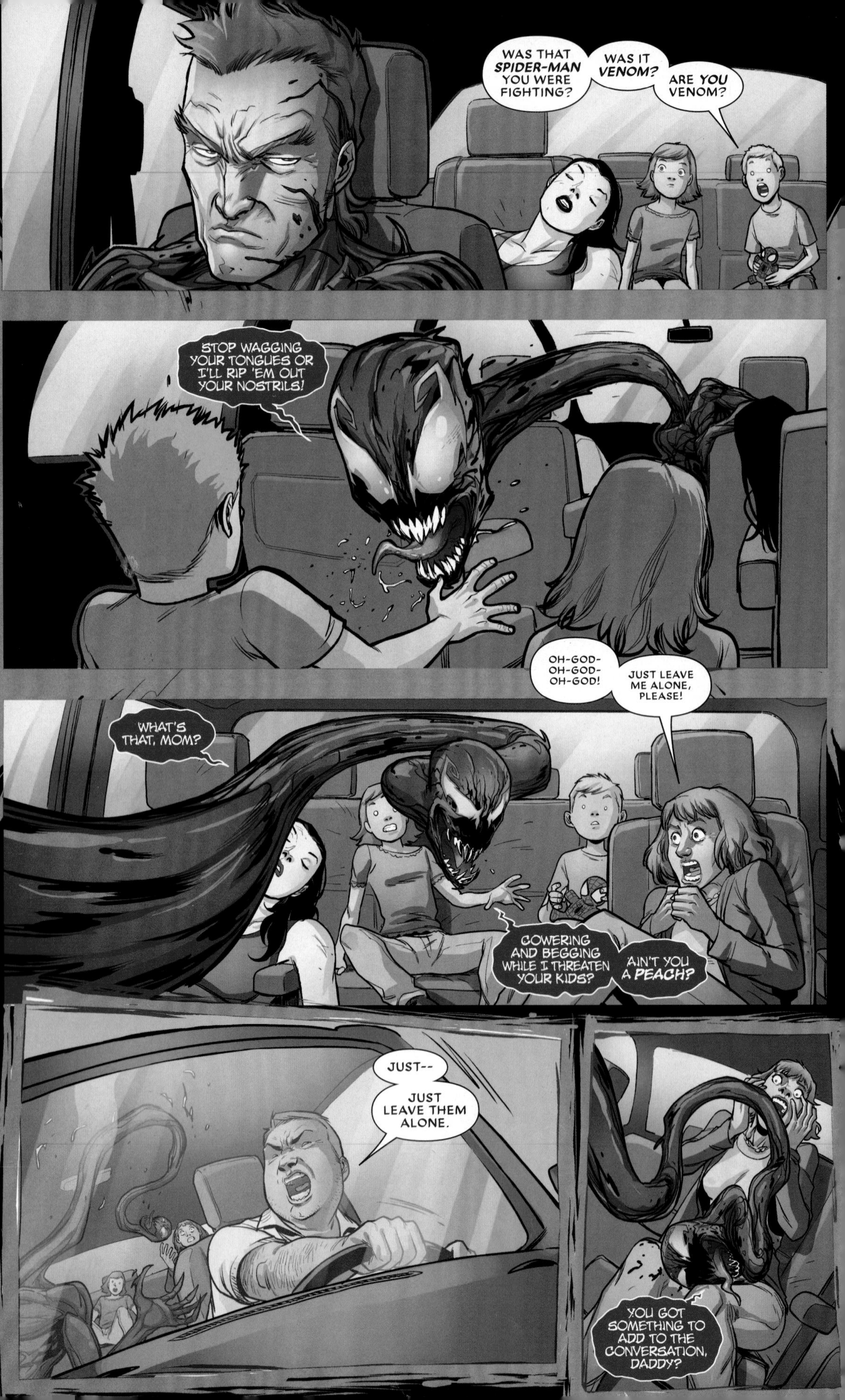
WAS THAT SPIDER-MAN YOU WERE FIGHTING?
WAS IT VENOM?
ARE YOU VENOM?
STOP WAGGING YOUR TONGUES OR I'LL RIP 'EM OUT YOUR NOSTRILS!
OH-GOD-OH-GOD-OH-GOD!
JUST LEAVE ME ALONE, PLEASE!
WHAT'S THAT, MOM?
COWERING AND BEGGING WHILE I THREATEN YOUR KIDS?
AIN'T YOU A PEACH?
JUST--
JUST LEAVE THEM ALONE.
YOU GOT SOMETHING TO ADD TO THE CONVERSATION, DADDY?

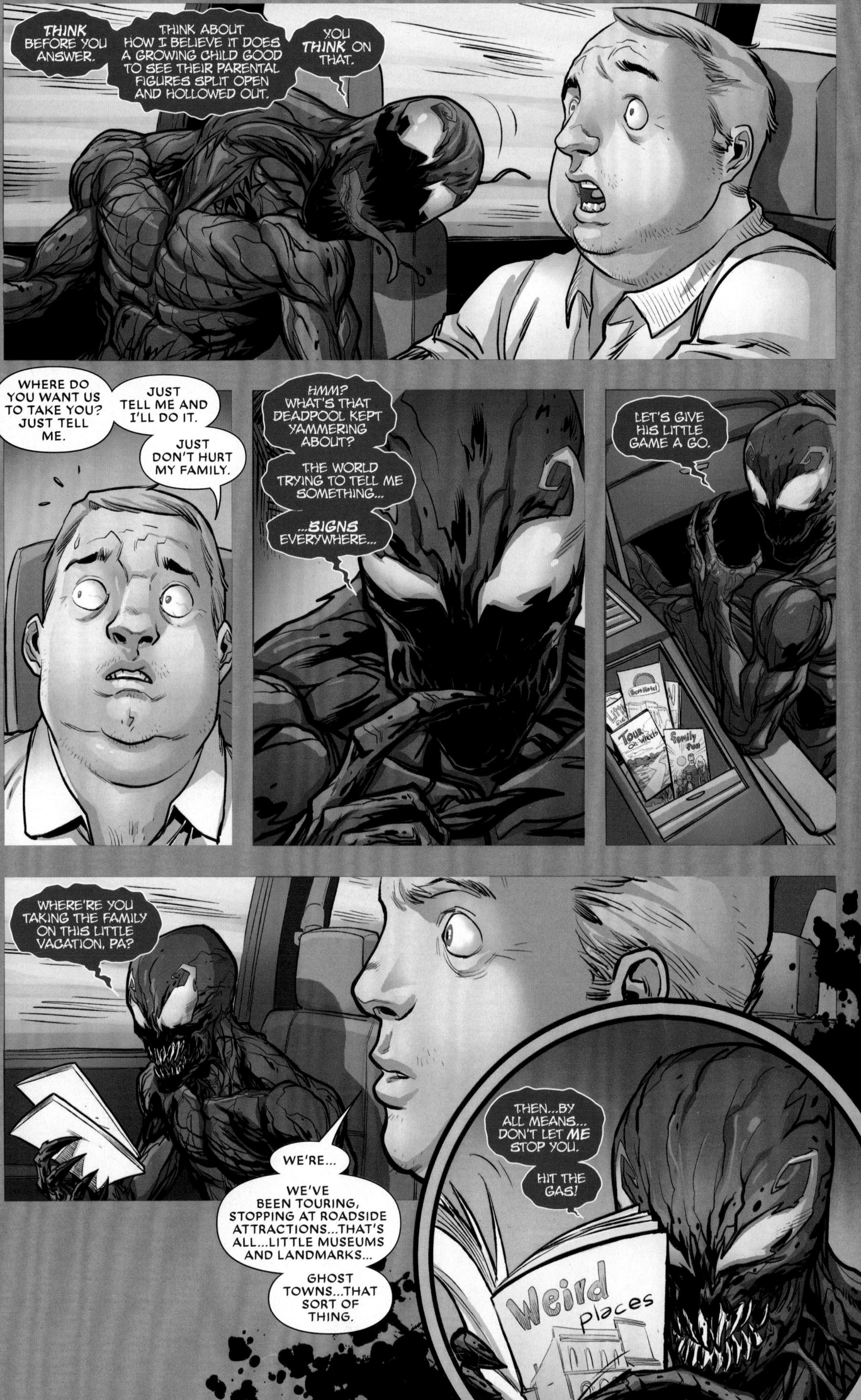
THINK BEFORE YOU ANSWER.
THINK ABOUT HOW I BELIEVE IT DOES A GROWING CHILD GOOD TO SEE THEIR PARENTAL FIGURES SPLIT OPEN AND HOLLOWED OUT.
YOU THINK ON THAT.
WHERE DO YOU WANT US TO TAKE YOU? JUST TELL ME.
JUST TELL ME AND I'LL DO IT.
JUST DON'T HURT MY FAMILY.
HMM? WHAT'S THAT DEADPOOL KEPT YAMMERING ABOUT?
THE WORLD TRYING TO TELL ME SOMETHING...
...SIGNS EVERYWHERE...
LET'S GIVE HIS LITTLE GAME A GO.
Tour on Wheels
Family Fun
WHERE'RE YOU TAKING THE FAMILY ON THIS LITTLE VACATION, PA?
WE'RE...
WE'VE BEEN TOURING, STOPPING AT ROADSIDE ATTRACTIONS...THAT'S ALL...LITTLE MUSEUMS AND LANDMARKS...
GHOST TOWNS...THAT SORT OF THING.
THEN...BY ALL MEANS... DON'T LET ME STOP YOU.
HIT THE GAS!
Weird places

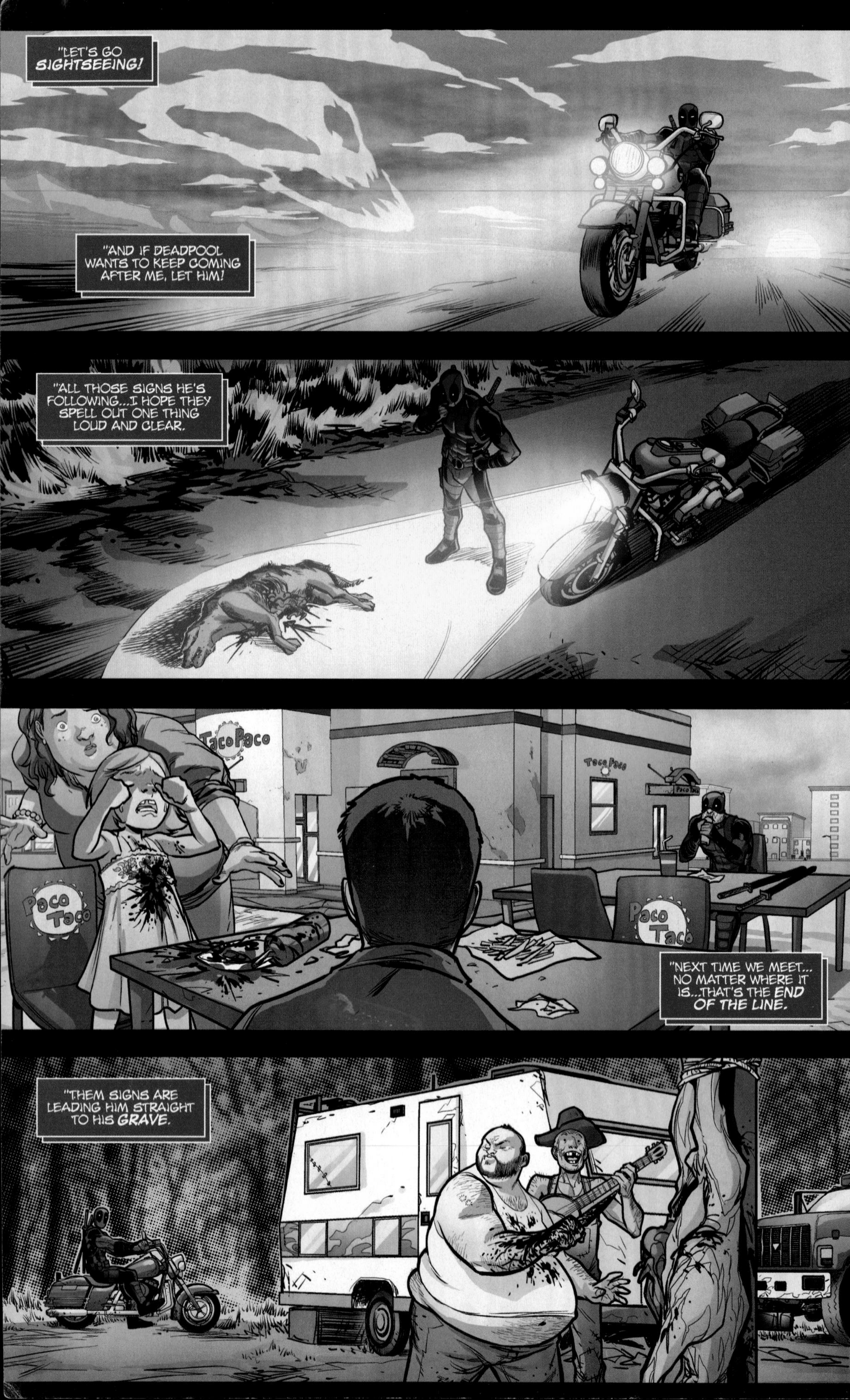
"LET'S GO SIGHTSEEING!
"AND IF DEADPOOL WANTS TO KEEP COMING AFTER ME, LET HIM!
"ALL THOSE SIGNS HE'S FOLLOWING...I HOPE THEY SPELL OUT ONE THING LOUD AND CLEAR.
Taco Paco
Paco Taco
Paco Taco
"NEXT TIME WE MEET... NO MATTER WHERE IT IS...THAT'S THE END OF THE LINE.
"THEM SIGNS ARE LEADING HIM STRAIGHT TO HIS GRAVE.

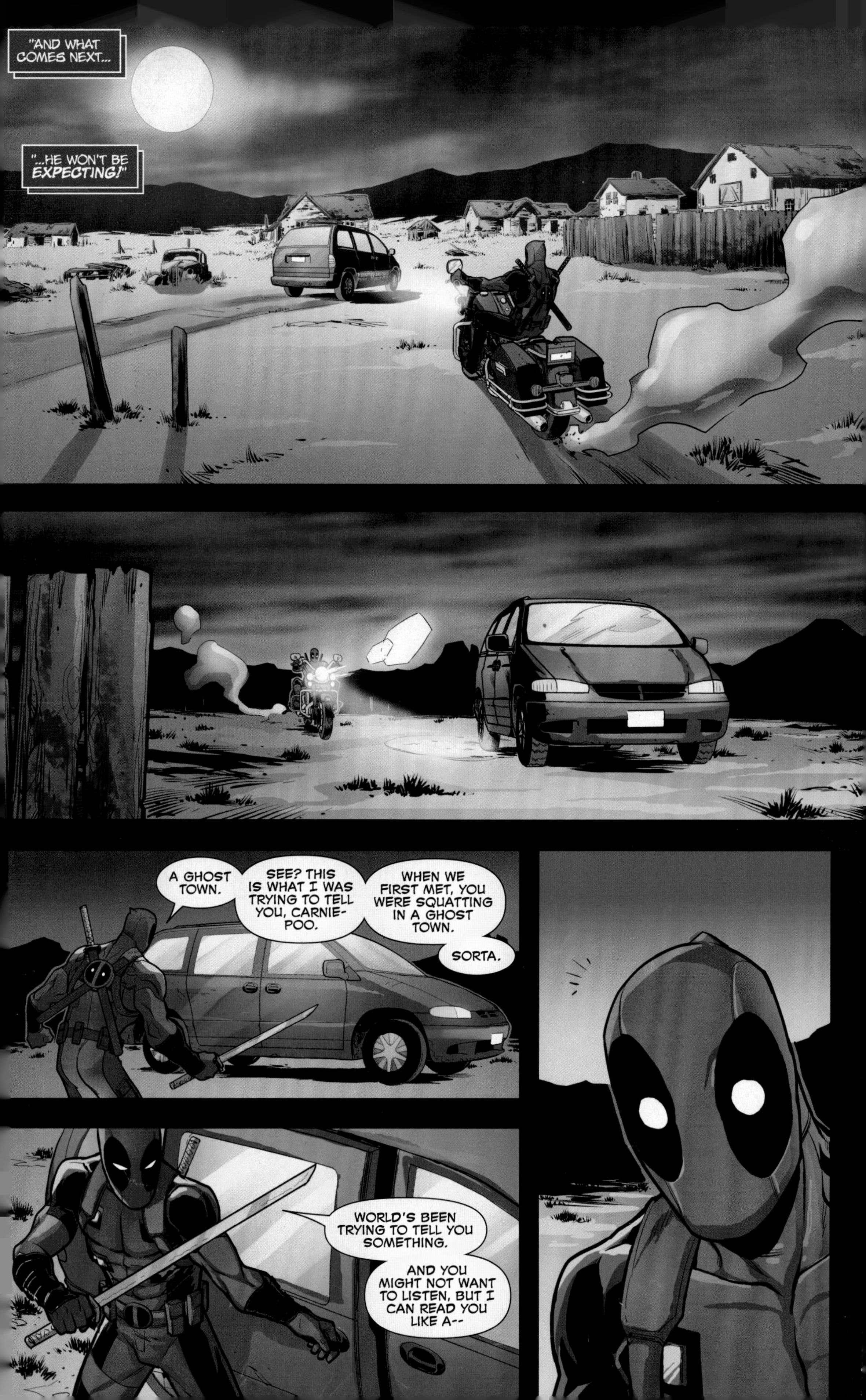
"AND WHAT COMES NEXT...
"...HE WON'T BE EXPECTING!"
A GHOST TOWN.
SEE? THIS IS WHAT I WAS TRYING TO TELL YOU, CARNIE-POO.
WHEN WE FIRST MET, YOU WERE SQUATTING IN A GHOST TOWN.
SORTA.
WORLD'S BEEN TRYING TO TELL YOU SOMETHING.
AND YOU MIGHT NOT WANT TO LISTEN, BUT I CAN READ YOU LIKE A--

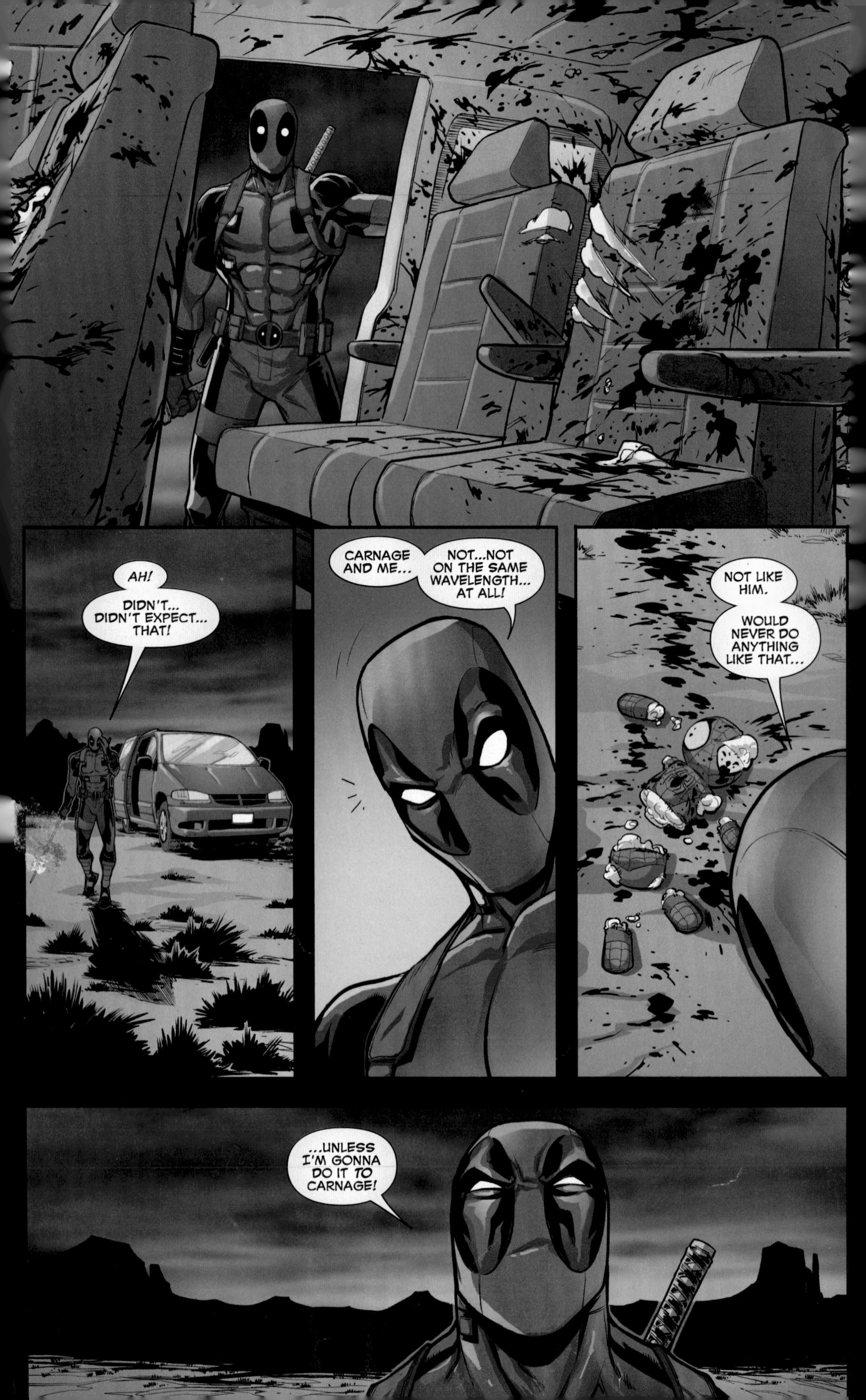
AH!
DIDN'T... DIDN'T EXPECT... THAT!
CARNAGE AND ME...
NOT...NOT ON THE SAME WAVELENGTH... AT ALL!
NOT LIKE HIM.
WOULD NEVER DO ANYTHING LIKE THAT...
...UNLESS I'M GONNA DO IT TO CARNAGE!

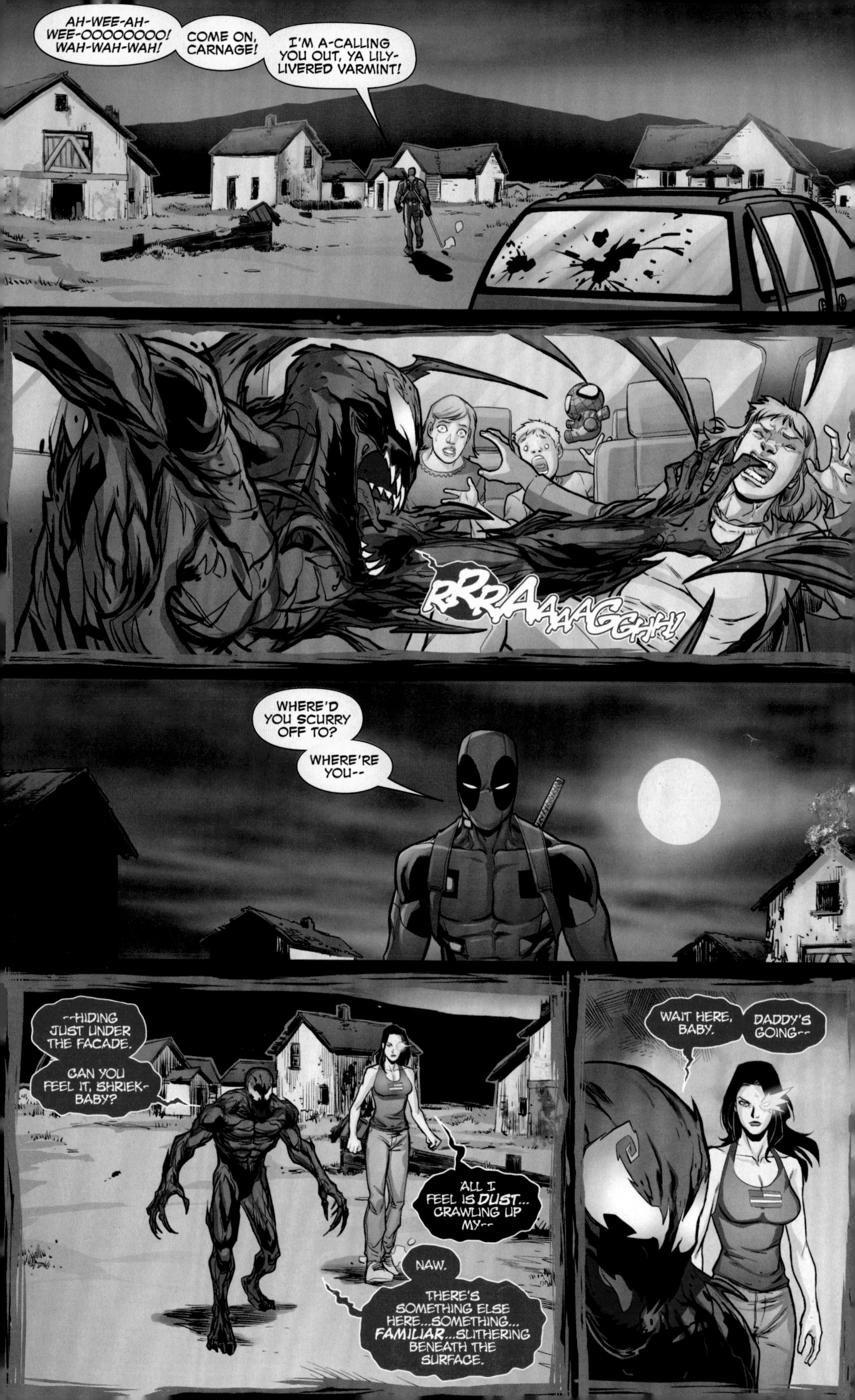
AH-WEE-AH-WEE-OOOOOOOO! WAH-WAH-WAH!
COME ON, CARNAGE!
I'M A-CALLING YOU OUT, YA LILY-LIVERED VARMINT!
RRRAAAAGGHH!
WHERE'D YOU SCURRY OFF TO?
WHERE'RE YOU--
--HIDING JUST UNDER THE FACADE.
CAN YOU FEEL IT, SHRIEK-BABY?
ALL I FEEL IS DUST... CRAWLING UP MY--
NAW.
THERE'S SOMETHING ELSE HERE...SOMETHING... FAMILIAR...SLITHERING BENEATH THE SURFACE.
WAIT HERE, BABY.
DADDY'S GOING--

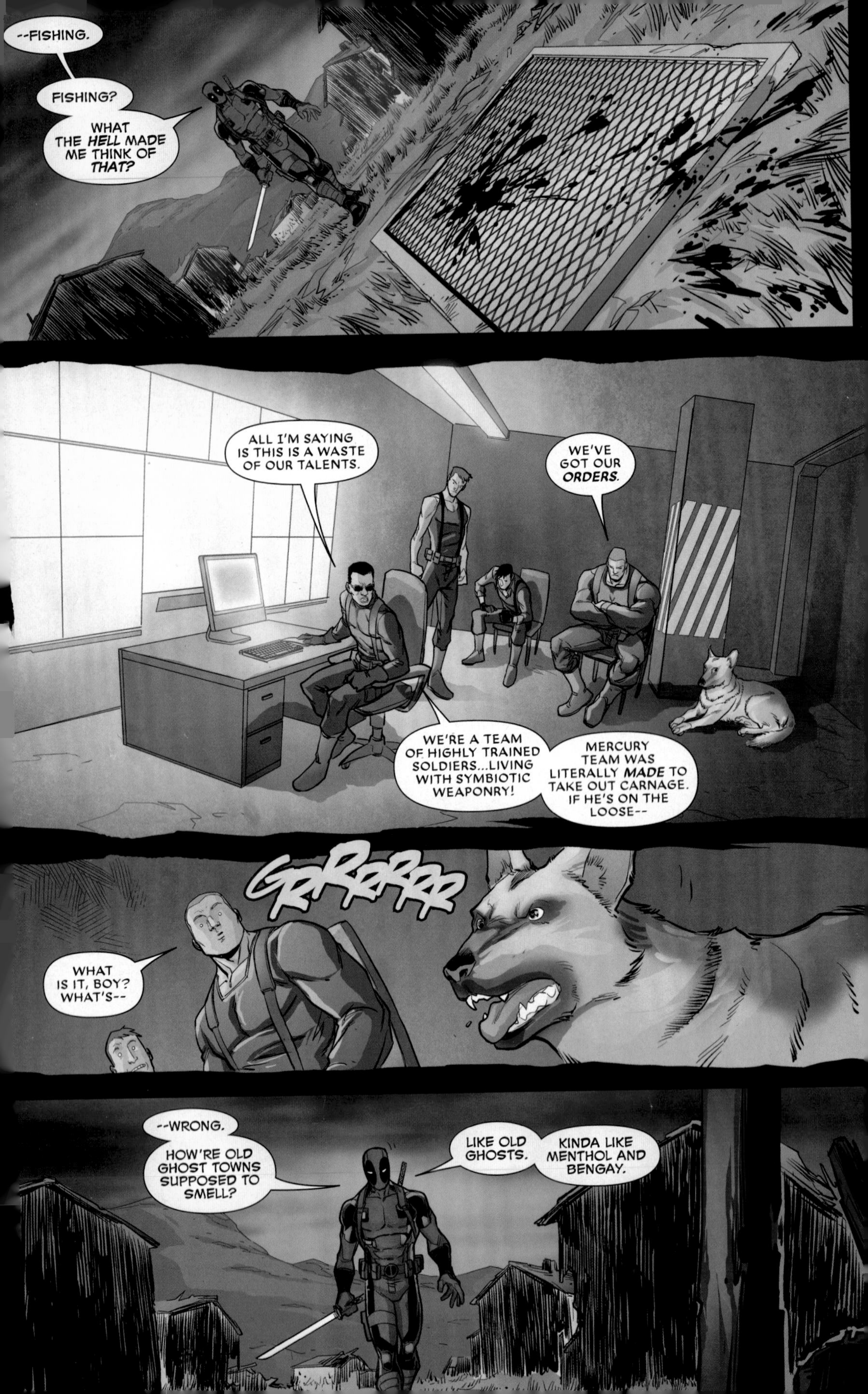
--FISHING.
FISHING?
WHAT THE HELL MADE ME THINK OF THAT?
ALL I'M SAYING IS THIS IS A WASTE OF OUR TALENTS.
WE'VE GOT OUR ORDERS.
WE'RE A TEAM OF HIGHLY TRAINED SOLDIERS...LIVING WITH SYMBIOTIC WEAPONRY!
MERCURY TEAM WAS LITERALLY MADE TO TAKE OUT CARNAGE. IF HE'S ON THE LOOSE--
GRRRRRR
WHAT IS IT, BOY? WHAT'S--
--WRONG.
HOW'RE OLD GHOST TOWNS SUPPOSED TO SMELL?
LIKE OLD GHOSTS.
KINDA LIKE MENTHOL AND BENGAY.

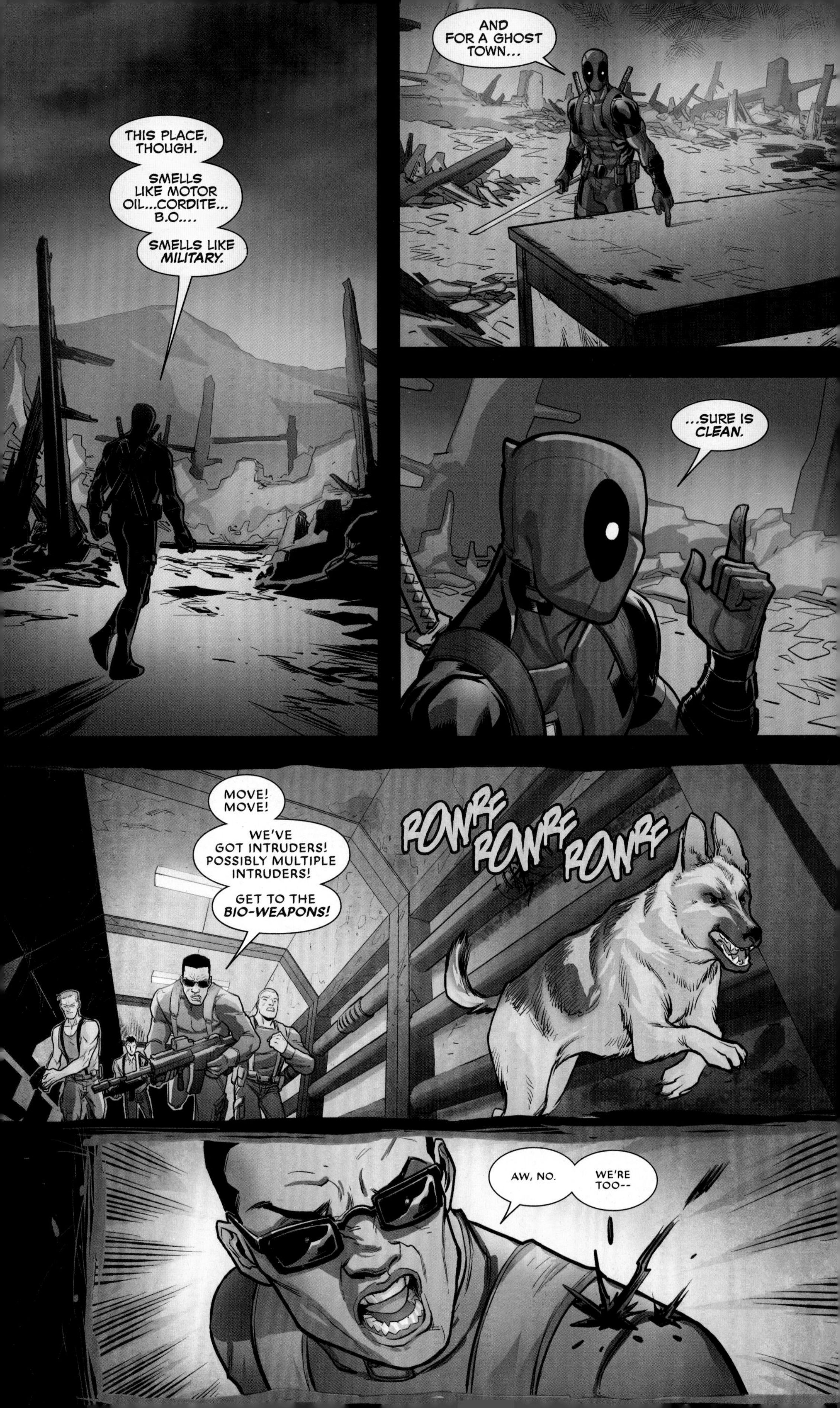
THIS PLACE, THOUGH.
SMELLS LIKE MOTOR OIL...CORDITE... B.O....
SMELLS LIKE MILITARY.
AND FOR A GHOST TOWN...
...SURE IS CLEAN.
MOVE! MOVE!
WE'VE GOT INTRUDERS! POSSIBLY MULTIPLE INTRUDERS!
GET TO THE BIO-WEAPONS!
ROWRF ROWRF ROWRF
AW, NO.
WE'RE TOO--

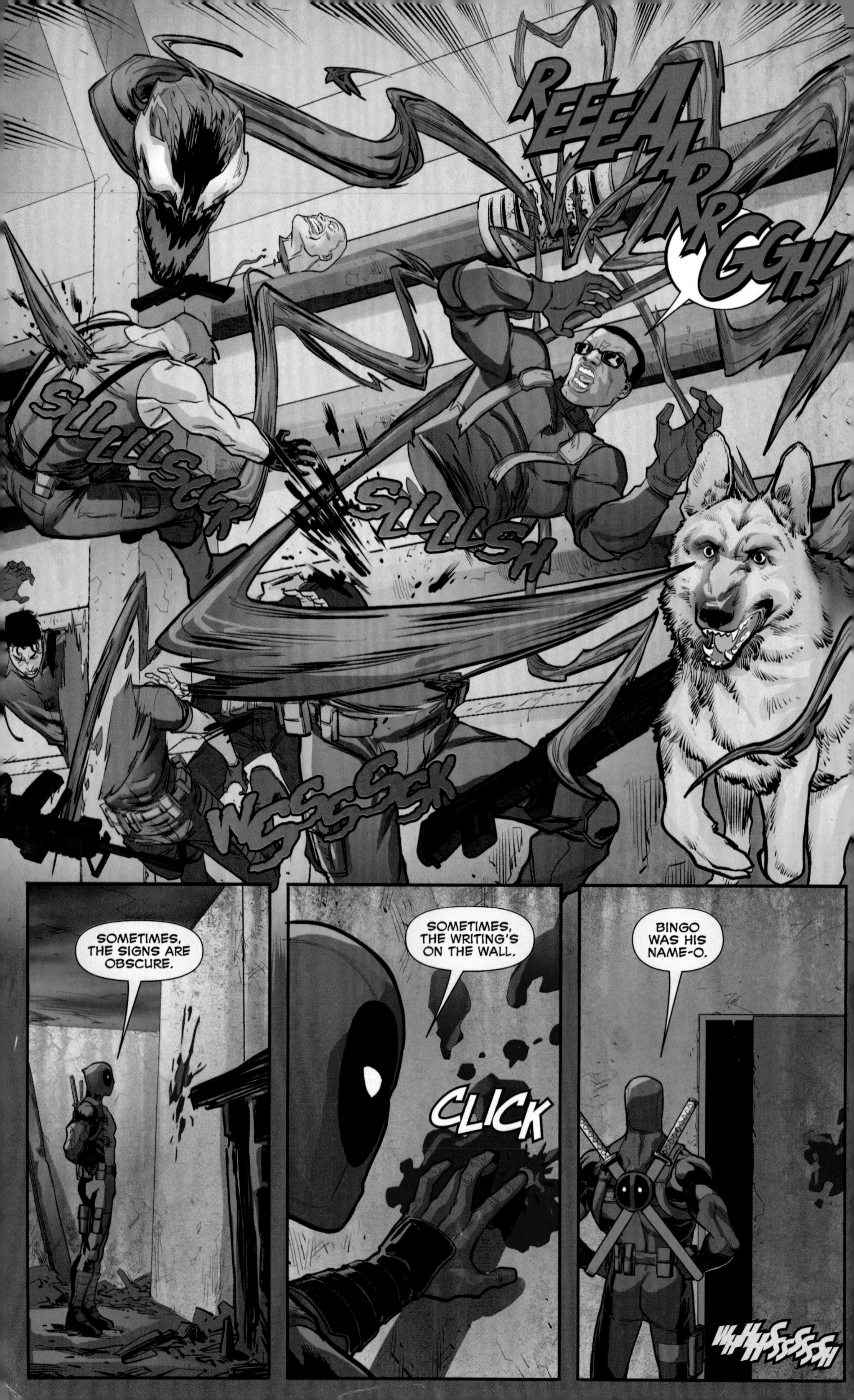
REEEAARRGGH!
SLLLLSCCK
SLLLLSH
WGSSSCK
SOMETIMES, THE SIGNS ARE OBSCURE.
SOMETIMES, THE WRITING'S ON THE WALL.
CLICK
BINGO WAS HIS NAME-O.
WHHSSSSH

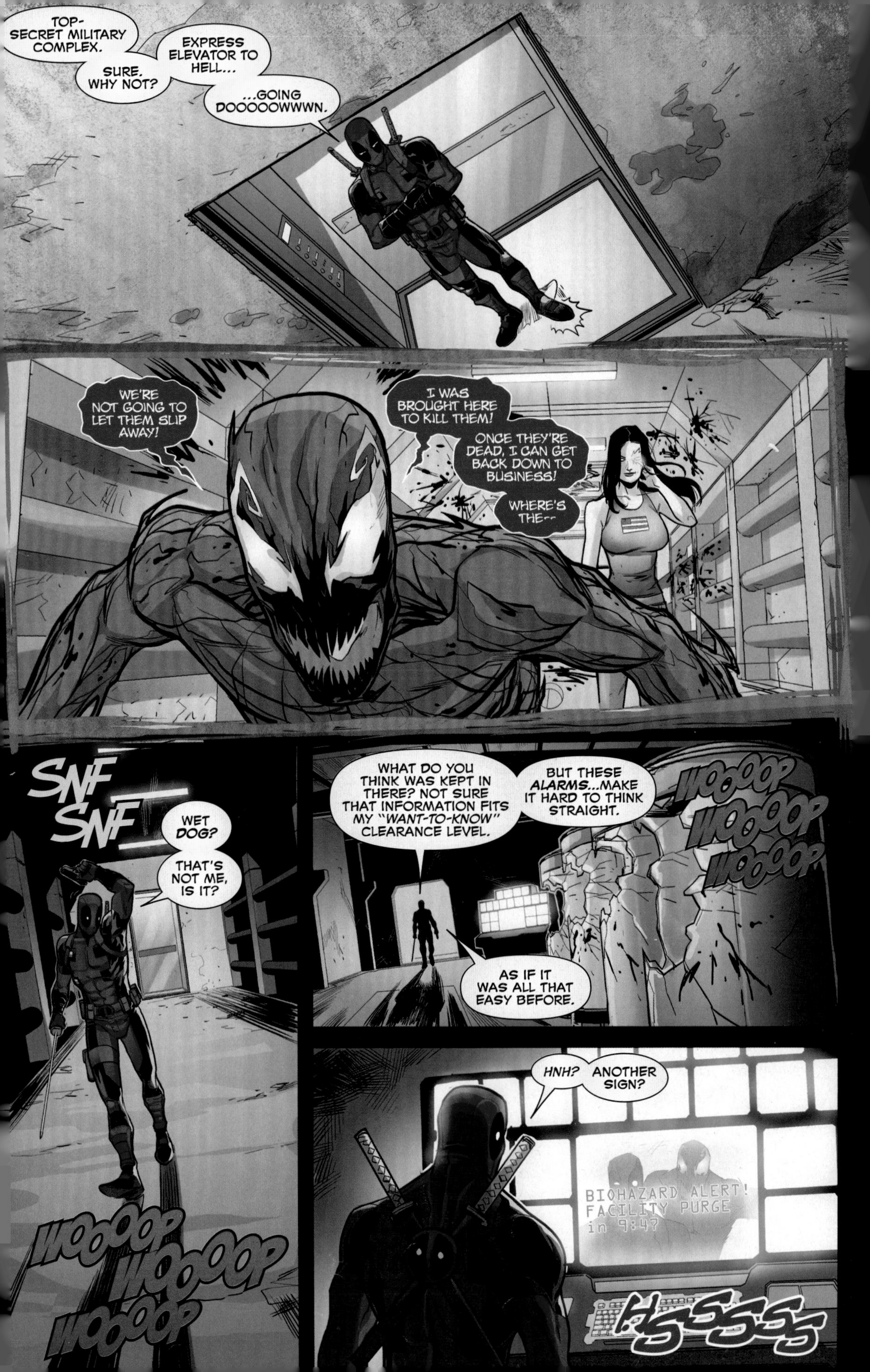
TOP-SECRET MILITARY COMPLEX.
SURE. WHY NOT?
EXPRESS ELEVATOR TO HELL...
...GOING DOOOOOWWWN.
WE'RE NOT GOING TO LET THEM SLIP AWAY!
I WAS BROUGHT HERE TO KILL THEM!
ONCE THEY'RE DEAD, I CAN GET BACK DOWN TO BUSINESS!
WHERE'S THE--
SNF SNF
WET DOG?
THAT'S NOT ME, IS IT?
WOOOOP WOOOOP WOOOOP
WHAT DO YOU THINK WAS KEPT IN THERE? NOT SURE THAT INFORMATION FITS MY "WANT-TO-KNOW" CLEARANCE LEVEL.
BUT THESE ALARMS...MAKE IT HARD TO THINK STRAIGHT.
WOOOOP WOOOOP WOOOOP
AS IF IT WAS ALL THAT EASY BEFORE.
HNH? ANOTHER SIGN?
BIOHAZARD ALERT! FACILITY PURGE in 9:47
HSSSSS

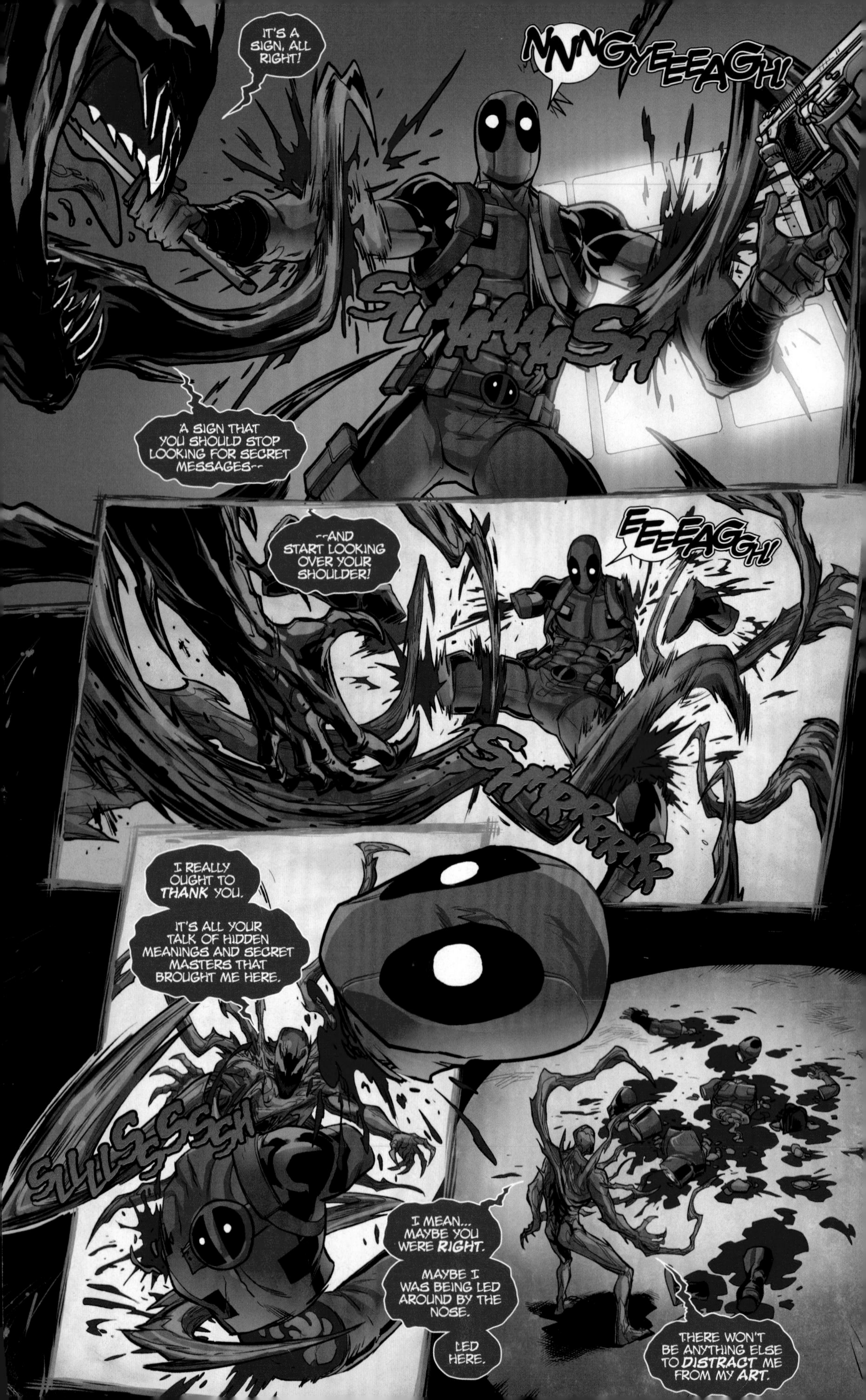
IT'S A SIGN, ALL RIGHT!
NNNGYEEEAGH!
SLAAAAASH
'A SIGN THAT YOU SHOULD STOP LOOKING FOR SECRET MESSAGES--
--AND START LOOKING OVER YOUR SHOULDER!
EEEEAGGH!
SHRRRRK
I REALLY OUGHT TO THANK YOU.
IT'S ALL YOUR TALK OF HIDDEN MEANINGS AND SECRET MASTERS THAT BROUGHT ME HERE.
SLLLSSSSH
I MEAN... MAYBE YOU WERE RIGHT.
MAYBE I WAS BEING LED AROUND BY THE NOSE.
LED HERE.
THERE WON'T BE ANYTHING ELSE TO DISTRACT ME FROM MY ART.

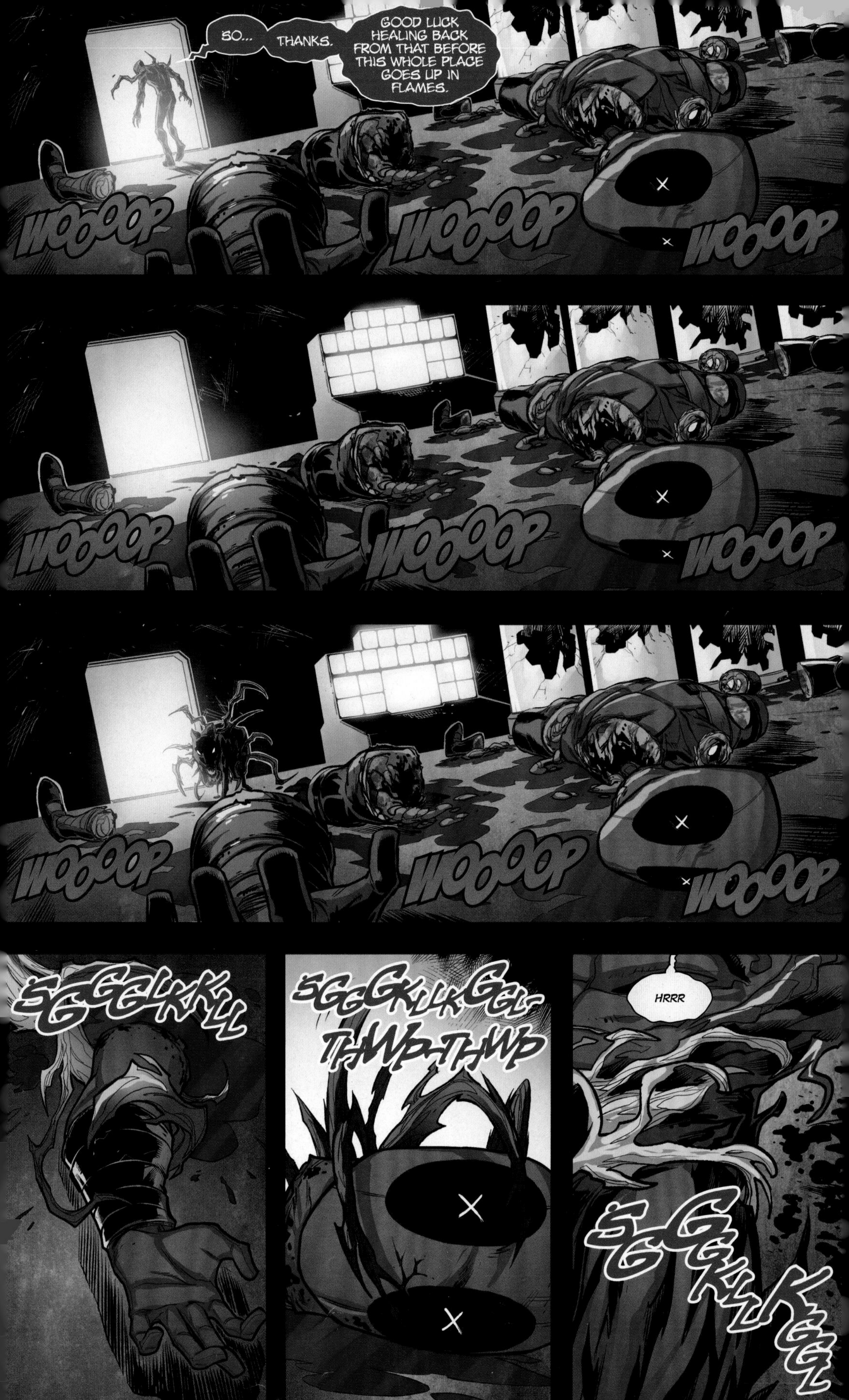
SO...
THANKS.
GOOD LUCK HEALING BACK FROM THAT BEFORE THIS WHOLE PLACE GOES UP IN FLAMES.
WOOOOP
WOOOOP
WOOOOP
WOOOOP
WOOOOP
WOOOOP
WOOOOP
WOOOOP
WOOOOP
SGGGLKKLL
SGGGKLLKGGL-
THWP-THWP
HRRR
SGGGKLLKGGL

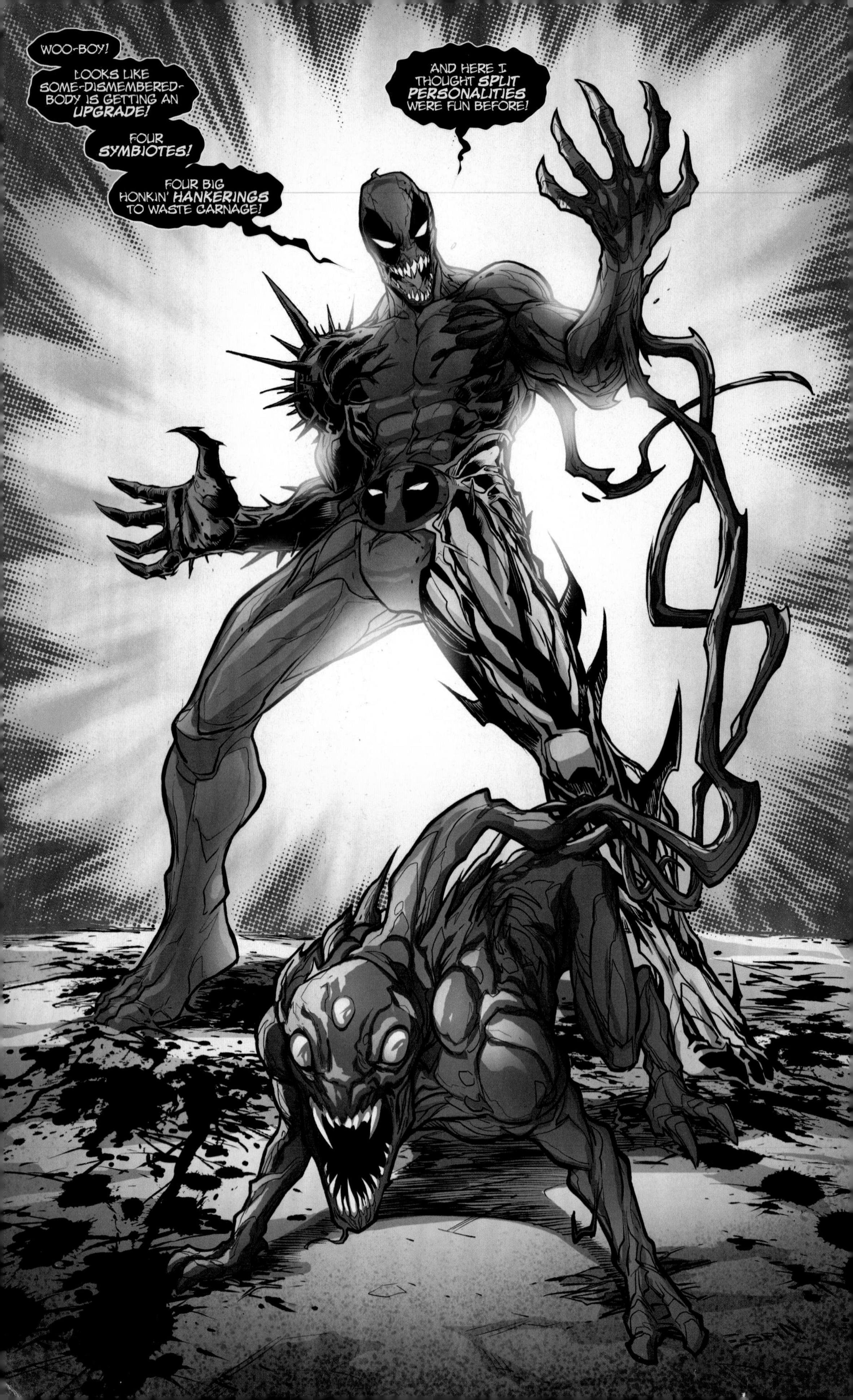
WOO-BOY!
LOOKS LIKE SOME-DISMEMBERED-BODY IS GETTING AN UPGRADE!
FOUR SYMBIOTES!
FOUR BIG HONKIN' HANKERINGS TO WASTE CARNAGE!
AND HERE I THOUGHT SPLIT PERSONALITIES WERE FUN BEFORE!

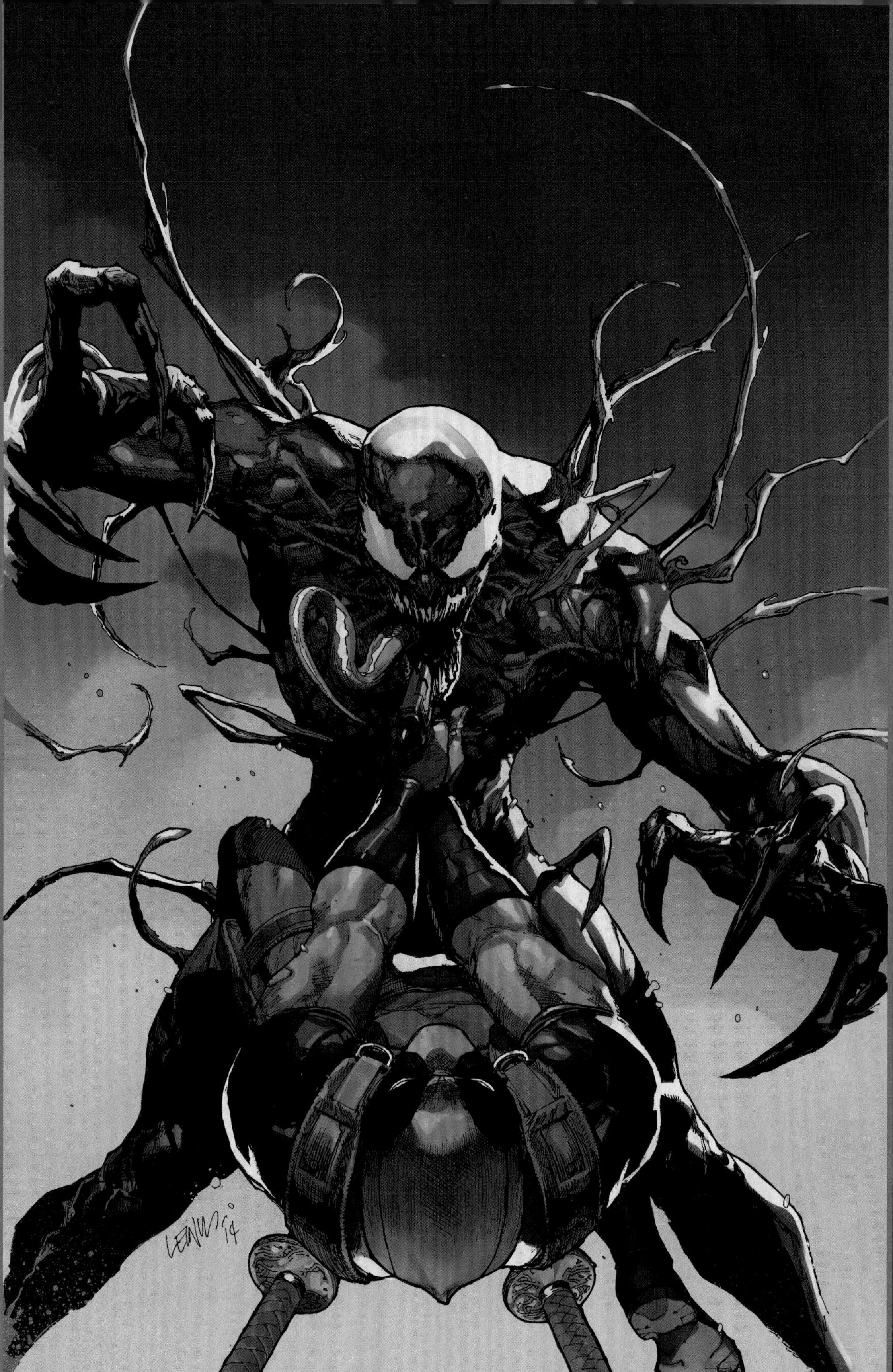
LEINIL '14

Deadpool vs. Carnage #1 Variant by Leinil Francis Yu

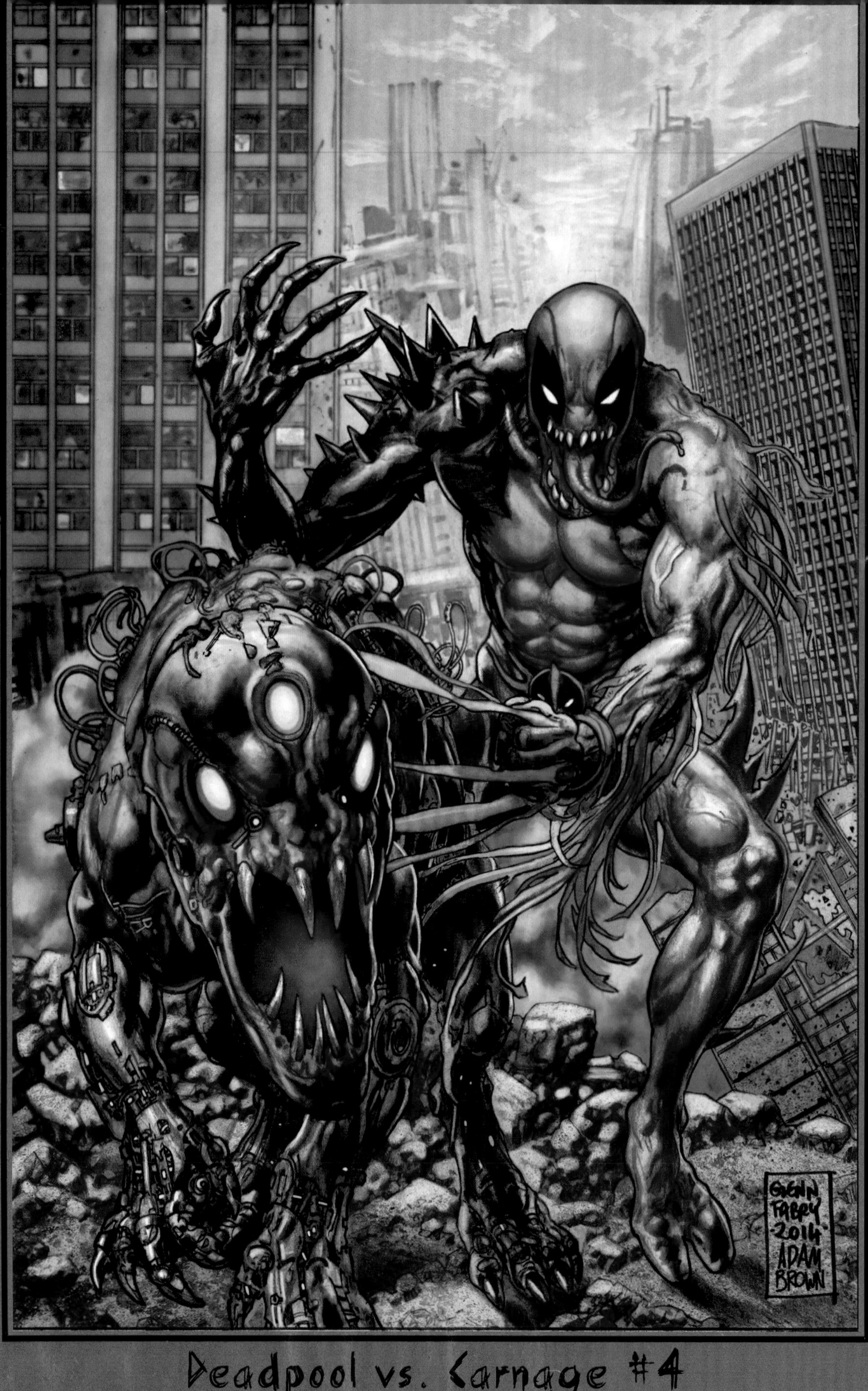
GLENN FABRY 2014 ADAM BROWN

Deadpool vs. Carnage #4

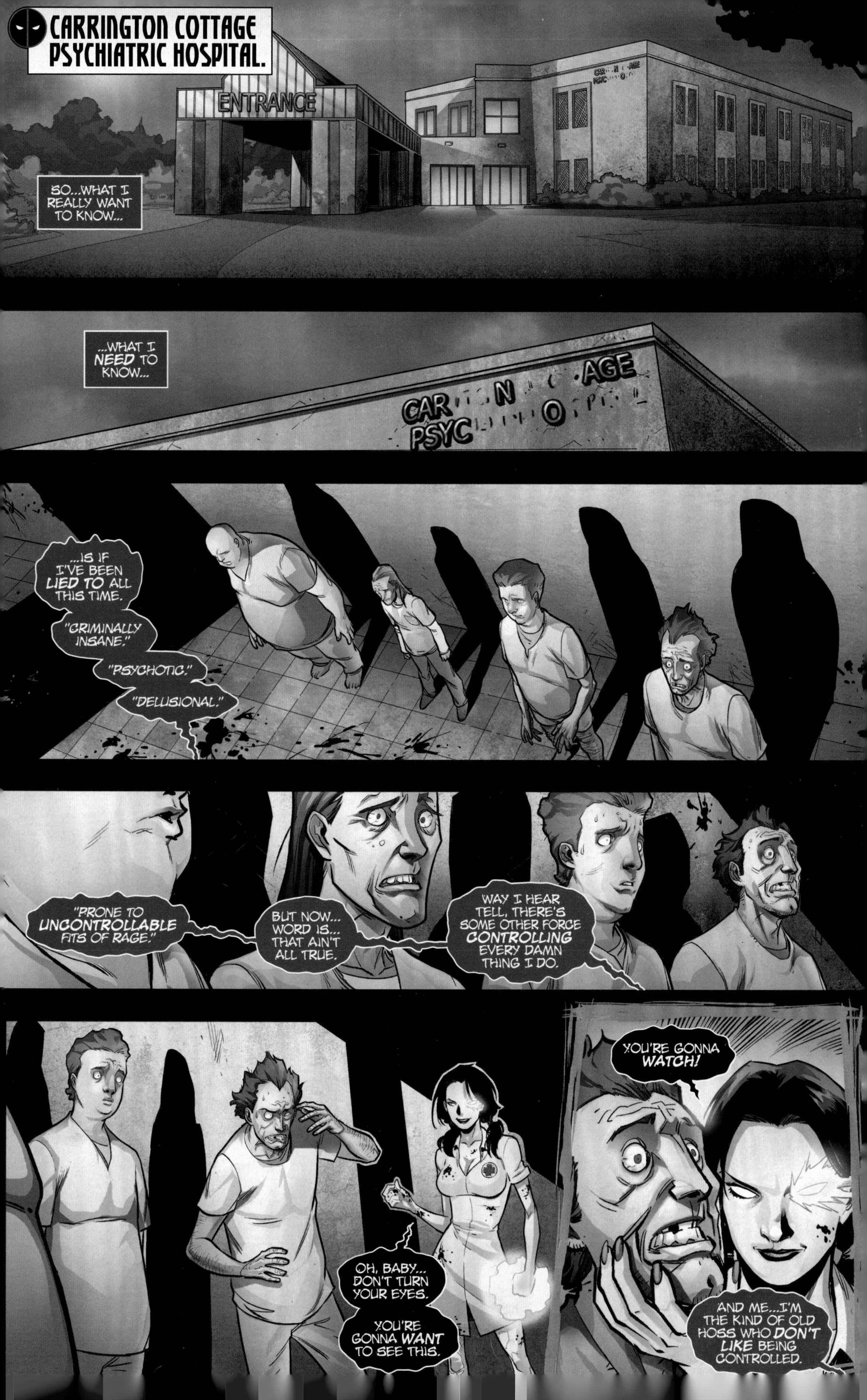
CARRINGTON COTTAGE PSYCHIATRIC HOSPITAL.
ENTRANCE
SO...WHAT I REALLY WANT TO KNOW...
...WHAT I NEED TO KNOW...
...IS IF I'VE BEEN LIED TO ALL THIS TIME.
"CRIMINALLY INSANE."
"PSYCHOTIC."
"DELUSIONAL."
"PRONE TO UNCONTROLLABLE FITS OF RAGE."
BUT NOW... WORD IS... THAT AIN'T ALL TRUE.
WAY I HEAR TELL, THERE'S SOME OTHER FORCE CONTROLLING EVERY DAMN THING I DO.
OH, BABY... DON'T TURN YOUR EYES.
YOU'RE GONNA WANT TO SEE THIS.
YOU'RE GONNA WATCH!
AND ME...I'M THE KIND OF OLD HOSS WHO DON'T LIKE BEING CONTROLLED.

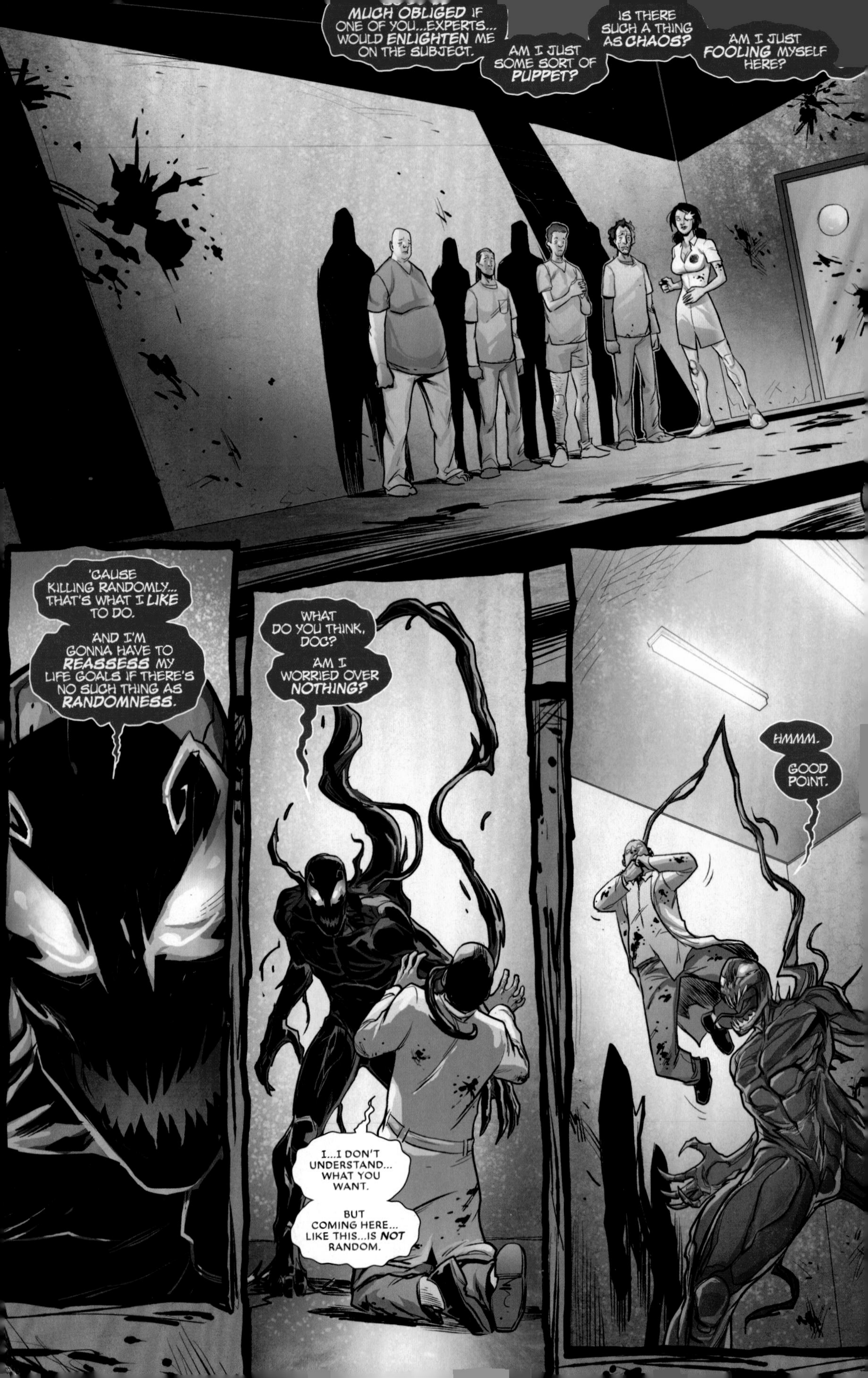
MUCH OBLIGED IF ONE OF YOU...EXPERTS... WOULD ENLIGHTEN ME ON THE SUBJECT.
AM I JUST SOME SORT OF PUPPET?
IS THERE SUCH A THING AS CHAOS?
AM I JUST FOOLING MYSELF HERE?
'CAUSE KILLING RANDOMLY... THAT'S WHAT I LIKE TO DO.
AND I'M GONNA HAVE TO REASSESS MY LIFE GOALS IF THERE'S NO SUCH THING AS RANDOMNESS.
WHAT DO YOU THINK, DOC?
AM I WORRIED OVER NOTHING?
I...I DON'T UNDERSTAND... WHAT YOU WANT.
BUT COMING HERE... LIKE THIS...IS NOT RANDOM.
HMMM.
GOOD POINT.

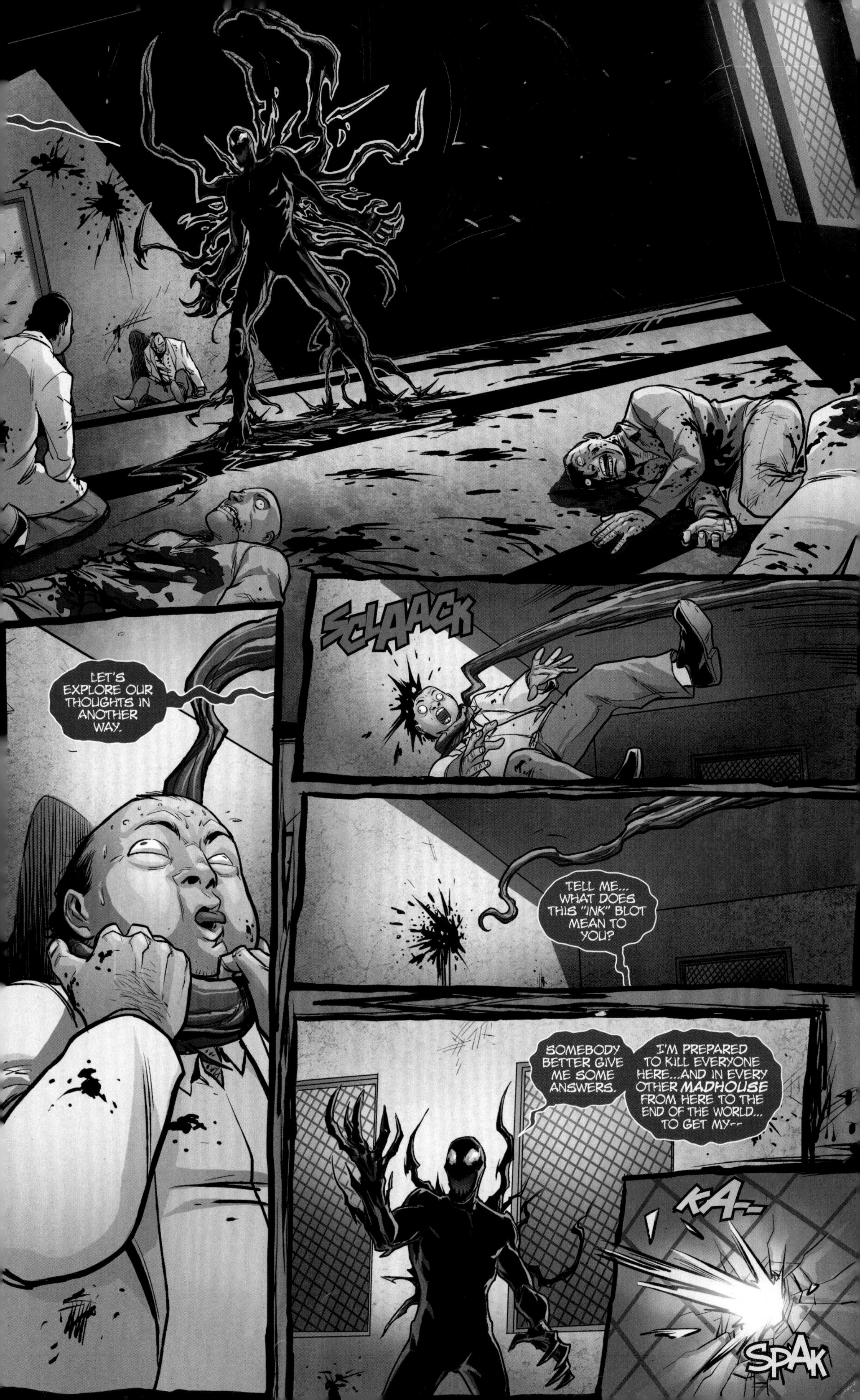
LET'S EXPLORE OUR THOUGHTS IN ANOTHER WAY.
SCLAACK
TELL ME... WHAT DOES THIS "INK" BLOT MEAN TO YOU?
SOMEBODY BETTER GIVE ME SOME ANSWERS.
I'M PREPARED TO KILL EVERYONE HERE...AND IN EVERY OTHER MADHOUSE FROM HERE TO THE END OF THE WORLD... TO GET MY--
KA--
SPAK

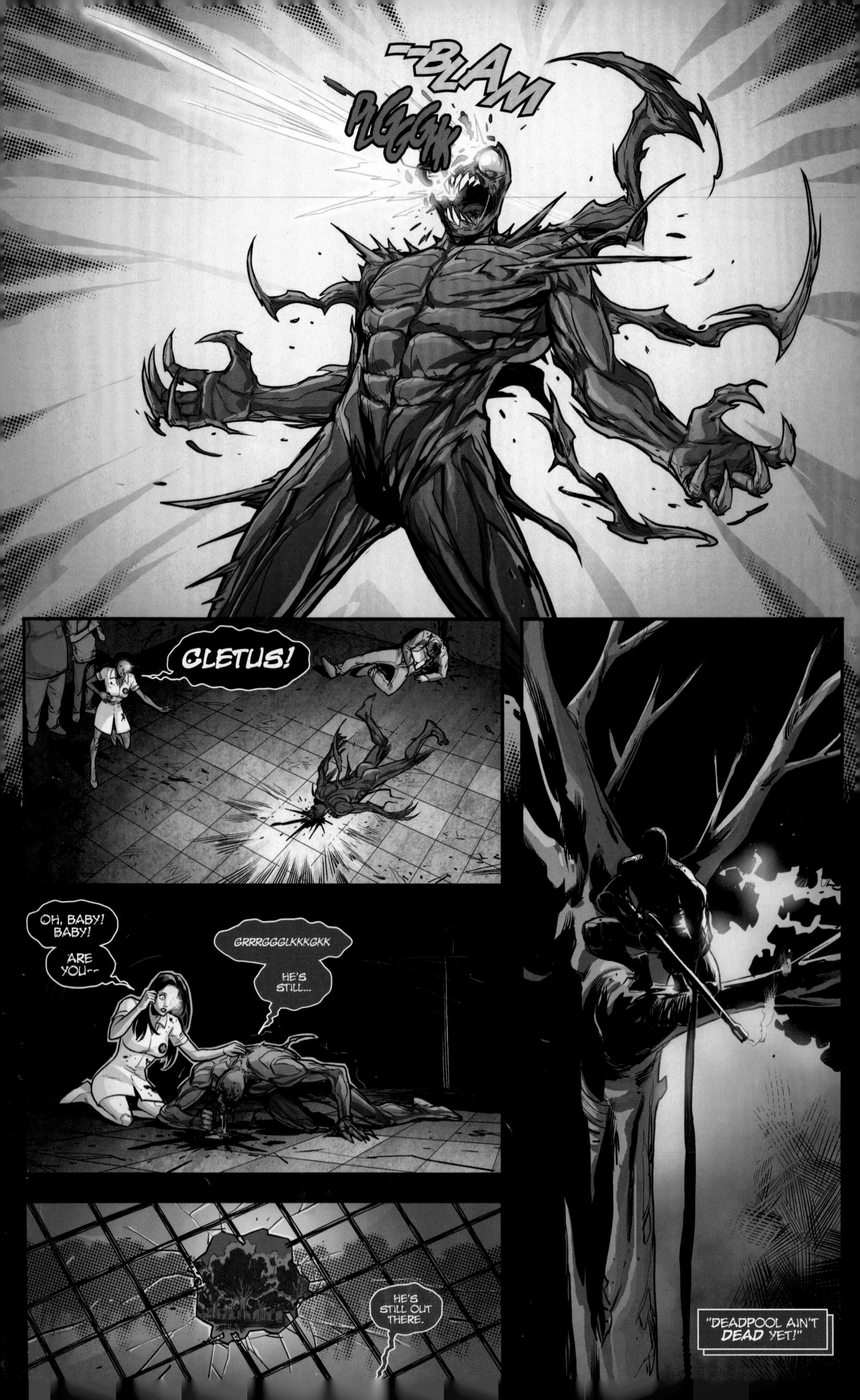

--BLAM
PLGGGHK
CLETUS!
OH, BABY! BABY!
ARE YOU--
GRRRGGGLKKKGKK
HE'S STILL...
HE'S STILL OUT THERE.
"DEADPOOL AIN'T DEAD YET!"

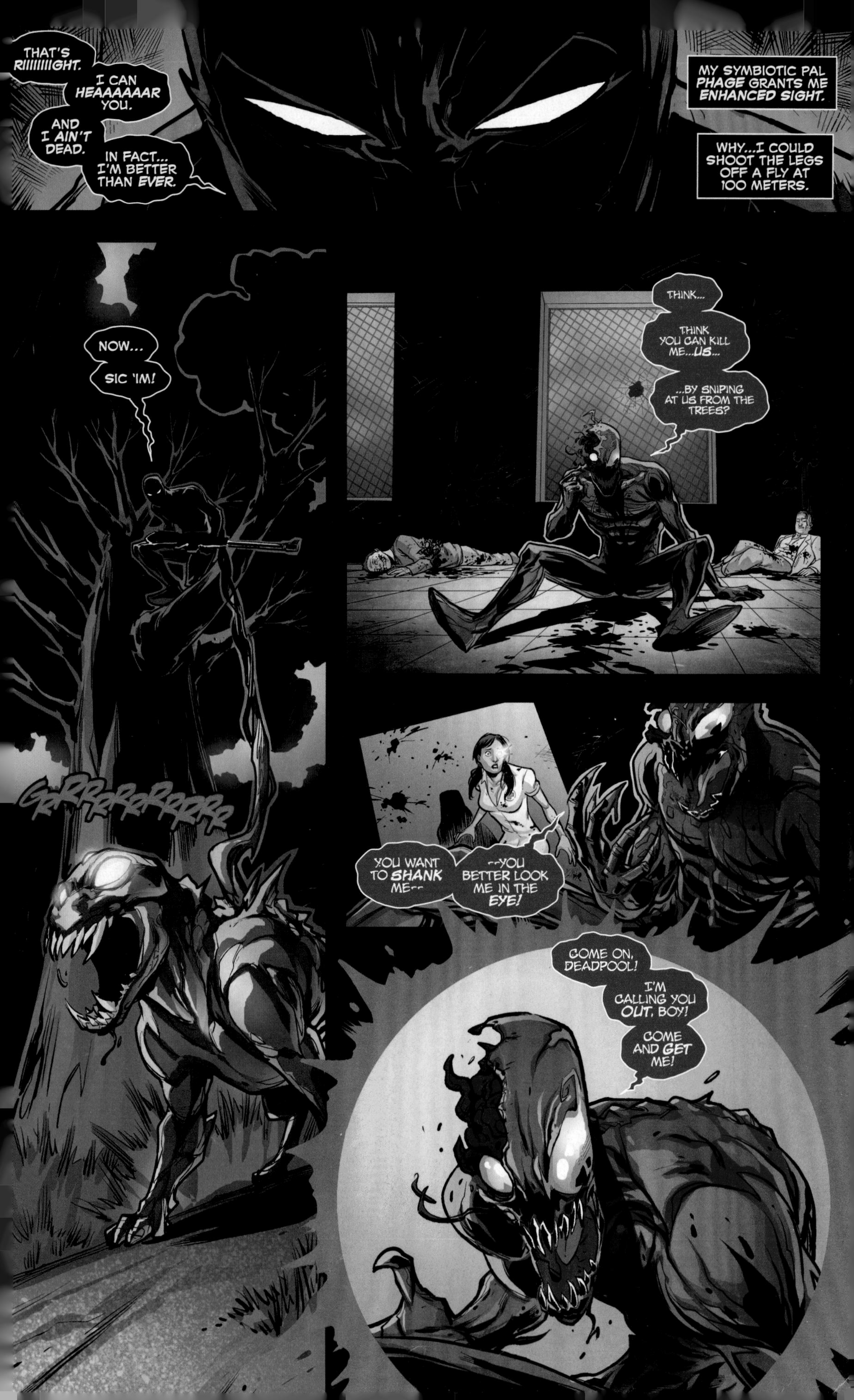

THAT'S RIIIIIIIGHT.
I CAN HEAAAAAAR YOU.
AND I AIN'T DEAD.
IN FACT... I'M BETTER THAN EVER.
MY SYMBIOTIC PAL PHAGE GRANTS ME ENHANCED SIGHT.
WHY...I COULD SHOOT THE LEGS OFF A FLY AT 100 METERS.
NOW...
SIC 'IM!
THINK...
THINK YOU CAN KILL ME...US...
...BY SNIPING AT US FROM THE TREES?
GRRRRRRRRRRR
YOU WANT TO SHANK ME--
--YOU BETTER LOOK ME IN THE EYE!
COME ON, DEADPOOL!
I'M CALLING YOU OUT, BOY!
COME AND GET ME!

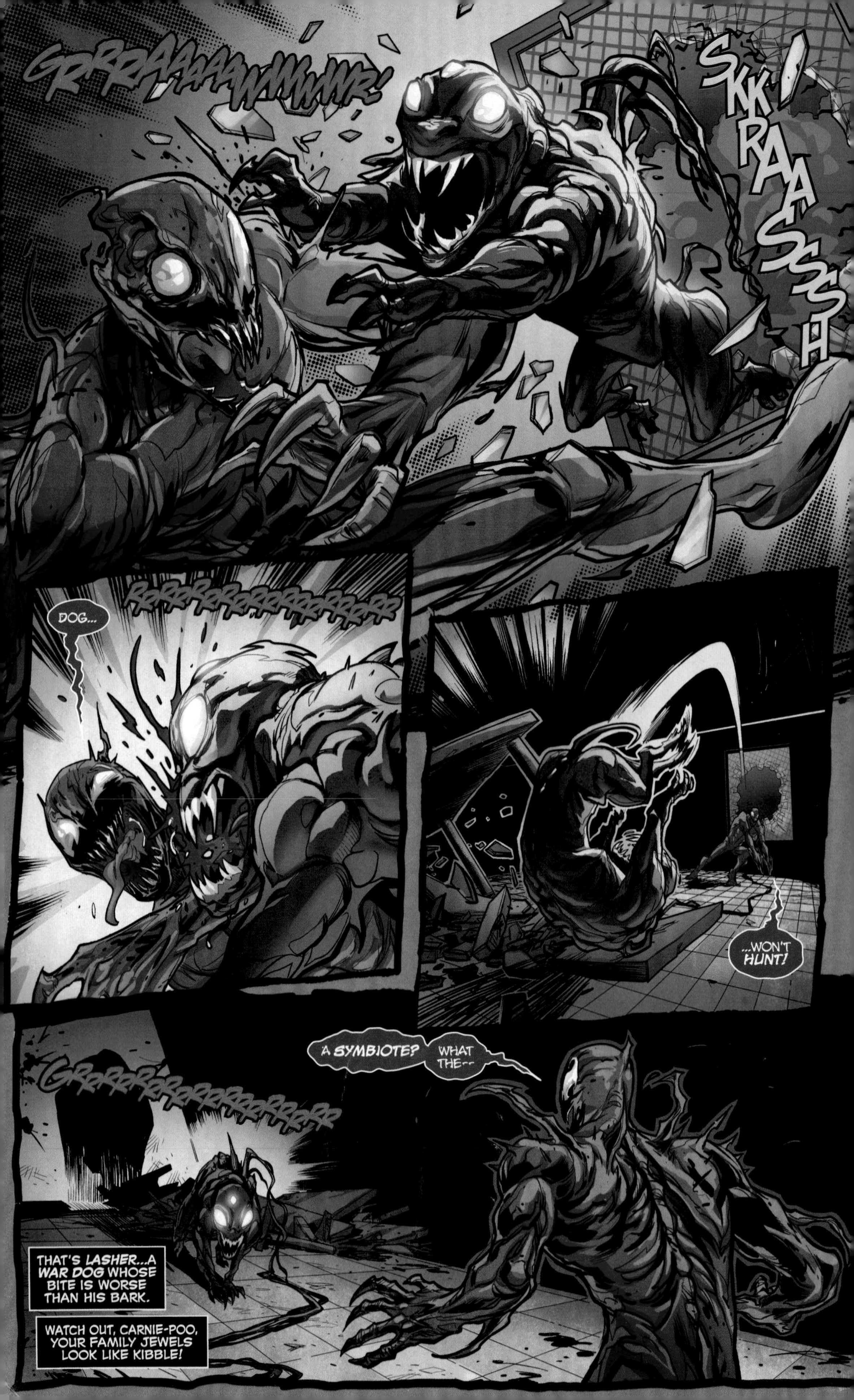
GRRRAAAAAWWWWR!
SKKRAASSSH
RRRRRRRRRRRRRRRRR
DOG...
...WON'T HUNT!
GRRRRRRRRRRRRRRRR
A SYMBIOTE? WHAT THE--
THAT'S LASHER...A WAR DOG WHOSE BITE IS WORSE THAN HIS BARK.
WATCH OUT, CARNIE-POO, YOUR FAMILY JEWELS LOOK LIKE KIBBLE!

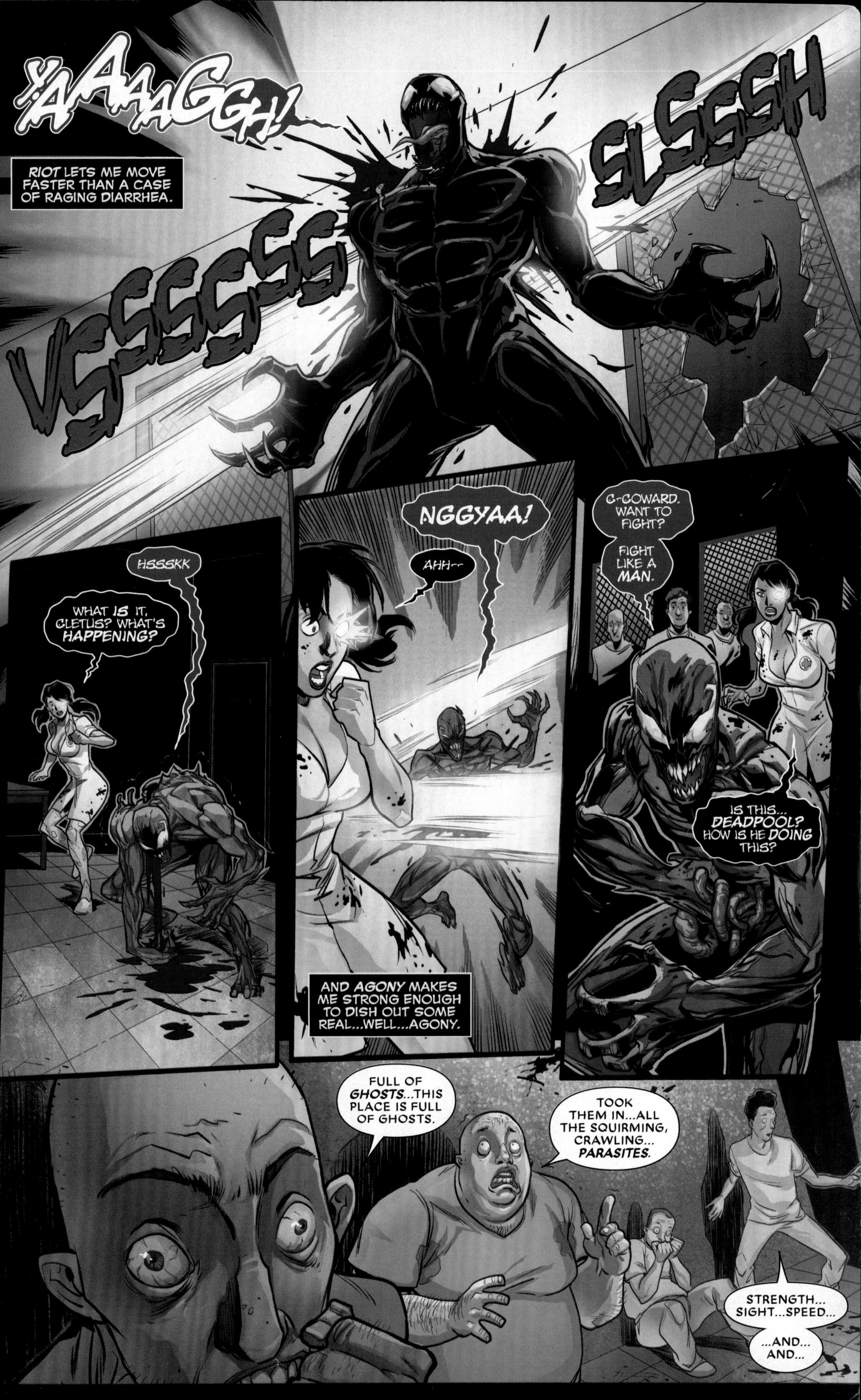
YAAAAAGGH!
RIOT LETS ME MOVE FASTER THAN A CASE OF RAGING DIARRHEA.
VSSSSSSS
SLSSSH
HSSSKK
WHAT IS IT, CLETUS? WHAT'S HAPPENING?
NGGYAA!
AHH--
AND AGONY MAKES ME STRONG ENOUGH TO DISH OUT SOME REAL...WELL...AGONY.
C-COWARD. WANT TO FIGHT?
FIGHT LIKE A MAN.
IS THIS... DEADPOOL? HOW IS HE DOING THIS?
FULL OF GHOSTS...THIS PLACE IS FULL OF GHOSTS.
TOOK THEM IN...ALL THE SQUIRMING, CRAWLING... PARASITES.
STRENGTH... SIGHT...SPEED...
...AND... AND...

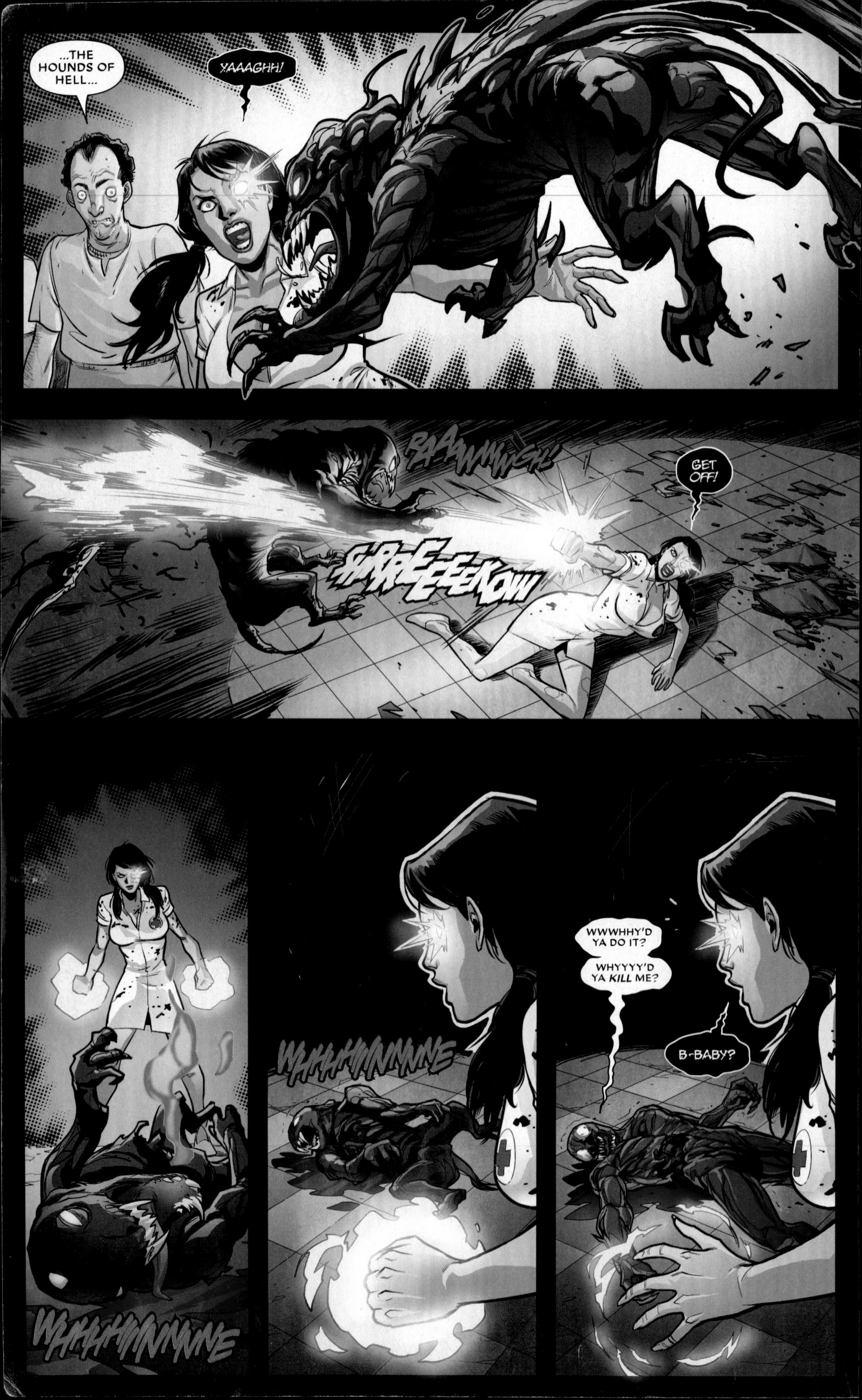
...THE HOUNDS OF HELL...
YAAAGHH!
RAAWWWGH!
GET OFF!
SHREEEEEKOW
WHHHHNNNNE
WHHHHNNNNE
WWWHHY'D YA DO IT?
WHYYYY'D YA KILL ME?
B-BABY?

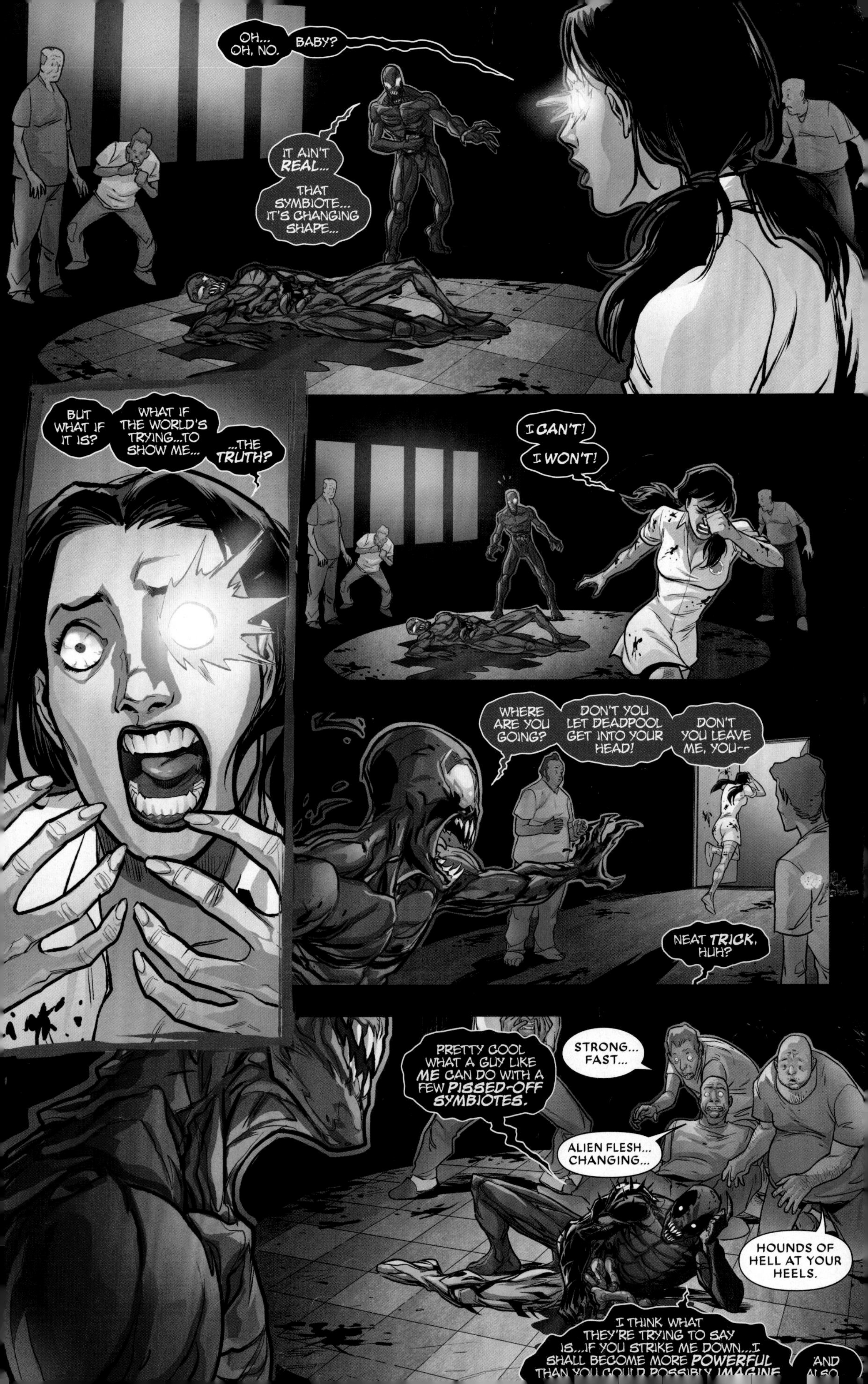
OH... OH, NO.
BABY?
IT AIN'T REAL...
THAT SYMBIOTE... IT'S CHANGING SHAPE...
BUT WHAT IF IT IS?
WHAT IF THE WORLD'S TRYING...TO SHOW ME...
...THE TRUTH?
I CAN'T!
I WON'T!
WHERE ARE YOU GOING?
DON'T YOU LET DEADPOOL GET INTO YOUR HEAD!
DON'T YOU LEAVE ME, YOU--
NEAT TRICK, HUH?
PRETTY COOL WHAT A GUY LIKE ME CAN DO WITH A FEW PISSED-OFF SYMBIOTES.
STRONG... FAST...
ALIEN FLESH... CHANGING...
HOUNDS OF HELL AT YOUR HEELS.
I THINK WHAT THEY'RE TRYING TO SAY IS...IF YOU STRIKE ME DOWN...I SHALL BECOME MORE POWERFUL THAN YOU COULD POSSIBLY IMAGINE.
'AND ALSO

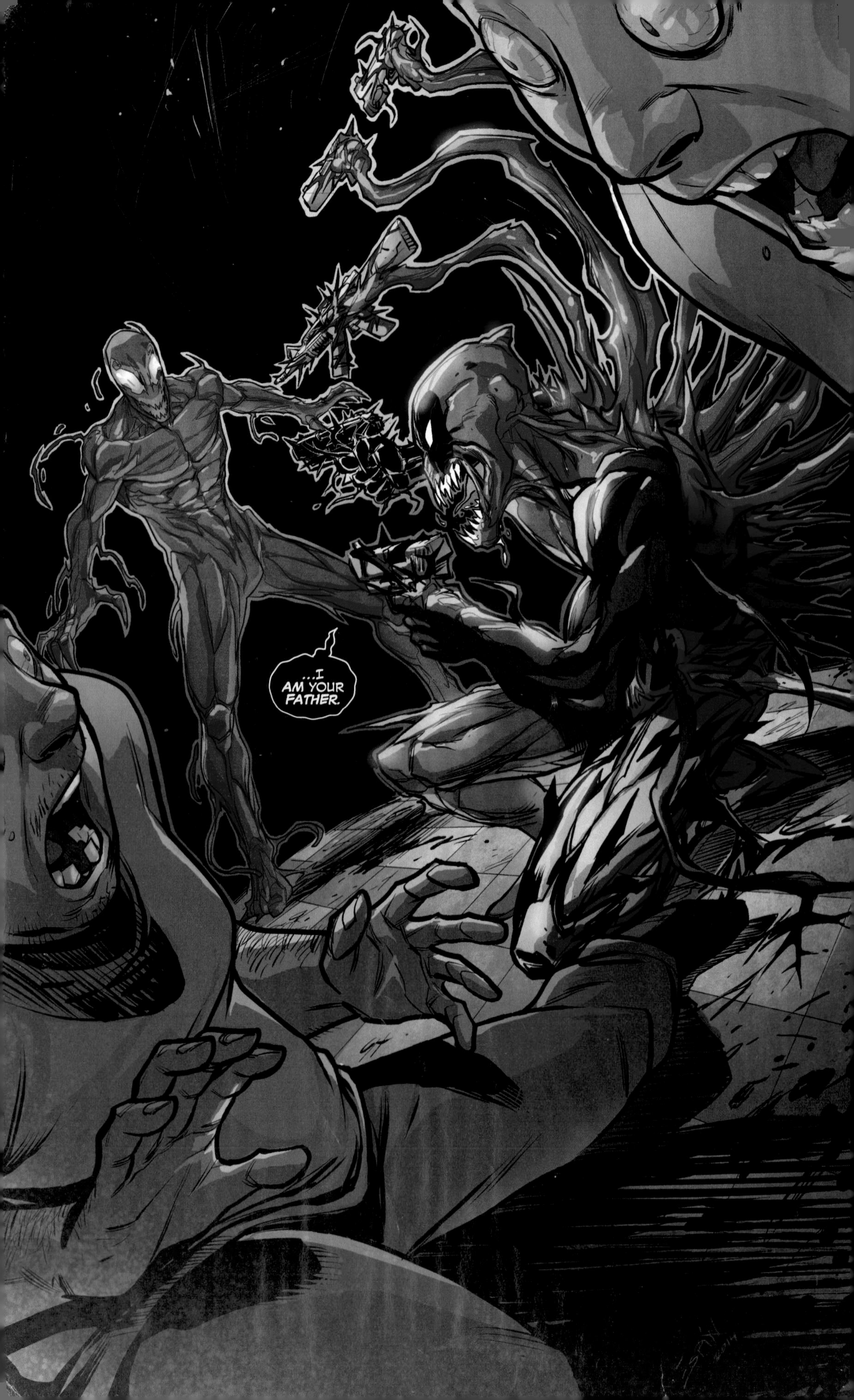
...I AM YOUR FATHER.

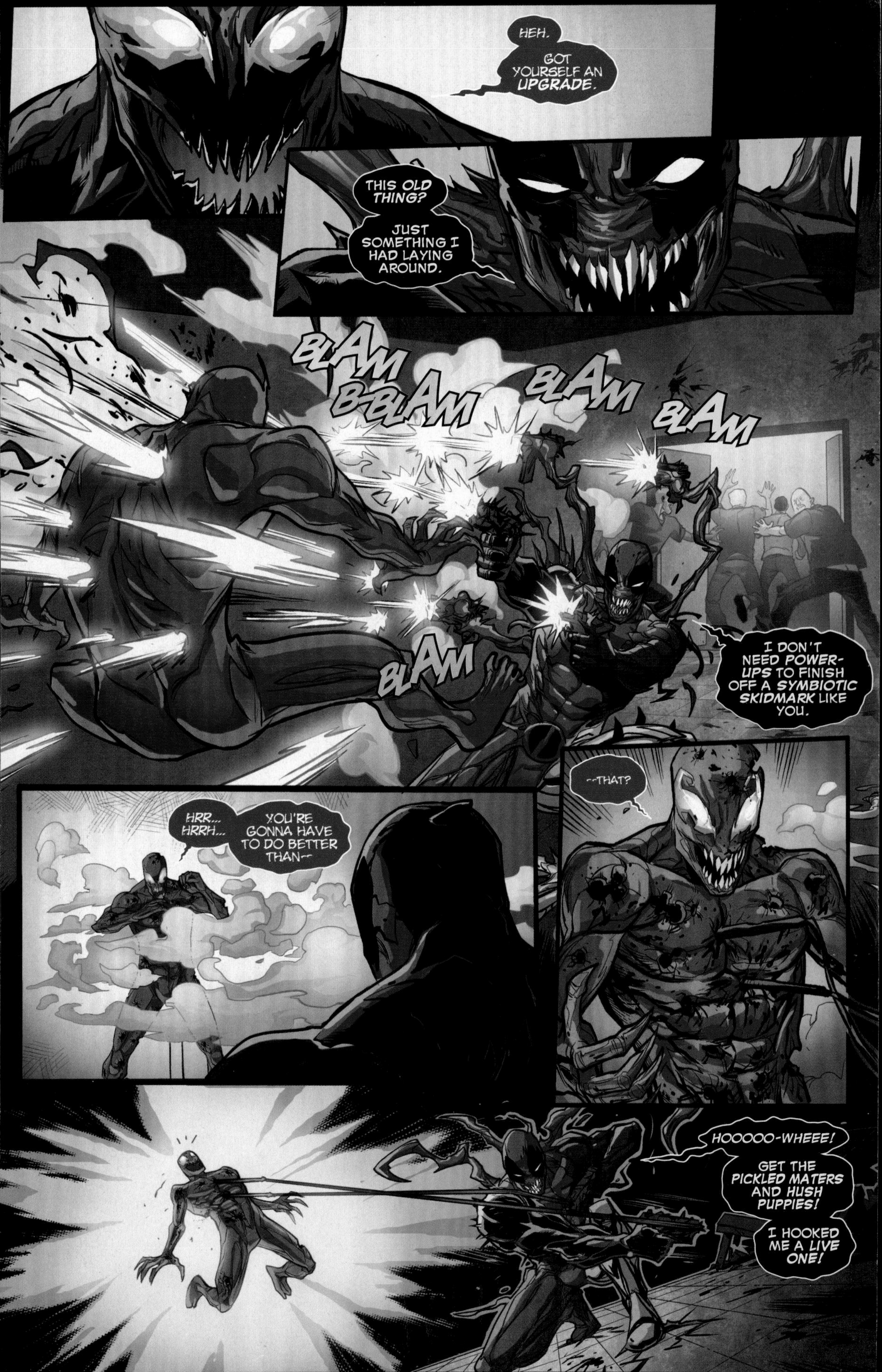
HEH.
GOT YOURSELF AN UPGRADE.
THIS OLD THING?
JUST SOMETHING I HAD LAYING AROUND.
BLAM
B-BLAM
BLAM
BLAM
BLAM
I DON'T NEED POWER-UPS TO FINISH OFF A SYMBIOTIC SKIDMARK LIKE YOU.
HRR... HRRH...
YOU'RE GONNA HAVE TO DO BETTER THAN--
--THAT?
HOOOOO-WHEEE!
GET THE PICKLED MATERS AND HUSH PUPPIES!
I HOOKED ME A LIVE ONE!

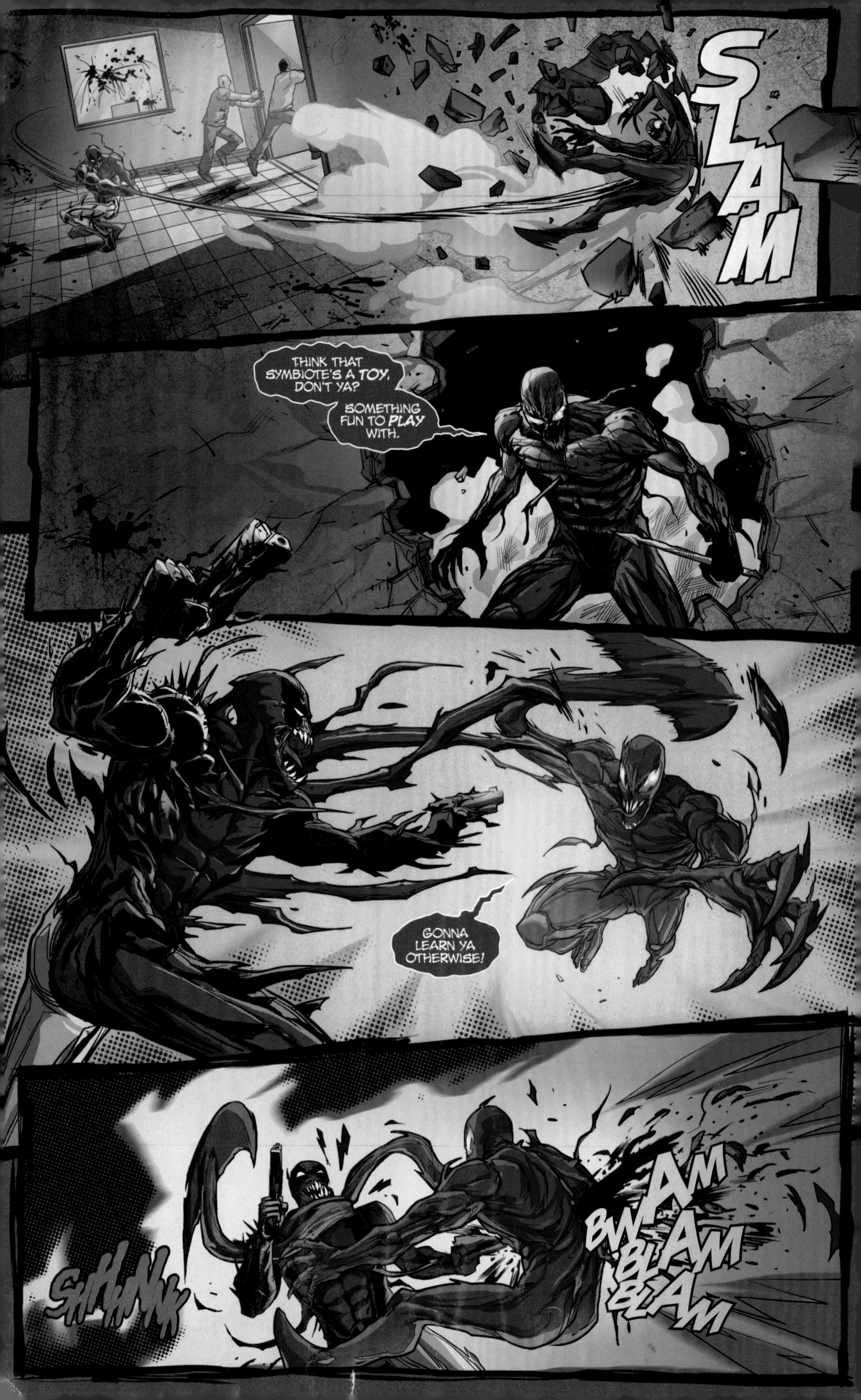
SLAM
THINK THAT SYMBIOTE'S A TOY, DON'T YA?
SOMETHING FUN TO PLAY WITH.
GONNA LEARN YA OTHERWISE!
SHHNKK
BWAM BLAM BLAM BLAM

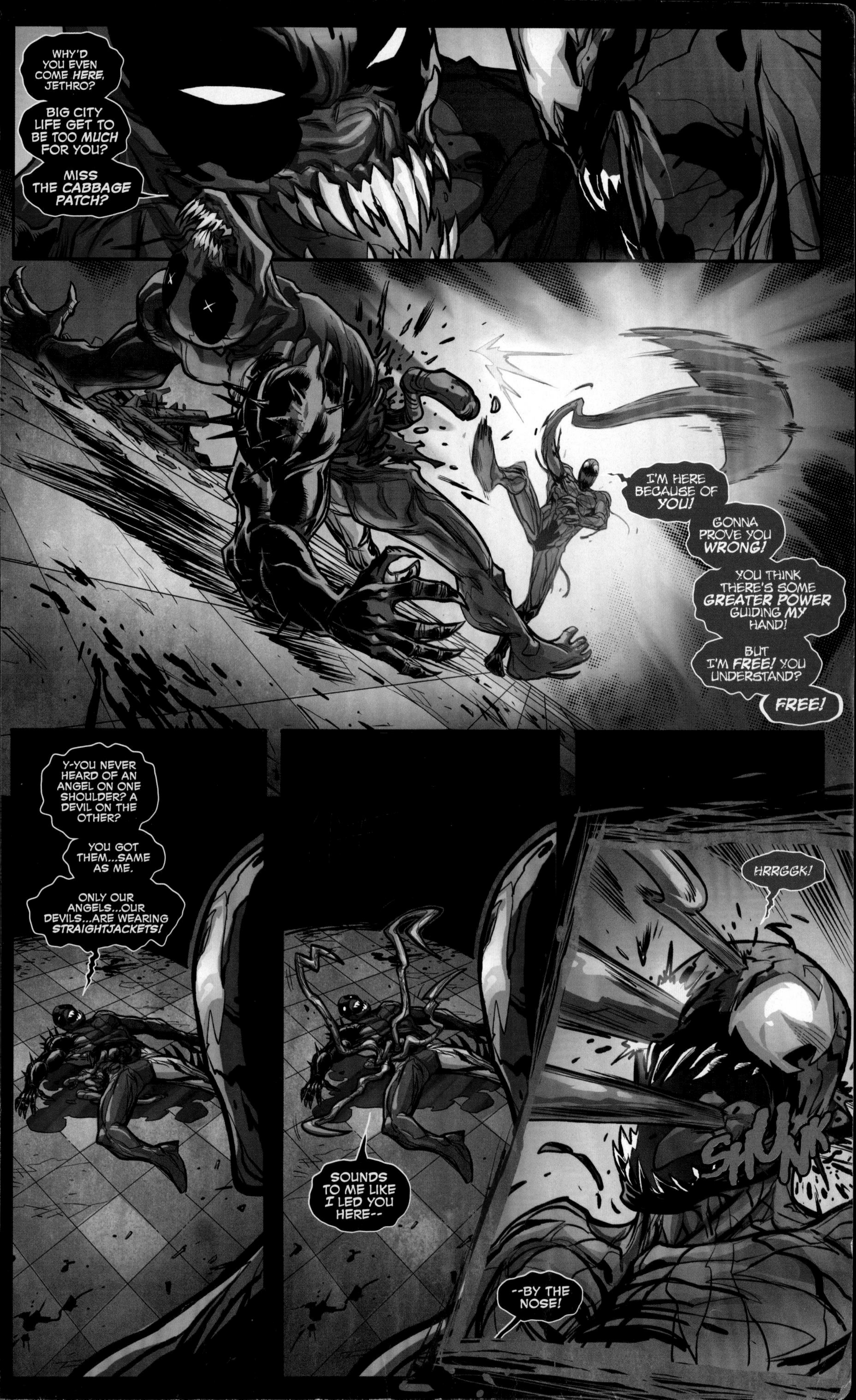
WHY'D YOU EVEN COME HERE, JETHRO?
BIG CITY LIFE GET TO BE TOO MUCH FOR YOU?
MISS THE CABBAGE PATCH?
I'M HERE BECAUSE OF YOU!
GONNA PROVE YOU WRONG!
YOU THINK THERE'S SOME GREATER POWER GUIDING MY HAND!
BUT I'M FREE! YOU UNDERSTAND?
FREE!
Y-YOU NEVER HEARD OF AN ANGEL ON ONE SHOULDER? A DEVIL ON THE OTHER?
YOU GOT THEM...SAME AS ME.
ONLY OUR ANGELS...OUR DEVILS...ARE WEARING STRAIGHTJACKETS!
SOUNDS TO ME LIKE I LED YOU HERE--
HRRGGK!
SHUNK
--BY THE NOSE!

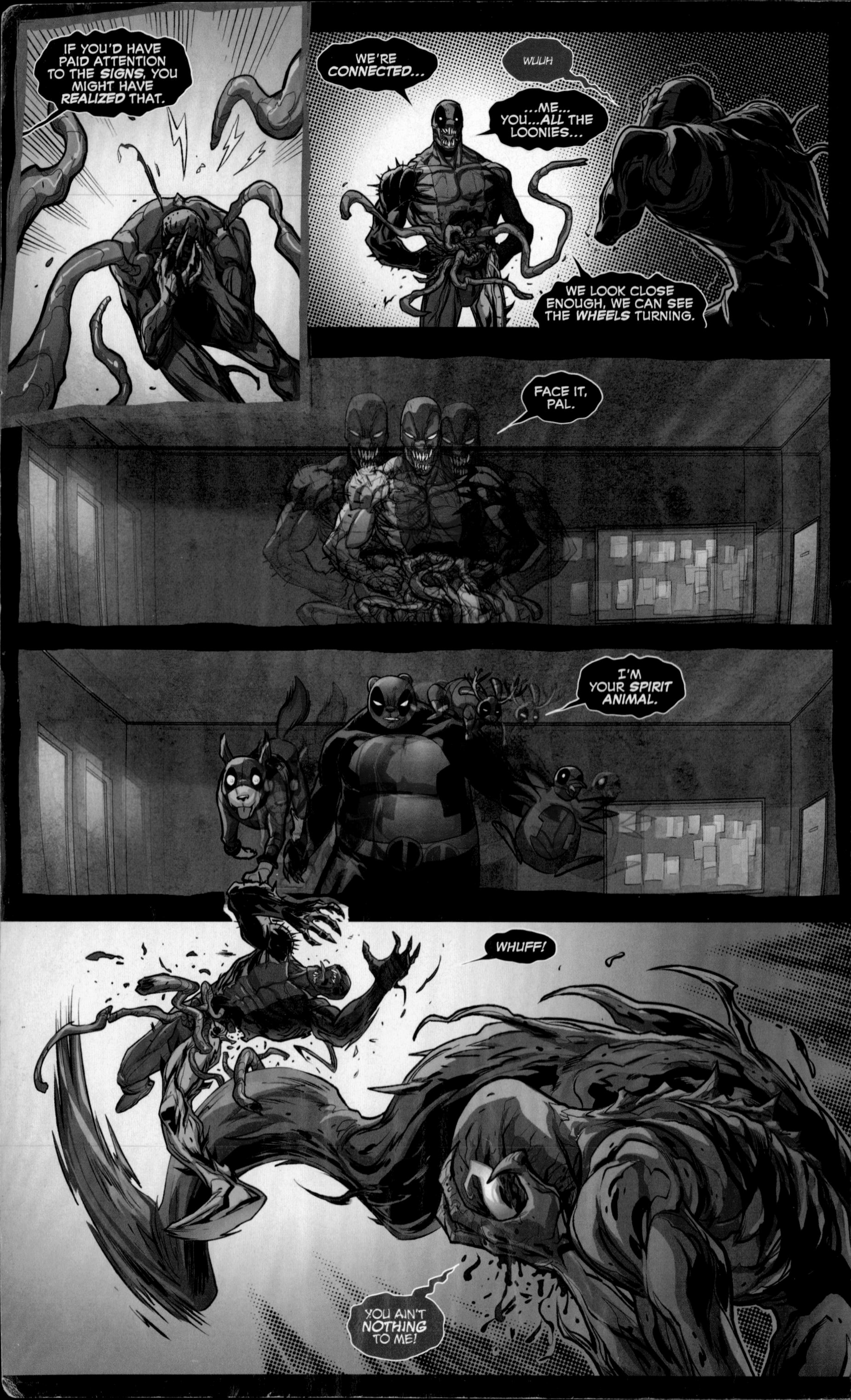
IF YOU'D HAVE PAID ATTENTION TO THE SIGNS, YOU MIGHT HAVE REALIZED THAT.
WE'RE CONNECTED...
WUUH
...ME... YOU...ALL THE LOONIES...
WE LOOK CLOSE ENOUGH, WE CAN SEE THE WHEELS TURNING.
FACE IT, PAL.
I'M YOUR SPIRIT ANIMAL.
WHUFF!
YOU AIN'T NOTHING TO ME!

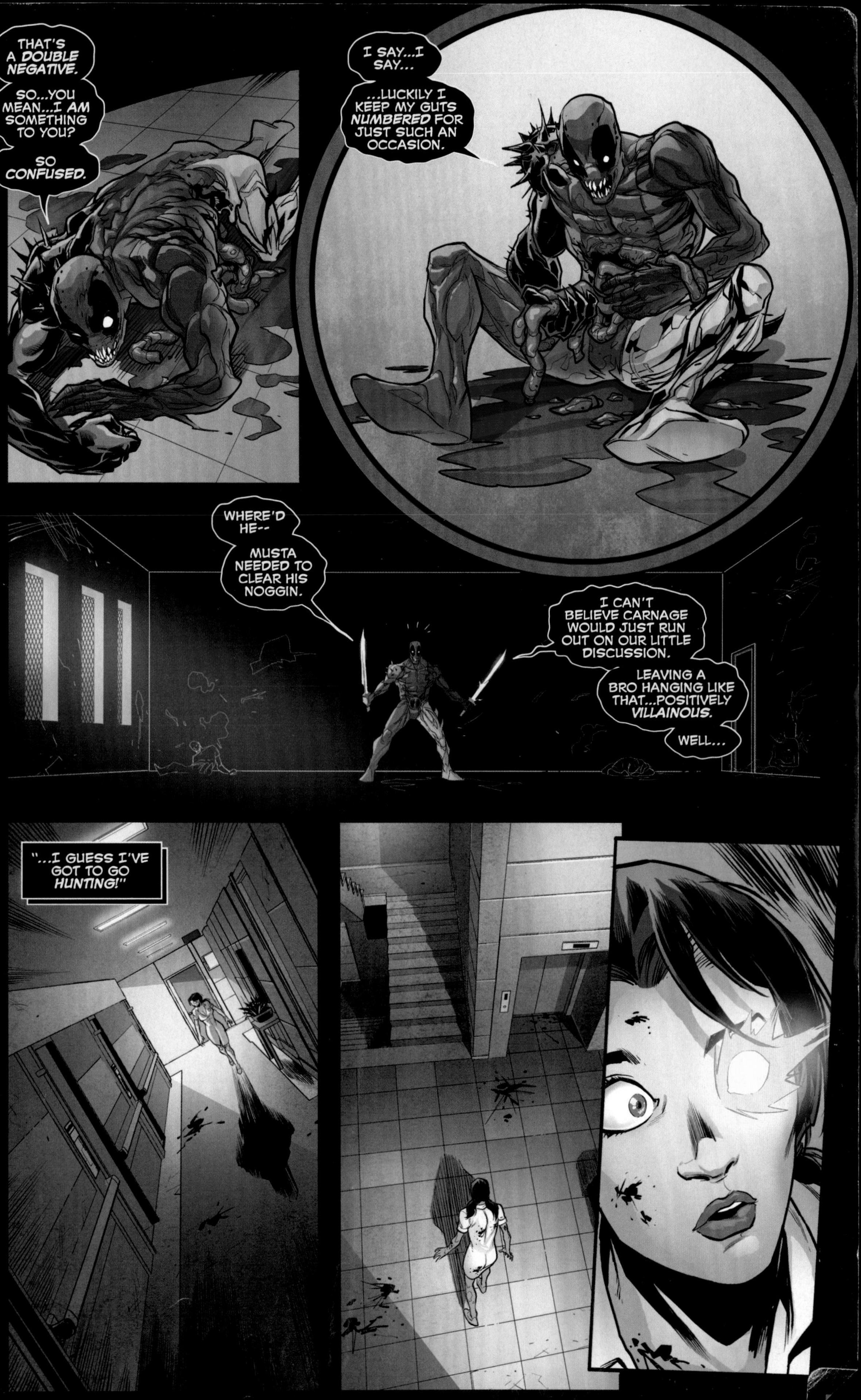
THAT'S A DOUBLE NEGATIVE.
SO...YOU MEAN...I AM SOMETHING TO YOU?
SO CONFUSED.
I SAY...I SAY...
...LUCKILY I KEEP MY GUTS NUMBERED FOR JUST SUCH AN OCCASION.
WHERE'D HE--
MUSTA NEEDED TO CLEAR HIS NOGGIN.
I CAN'T BELIEVE CARNAGE WOULD JUST RUN OUT ON OUR LITTLE DISCUSSION.
LEAVING A BRO HANGING LIKE THAT...POSITIVELY VILLAINOUS.
WELL...
"...I GUESS I'VE GOT TO GO HUNTING!"

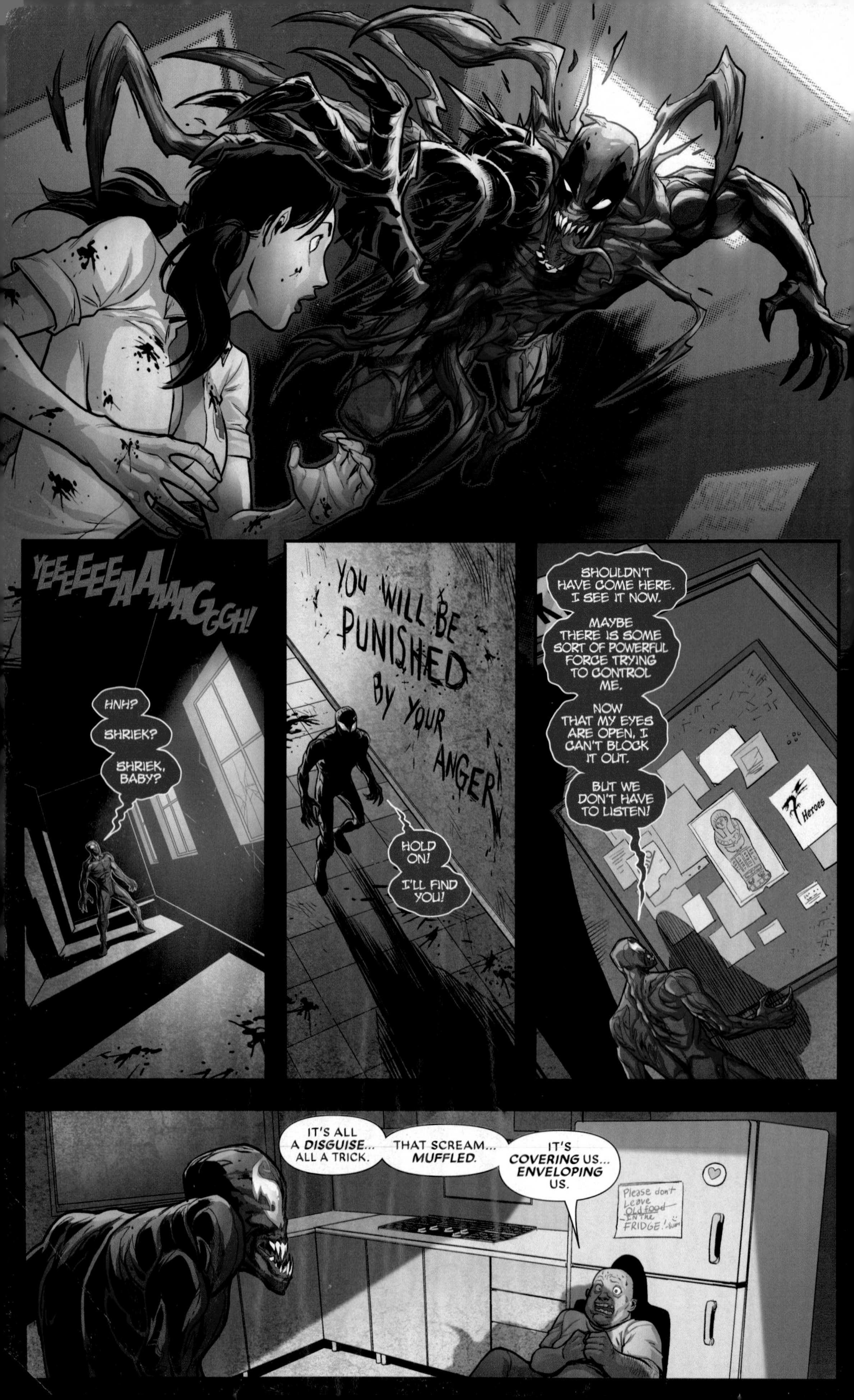
YEEEEEEAAAAAGGGH!
HNH?
SHRIEK?
SHRIEK, BABY?
YOU WILL BE PUNISHED BY YOUR ANGER!
HOLD ON!
I'LL FIND YOU!
SHOULDN'T HAVE COME HERE. I SEE IT NOW.
MAYBE THERE IS SOME SORT OF POWERFUL FORCE TRYING TO CONTROL ME.
NOW THAT MY EYES ARE OPEN, I CAN'T BLOCK IT OUT.
BUT WE DON'T HAVE TO LISTEN!
Heroes
IT'S ALL A DISGUISE... ALL A TRICK.
THAT SCREAM... MUFFLED.
IT'S COVERING US... ENVELOPING US.
Please don't Leave Old food in the FRIDGE!

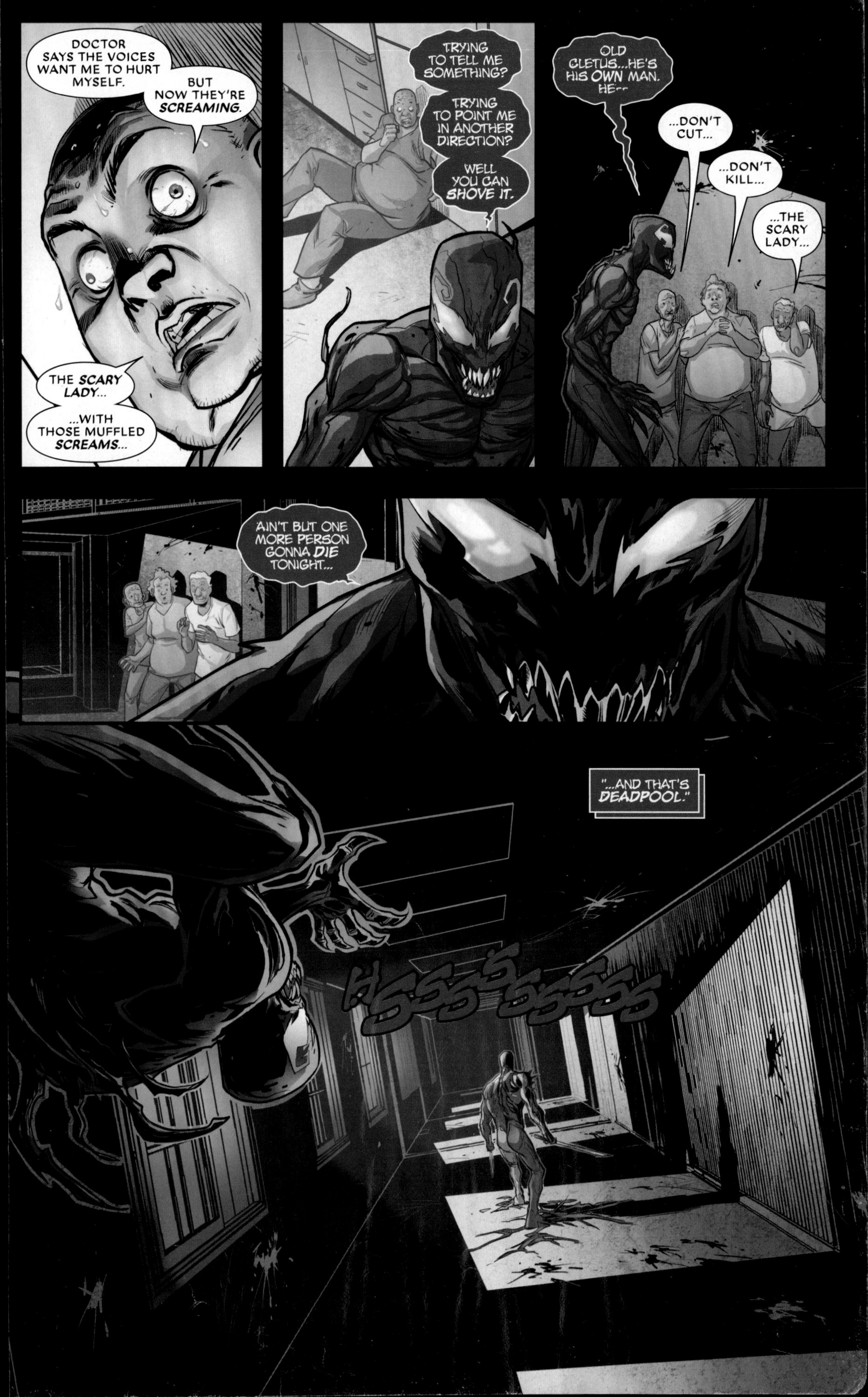
DOCTOR SAYS THE VOICES WANT ME TO HURT MYSELF.
BUT NOW THEY'RE SCREAMING.
THE SCARY LADY...
...WITH THOSE MUFFLED SCREAMS...
TRYING TO TELL ME SOMETHING?
TRYING TO POINT ME IN ANOTHER DIRECTION?
WELL YOU CAN SHOVE IT.
OLD CLETUS...HE'S HIS OWN MAN. HE--
...DON'T CUT...
...DON'T KILL...
...THE SCARY LADY...
AIN'T BUT ONE MORE PERSON GONNA DIE TONIGHT...
"...AND THAT'S DEADPOOL."
HSSSSSSSSSS

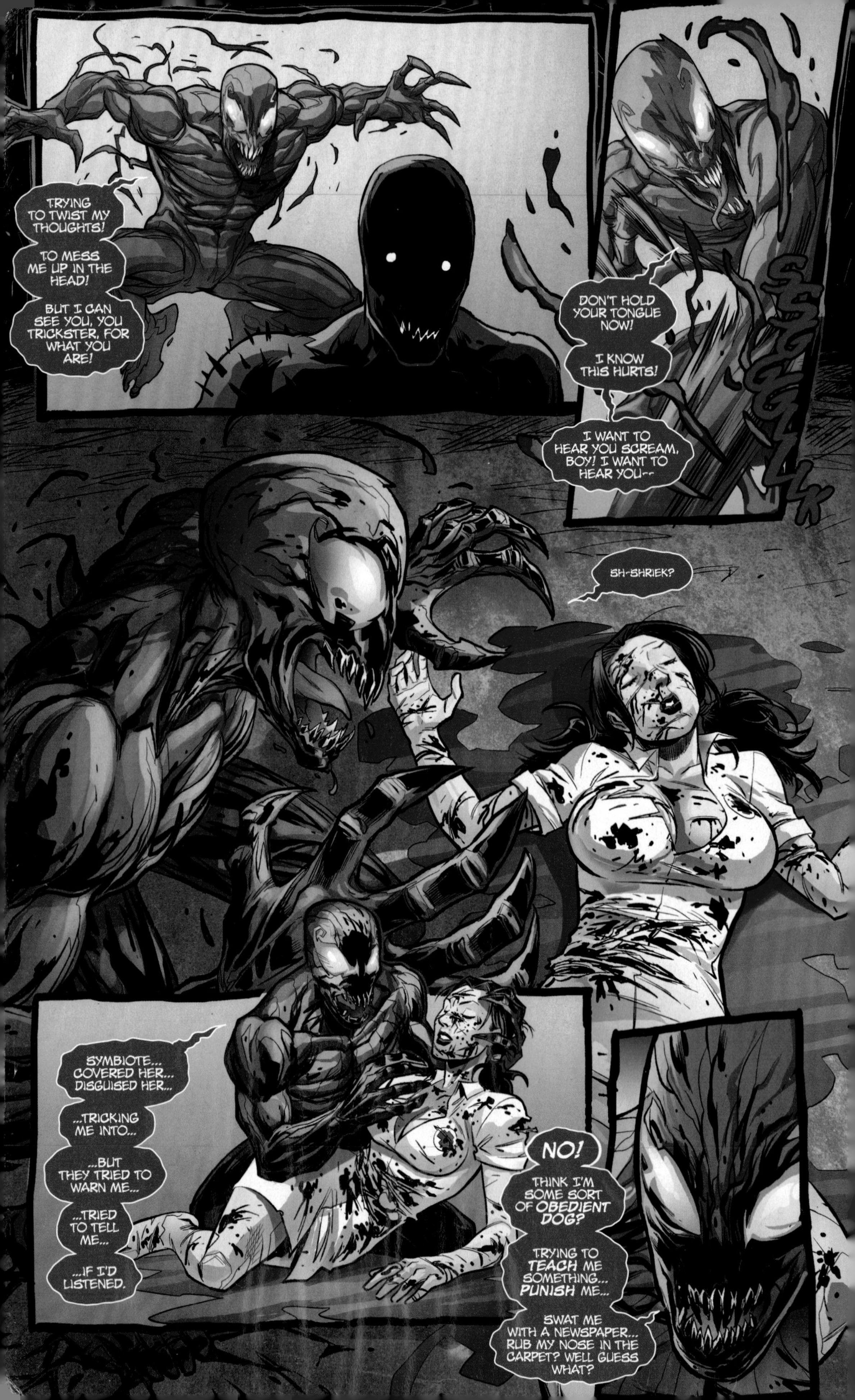
TRYING TO TWIST MY THOUGHTS!
TO MESS ME UP IN THE HEAD!
BUT I CAN SEE YOU, YOU TRICKSTER, FOR WHAT YOU ARE!
DON'T HOLD YOUR TONGUE NOW!
I KNOW THIS HURTS!
I WANT TO HEAR YOU SCREAM, BOY! I WANT TO HEAR YOU--
SSGGLLK
SH-SHRIEK?
SYMBIOTE... COVERED HER... DISGUISED HER...
...TRICKING ME INTO...
...BUT THEY TRIED TO WARN ME...
...TRIED TO TELL ME...
...IF I'D LISTENED.
NO!
THINK I'M SOME SORT OF OBEDIENT DOG?
TRYING TO TEACH ME SOMETHING... PUNISH ME...
SWAT ME WITH A NEWSPAPER... RUB MY NOSE IN THE CARPET? WELL GUESS WHAT?

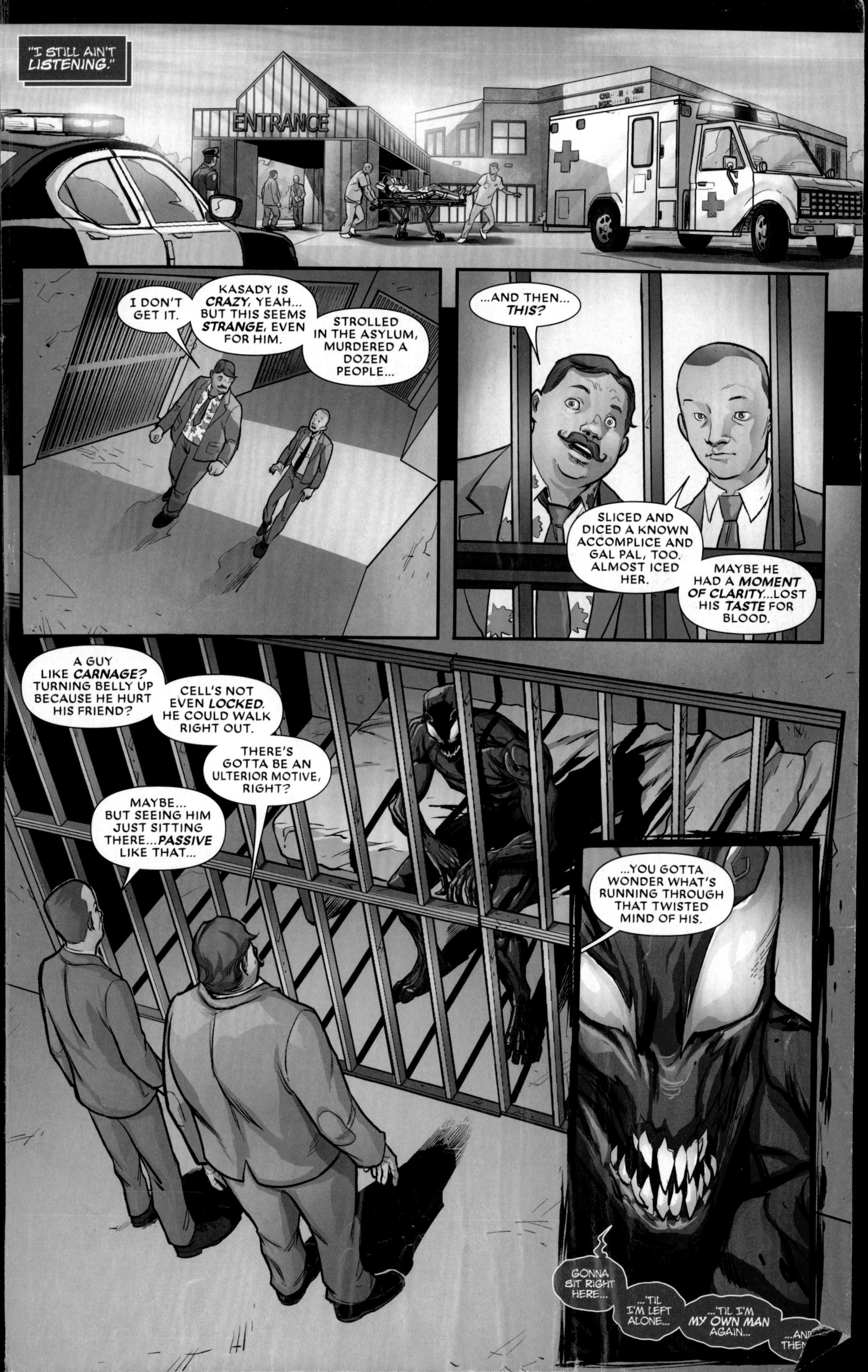
"I STILL AIN'T LISTENING."
I DON'T GET IT.
KASADY IS CRAZY, YEAH... BUT THIS SEEMS STRANGE, EVEN FOR HIM.
STROLLED IN THE ASYLUM, MURDERED A DOZEN PEOPLE...
...AND THEN... THIS?
SLICED AND DICED A KNOWN ACCOMPLICE AND GAL PAL, TOO. ALMOST ICED HER.
MAYBE HE HAD A MOMENT OF CLARITY...LOST HIS TASTE FOR BLOOD.
A GUY LIKE CARNAGE? TURNING BELLY UP BECAUSE HE HURT HIS FRIEND?
CELL'S NOT EVEN LOCKED. HE COULD WALK RIGHT OUT.
THERE'S GOTTA BE AN ULTERIOR MOTIVE, RIGHT?
MAYBE... BUT SEEING HIM JUST SITTING THERE...PASSIVE LIKE THAT...
...YOU GOTTA WONDER WHAT'S RUNNING THROUGH THAT TWISTED MIND OF HIS.
GONNA SIT RIGHT HERE...
...'TIL I'M LEFT ALONE...
...'TIL I'M MY OWN MAN AGAIN...
...AN THE

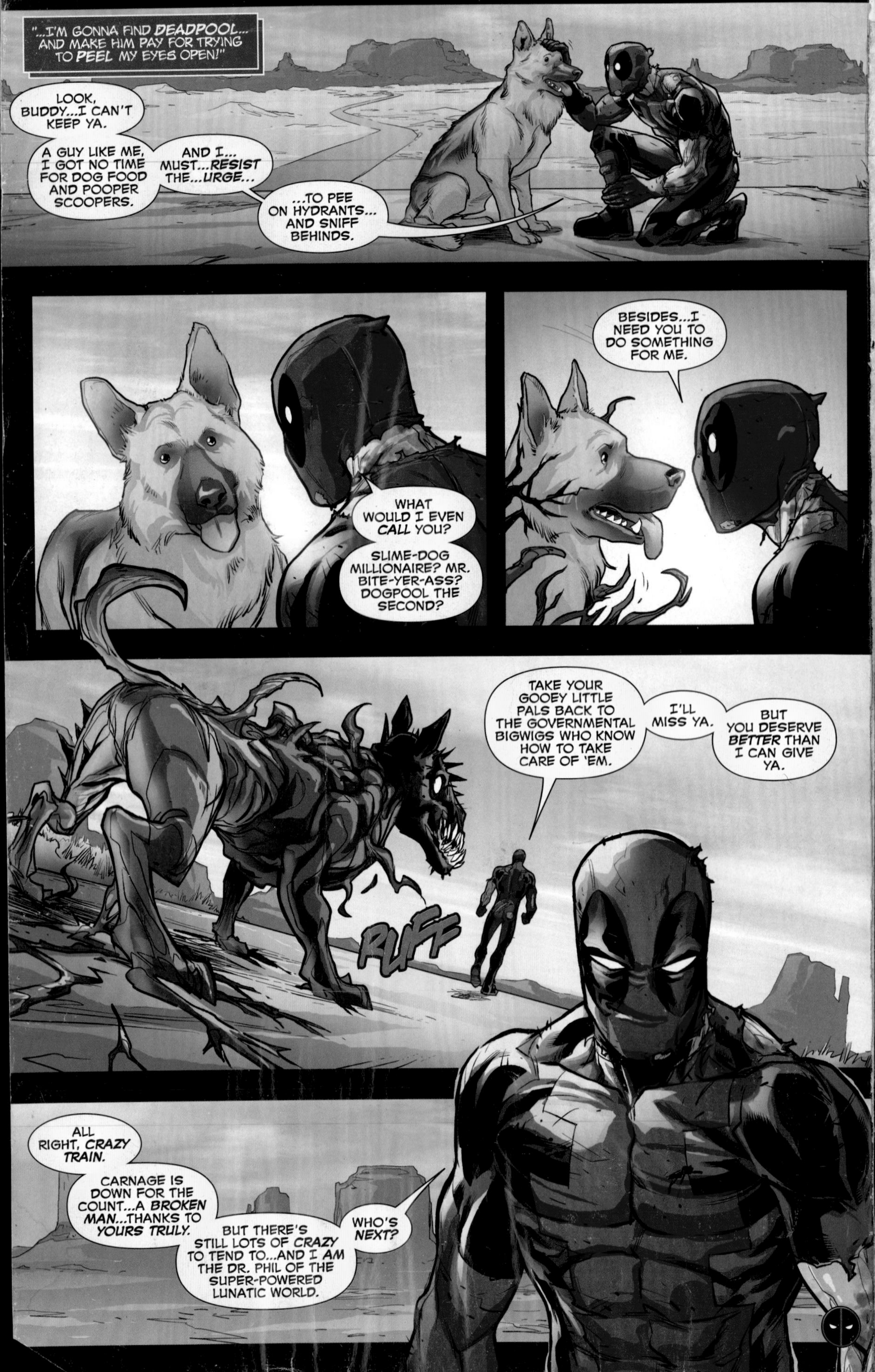
"...I'M GONNA FIND DEADPOOL... AND MAKE HIM PAY FOR TRYING TO PEEL MY EYES OPEN!"
LOOK, BUDDY...I CAN'T KEEP YA.
A GUY LIKE ME, I GOT NO TIME FOR DOG FOOD AND POOPER SCOOPERS.
AND I... MUST...RESIST THE...URGE...
...TO PEE ON HYDRANTS... AND SNIFF BEHINDS.
WHAT WOULD I EVEN CALL YOU?
SLIME-DOG MILLIONAIRE? MR. BITE-YER-ASS? DOGPOOL THE SECOND?
BESIDES...I NEED YOU TO DO SOMETHING FOR ME.
TAKE YOUR GOOEY LITTLE PALS BACK TO THE GOVERNMENTAL BIGWIGS WHO KNOW HOW TO TAKE CARE OF 'EM.
I'LL MISS YA.
BUT YOU DESERVE BETTER THAN I CAN GIVE YA.
RUFF
ALL RIGHT, CRAZY TRAIN.
CARNAGE IS DOWN FOR THE COUNT...A BROKEN MAN...THANKS TO YOURS TRULY.
BUT THERE'S STILL LOTS OF CRAZY TO TEND TO...AND I AM THE DR. PHIL OF THE SUPER-POWERED LUNATIC WORLD.
WHO'S NEXT?